SCHOLASTIC

Rhyming
Dictionary

Foreword by Paul B. Janeczko

SUE YOUNG

SCHOLASTIC REFERENCE
An imprint of
SCHOLASTIC

0-439-79642-3

Cover Design: Tatiana Sperhacke
Art Direction: Tatiana Sperhacke
Interior Design: Kay Petronio
Illustration: David Sheldon

10 9 8 7 6 5 4 3 2 1   06 07 08 09 10

Printed in the U.S.A.

This edition first printing, July 2006

CONTENTS

Index

FOREWORD

by Paul B. Janeczko

recall the first time I mentioned to a class of young writers that there was such a thing as a rhyming dictionary. They looked at me and at one another in disbelief. "You mean a book that has rhymes for other words in it?" they asked. "Exactly," I said, but they needed convincing. The next day I brought in three or four different pocket rhyming dictionaries. Big mistake. From that point on, the students didn't want to write poems. They wanted to read to one another from the dictionaries!

Even though I wasn't thrilled that these kids didn't want to write, I was thrilled that they were so delighted with the words in the dictionary. And, if you like the sounds of words, if you like to roll words around in your mouth like hard candies as you taste each one, this book is for you. It's filled with delicious words that you can use to make your poems come alive.

This rhyming dictionary can be a valuable tool. A word of caution, however. Don't become a slave to this book. Rely on your own imagination when you write poems. Don't let the rhyme control your poem. Your poem needs, first of all, to say what you want it to say. Then you can use the rhyming dictionary to help you work out a rhyme or two for a couple of trouble spots in the poem. I've seen a number of young writers who write poems with the rhyming dictionary open on their desks. These students usually write poetry that doesn't make a lot of sense. Oh, it rhymes, but readers won't care much about the rhymes if the poem doesn't make sense.

On the other hand, you can use the rhyming dictionary to get ideas for poems. You could thumb through it, looking for appealing, fascinating, and tantalizing words that might give you an idea for a poem. X. J. Kennedy, author of many books of humorous poetry, once told me how the rhyming dictionary worked for him. He was writing a poem about dogs and was stuck on finding a rhyme for *poodle* (other than the obvious: *noodle*). So, he turned to his rhyming dictionary and looked up the *-oodle* sound. Among the words listed with that sound, he found *strudel*. Captivated by that name for a German pastry, Kennedy put his dog poem into a drawer and began working on a poem about food!

Writing good rhyming poems can be lots of fun as well as a challenge. This rhyming dictionary can help you write poems that are more fun to write and read. I know that the copy that I own is starting to look shabby from so much use. But I have come to rely on it when I'm looking for the perfect rhyme. And you can, too. The rhyming dictionary that you're holding in your hands is one of the tools that can help you become a better poet.

Paul B. Janeczko is an award-winning poet and anthologist. He has written more than thirty books of poetry, fiction, and nonfiction, including *How to Write Poetry*, *Writing Winning Reports and Essays*, and *Blushing: Expressions of Love in Poems and Letters*.

cheer ....> fear

HOW TO USE THIS DICTIONARY

Welcome to the world of rhymes. We encounter rhyming sounds everywhere — in song lyrics, advertising jingles, rap, greeting card messages, poetry, and verse of all kinds. In all of these, the sounds of rhyme can please and tickle our ears. This book helps you write verse that rhymes.

There are different kinds of rhymes: **perfect**, **imperfect**, and **slant**. Some poets use only perfect rhyme, but you can be more casual, especially if you're rhyming for fun.

Words that sound exactly the same, such as *wait* and *weight*, are not considered rhymes at all — even though the two words sound alike and are spelled differently.

A perfect rhyme is formed by two words that have different consonant sounds before identical rhyming sounds. *Cake* and *lake* form a perfect rhyme.

An imperfect rhyme has the same consonant before the rhyming sound, such as *therefore* and *before*. (The rhyming sound is *ore* and the consonant is *f*.)

A slant rhyme is one in which the sounds are pronounced alike even when they are technically different. For instance, the words *daddy* and *chatty* are frequently spoken with the same rhyming sound: *addy*. Slant rhymes are not true rhymes, but they often sound the same to our ears.

Locating a rhyming sound

Unlike other dictionaries that list words by the beginning letter of the word, a rhyming dictionary lists words by the beginning vowel of the rhyming sound.

RHYMING SOUNDS ALWAYS START WITH A VOWEL. The vowels are *A*, *E*, *I*, *O*, *U*, and sometimes *Y*. All rhyming sounds will start with one of these vowels. Therefore, the main part of this book is divided into six sections — one for each vowel. The sounds are listed alphabetically under the starting vowel.

There are two ways to locate a rhyme in this book. For instance, if you are looking for a rhyme for the word *self*, you can do one of two things:

1. Go directly to the *elf* sound in the rhyming dictionary.

2. Look up the word *self* in the **index** at the back of the book. There the words are listed alphabetically by the beginning letter of the word. There you will see: **self/**elf.

What is the rhyming sound of a word?

Which sound toward the end of the word is louder, or has more stress? One-syllable words have only one sound in them, like *snake* and *cake*. Their rhyming sound is *ake*. But, what if you wanted something to rhyme with a two-syllable word like *silly*? Listen to the sound that you stress the most in *silly* — *ill*. The rhyming sound includes the stressed syllable plus the rest of the word. So, to rhyme *silly*, you would look up the sound *illy* in the **i** section. There you would find words that end with the same sound, such as *chili*, *frilly*, and *hilly*.

One sound, different spellings

Sometimes you might look up a rhyming sound in the dictionary, but instead of finding a list of words that rhyme, you are sent to another sound. This is a **cross-reference**. For instance, if you are looking for words that rhyme with *jacks* and you go to *acks* in the dictionary, you won't find a list. Instead you'll find a cross-reference:

acks as in jacks, see ax

The *ax* list contains *jacks*, *tax*, *kayaks*, *lilacs* — all the words with different spellings of the same sound. Without cross-references, the dictionary would contain many duplicated lists. It would be a very heavy book!

One word, many sounds

Some words end in the same spelling but have totally different sounds. When this happens, the spelling may be listed two or three times, once for each pronunciation of the sound. Each sound will be marked with a number. For instance, you will find three listings for the spelling *ard*. Each stands for a different sound that **ard** makes:

ard 1 stands for sounds like *card* and *guard*.

ard 2 stands for sounds like *reward* and *cord*.

ard 3 stands for sounds like *backward* and *bird*.

The way you hear a word's sound may depend on the region of the country in which you live. That's why in this dictionary you may find some words on a list that don't seem to you to rhyme. The same word may appear on another list under the sound familiar to you.

The point of this book is that you can have fun writing rhymes. As you begin to write your own verse, you may think of rhymes that are not in this or any other book. We encourage you to use your imagination to its fullest.

One word, no rhyme

What if the word you want to rhyme with has no rhyme? *Orange* and *pint* don't have a rhyme. It would be very difficult to complete a two-line rhyme that began:

Every day I eat an orange

If you wanted a rhyme, you could try instead:

I always eat an orange a day
It's good for me, or so they say

By not placing the hard-to-rhyme word at the end, you made it easier to find a rhyme.

Whether you want to write a rap or a sonnet, the world of verse is yours for the rhyming. Rhyming sounds, together with the melody of meter, ensure that what we write will be pleasing to the ear.

a

a **1** as in USA, see ay

a **2** as in spa, see aw

ab 1

blab
cab
crab
dab
drab
fab
flab
gab
grab
jab
lab
nab
scab
stab
tab

backstab
rehab
sand crab

taxicab

ab 2 as in swab, see ob

abber

blabber
drabber
gabber
grabber
jabber

backstabber

money grabber

abble

babble
dabble
rabble
Scrabble

Tower of Babel

abby

abbey
blabby
cabby
crabby
drabby
flabby
gabby
grabby
shabby
tabby

Dear Abby

able

able
cable

fable
label
sable
stable
table

disable
enable
mislabel
times table
timetable
unable
unstable

Aesop's fable
Cain and Abel
warning label

willing and able

aby

baby

baby

maybe

ac as in almanac, see ack

ace

ace

base
bass
brace
case
chase
face
grace
lace
pace
place
race
space
trace
vase

birthplace
bookcase
briefcase
deface
disgrace
embrace
erase
fireplace
home base
horse race
misplace
neck brace
replace
retrace
sack race
shoelace
staircase
suitcase
unlace

workplace
anyplace
breathing space
change of pace
database
double-space
everyplace
face-to-face
freckle face
human race
just in case
outer space
out of place
poker face
saving grace
wild-goose chase

aced as in laced,
   see **aste**

ach as in attach,
   see **atch 1**

ache 1 as in
   headache,
   see **ake**

ache 2 as in
   mustache,
   see **ash 1**

acial

facial
glacial
racial

spatial
interracial

acious

gracious
spacious
audacious
curvacious
flirtatious
Horatius
loquacious
tenacious
vivacious

ostentatious

acity

audacity
capacity
sagacity
tenacity
veracity

ack

back
black
crack
flack
hack
jack
knack
lack
pack
plaque

3

quack
rack
sack
shack
slack
smack
snack
stack
tack
track
whack
yak

attack
backpack
backtrack
blackjack
drawback
feedback
flapjack
flashback
fullback
haystack
hijack
icepack
Iraq
kayak
knapsack
laugh track
offtrack
one-track
racetrack
ransack
setback

sidetrack
six-pack
soundtrack
thumbtack
Tic Tac
unpack
wisecrack
wrong track

almanac
back-to-back
Cadillac
camelback
crackerjack
cul-de-sac
gunnysack
heart attack
hit the sack
jumping jack
lumberjack

lumberjack

maniac
paperback
piggyback
quarterback
railroad track

amnesiac
insomniac
panic attack
yakkity-yak

acked as in
    cracked,
    see **act**

ackle

cackle
crackle
jackal
shackle
spackle
tackle

debacle
ramshackle

fishing tackle
tabernacle

acks as in jacks,
    see **ax**

acs as in maniacs,
    see **ax**

act

act
backed
cracked
fact
lacked
packed

pact
quacked
sacked
smacked
snacked
stacked
tacked
tact
tracked
tract
whacked
yakked

abstract
attacked
attract
backpacked
compact
contract
distract
enact
exact
extract
hijacked
impact
in fact
jam-packed
ransacked
react
sidetracked
subtract
transact
unpacked
wisecracked

artifact
interact
overact
riot act
vacuum-packed

matter of fact
overreact

actical

practical
tactical

impractical

action

action
faction
fraction
traction

abstraction
attraction
contraction
distraction
extraction
inaction
infraction
reaction
subtraction
transaction

chain reaction
interaction
satisfaction
star attraction

dissatisfaction
affirmative action

active

active

attractive
inactive
reactive

hyperactive
overactive
retroactive

radioactive

acts as in facts,
see ax

acy

Casey
Gracie
lacy
spacey
Tracy

ad 1

ad
add
bad
cad
Chad
clad
dad
fad
grad

had
lad
mad
pad
plaid
sad
tad

comrade
doodad
egad
granddad
ink pad
nomad
Sinbad
too bad

Galahad
ironclad
launching pad
mom and dad
not so bad
shoulder pad
Trinidad
undergrad

Olympiad
stark-raving mad

ad 2 as in squad,
see awed

ada

armada
cicada
Granada

piñata
regatta
tostada

enchilada

aficionada

adder as in
ladder,
see atter

addle as in
paddle,
see attle

addy as in daddy,
see atty

ade 1

aid
aide
blade
braid
fade
frayed
grade
grayed
jade
laid
made
maid
neighed
paid
played
prayed

raid
shade
spade
sprayed
stayed
suede
swayed
trade
wade
weighed

afraid
arcade
Band-Aid
betrayed
blockade
bridesmaid
charade
crusade
decade
decayed
delayed
displayed
first aid
grenade
homemade
invade
Kool-Aid
lampshade
mermaid
nursemaid
obeyed
okayed
outweighed

parade
persuade
portrayed
repaid
surveyed
tirade
unmade
unpaid
upgrade
x-rayed

accolade
barricade
cavalcade
centigrade
custom-made
disobeyed
escapade
foreign aid
Gatorade
hearing aid
hit parade
lemonade
make the grade
marmalade
masquerade
overpaid
promenade
razor blade
ready-made
renegade
ricocheted
Rose Parade
serenade

shoulder blade
unafraid
underpaid

penny arcade
visual aid

ade 2 as in facade,
see awed

ader

cater
crater
freighter
gator
greater
hater
later
nadir
raider
skater
straighter
trader
traitor
waiter

creator
crusader
debater
dictator
equator
ice skater

invader
narrator
persuader
spectator
tailgater
translator

agitator
alligator

alligator

animator
aviator
calculator
decorator
demonstrator
detonator
duplicator
educator
elevator
escalator
generator
illustrator
imitator
indicator
innovator
instigator
legislator
liberator
masquerader
mediator

moderator
navigator
operator
perpetrator
radiator
regulator
roller skater
see you later
serenader
speculator
terminator
ventilator

assassinator
coordinator
exaggerator
exterminator
facilitator
impersonator
investigator
manipulator
negotiator
procrastinator
refrigerator
sooner or later

ady

eighty
Haiti
Katie
lady
matey
shady
weighty

aff

calf
graph
half
laugh
staff

behalf
decaf
giraffe
riffraff

autograph
belly laugh
better half
chief of staff
paragraph
phonograph
photograph
telegraph

aft

craft
draft
graft
laughed
raft
shaft
staffed

aircraft
life raft
mine shaft
spacecraft
witchcraft

autographed
fore and aft
photographed

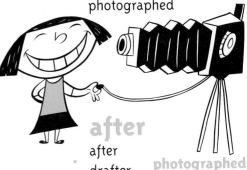
photographed

after

after
drafter
laughter
rafter

hereafter
thereafter

forever after

afty

crafty
drafty

ag

bag
brag
drag
flag
gag
jag
lag
nag
rag
sag
shag

snag
stag
tag
wag
zag

beanbag
dishrag
dog tag
grab bag
jet lag
mailbag
name tag
price tag
ragtag
sandbag
tea bag
trash bag
washrag
windbag
zigzag

doggie bag
litterbag
lollygag
saddlebag
sleeping bag

age 1

age
cage
gauge
page
rage
sage

stage
wage

backstage
birdcage
Bronze Age
engage
enrage
front page
Ice Age
offstage
old age
outrage
rampage
rib cage
space age
Stone Age
teenage
upstage

middle age
underage
minimum wage

age 2

barrage
collage
corsage
garage
massage
mirage

bon voyage
camouflage
entourage
sabotage

espionage

ageous

contagious
courageous
enrage us
outrageous
rampageous
upstage us

advantageous

aggy

baggy
draggy
Maggie
saggy
shaggy

ah as in hah,
  see **aw**

ai as in bonzai,
  see **y**

aid as in paid,
  see **ade** 1

aider as in raider,
  see **ader**

ail as in mail,
  see **ale** 1

aily

daily
gaily

scaly

Israeli
shillelagh
ukulele

Barnum and Bailey

aim

aim
blame
came
claim
fame
flame
frame
game
lame
maim
name
same
shame
tame

acclaim
aflame
ball game
became
defame
exclaim
for shame
inflame
nickname
reclaim
surname

take aim
claim to fame
Hall of Fame
Notre Dame
overcame
put to shame

ain

brain
cane
chain
crane
drain
gain
grain
Jane
lane
main
Maine
mane
pain
pane
plain
plane
rain
reign
rein
sane
slain
Spain
sprain
stain
strain

train
vain
vane
vein
wane

abstain
airplane
birdbrain
bloodstain
campaign
champagne
chow mein
complain
contain
disdain
domain
Elaine
explain
freight train
Great Dane

Great Dane

humane
insane

in vain
Lorraine
maintain
Mark Twain
migraine
mundane
obtain
profane
refrain
regain
remain
restrain
retain
sustain
tearstain
terrain
Ukraine
unchain

acid rain
ascertain
candy cane
cellophane
down the drain
entertain
featherbrain
hurricane
inhumane
lovers' lane
Novocain
potty train
scatterbrain
Solarcaine
wagon train

weather vane
windowpane

memory lane
no pain, no gain

air

air
bare
bear
blare
care
chair
dare
fair
fare
flair
flare
glare
hair
hare
heir
lair
mare
pair
pear
prayer
rare
scare
share
snare
spare
square
stair

stare
swear
tear
their
there
ware
wear
where

affair
airfare
aware
Bel Air
beware
bus fare
child care
compare
declare
despair
elsewhere
fanfare
fresh air
health care
high chair
impair
midair
nightmare
no fair
nowhere
outwear
Pierre
prepare
repair
somewhere

threadbare
Times Square
unfair
warfare
welfare
wheelchair

anywhere
billionaire
county fair
debonair
Delaware
dentist chair
everywhere
fair and square
here and there
millionaire
not all there
on the air
over there
questionnaire
rocking chair
silverware
solitaire
teddy bear

unaware
underwear
wash and wear

electric chair
intensive care
Smokey the Bear

aire as in
   millionaire,
   see **air**
airy as in fairy,
   see **ary**
aise as in praise,
   see **aze**
ait as in bait,
   see **ate**
ak as in yak,
   see **ack**

ake
ache
bake
Blake
brake
break
cake
fake
flake
Jake
lake
make

quake
rake
sake
shake
snake
stake

snake

steak
take
wake

awake
backache
beefsteak
cheesecake
clambake
cupcake
daybreak
earache
earthquake
fruitcake
handshake
headache
heartache
heartbreak
housebreak
intake
jailbreak
keepsake
milk shake

teddy bear

mistake
namesake
newsbreak
opaque
outbreak
pancake
remake
shortcake
snowflake
toothache

bellyache
birthday cake
coffee break
double take
give and take
overtake
pat-a-cake
rattlesnake
Shake 'n Bake
stomachache
take a break
wide-awake

for goodness' sake
for pity sake
gimme a break
jump in the lake

aks as in kayaks,
see ax

al

Al
gal

Hal
pal
shall

canal
chorale
corral
decal
locale
low-cal
morale
pen pal

musicale
rationale
root canal

ald as in bald,
see alled

ale 1

ail
ale
bail
Braille
fail
frail
gale
hail
jail
mail
male
nail
pail
pale

quail
rail
sail
sale
scale
snail
stale
tail
tale
trail
veil
wail
whale
Yale

airmail
blackmail
cocktail
curtail
derail
detail
dovetail
exhale
fan mail
female
for sale
hangnail
impale
inhale
pigtail
prevail
retail
shirttail
telltale

pen pal

thumbnail
toenail
unveil
upscale
wholesale

Abigail
cottontail
fairy tale
fingernail
garage sale
ginger ale
Holy Grail
killer whale
monorail
nature trail
nightingale
rummage sale
tattletale
without fail

ale 2 as in morale,
  see al

ale 3 as in finale,
  see olly

alf as in calf,
  see aff

ality 1

brutality
fatality
finality
formality

legality
locality
mentality
morality
mortality
neutrality
normality
reality
totality
vitality

abnormality
hospitality
illegality
immorality
immortality
informality
joviality
nationality
personality
practicality
principality
punctuality
rationality
technicality
triviality

congeniality
municipality
originality
sentimentality

confidentiality
constitutionality
individuality

ality 2

quality
equality
frivolity
inequality

alk as in talk,
  see ock

alker as in walker,
  see ocker

alks as in walks,
  see ox

all

all
ball
bawl
brawl
call
crawl
doll
drawl
fall
gall
hall
haul
loll
mall
maul
Paul
Saul
scrawl

shawl
small
sprawl
squall
stall
tall
wall

appall
baseball
birdcall
blackball
close call
downfall
enthrall
eyeball
football
free fall
goofball
gum ball
handball
install
meatball
nightfall
oddball
phone call
pinball
pitfall
rag doll
rainfall
recall
snowball
snowfall
spitball

baseball

stonewall
toll call

aerosol
alcohol
Barbie doll
basketball
butterball
cannonball
caterwaul
city hall
cotton ball
crystal ball
curtain call
free-for-all
know-it-all
Montreal
off-the-wall
overall
overhaul
paper doll
parasol
protocol
shopping mall
study hall
Taj Mahal
Tylenol
volleyball
wake-up call
wall-to-wall
waterfall

cholesterol
justice for all

Neanderthal

alled
bald
bawled
brawled
called
crawled
drawled
hauled
lolled
mauled
scald
scrawled
sprawled
squalled
stalled
walled

appalled
blackballed
enthralled
installed
recalled
snowballed
so-called

overhauled

aller
brawler
caller
collar
dollar
holler

15

scholar
smaller
squalor
taller

bird caller
blue-collar
flea collar
free-faller
installer
name-caller
white-collar

creepy crawler
hoot and holler
million-dollar

million-dollar

alley

alley
Bali
dally
galley
rally
Sally
tally

valley
blind alley
Death Valley
pep rally

allow 1

aloe
hallow
shallow

marshmallow

allow 2

follow
hollow
swallow
wallow

Apollo

ally as in rally,
see alley

alm

balm
calm
palm
psalm
qualm

embalm
napalm

alt

fault
halt

malt
salt
vault

asphalt
assault
default
exalt
pole-vault

somersault

alter

altar
alter
falter
halter
vaulter
Walter

assaulter
Gibraltar

alts

faults
halts
malts
salts
vaults
waltz

assaults
defaults

smelling salts
somersaults

am

am
clam
cram
dam
gram
ham
jam
lamb
ma'am
Pam
ram
Sam
scam
scram
sham
slam
swam
tram
wham
yam

exam
flimflam
grand slam
madame
outswam
program
toe jam

Abraham
Amsterdam
anagram
Birmingham
diagram
in a jam
leg of lamb
milligram
telegram
traffic jam
Uncle Sam

Uncle Sam

ama 1

comma
drama
llama
mama
Rama
trauma

pajama

cinerama
melodrama
Yokohama

ama 2

pajama

Alabama
cinerama
panorama

ame as in fame,
   see aim

ami as in pastrami,
   see ommy

ammy

clammy
Grammy
Tammy
whammy

Miami

amp

amp
camp
champ
clamp
cramp
damp
lamp
ramp
scamp
stamp
tramp
vamp

postage stamp
summer camp
writer's cramp

amper

camper
damper
hamper
pamper
scamper
tamper

an 1

an
Anne

ban
bran
can
clan
fan
Fran
Jan
man
Nan
pan
plan
ran
scan
span
Stan
tan
than
van

Batman
began
cancan
caveman

Chopin
deadpan
dishpan
dustpan
hangman
Japan
lawman
life span
madman
oat bran
outran
Pac-Man
sandman
sedan
Spokane
suntan
time span
trash can

caravan
frying pan
handyman
man-to-man
moving van
overran
Pakistan
Peter Pan
spic-and-span
Superman

Afghanistan
attention span
catamaran
flash-in-the-pan

medicine man
orangutan

an 2 as in pecan, see **awn**

ana 1
Anna

banana
bandanna
Diana
Havana
Montana
Savannah
Susanna

Indiana
Pollyanna

Louisiana

ana 2 as in iguana, see **onna**

ance
ants
aunts
chance
chants
dance
France
glance
grants
lance

caveman

pants
plants
prance
stance
trance

advance
break-dance
by chance
enchants
enhance
entrance
expanse
fat chance
finance
folk dance
freelance
last chance
rain dance
romance
square dance
sweat pants
tap dance
transplants

circumstance
disenchants
fighting chance
song and dance
underpants

and

and
band
banned

bland
brand
canned
fanned
gland
grand
hand
land
panned
planned
sand
spanned
stand
strand
tanned

armband
backhand
bandstand
command
cowhand
crash-land
demand
disband
dreamland
expand
firsthand
grandstand
handstand
headband
homeland
kickstand
Lapland
longhand

namebrand
offhand
quicksand
shorthand
suntanned
Thailand
wasteland

baby grand
beforehand
close at hand
contraband
Disneyland
Dixieland
fairyland
hand-in-hand
helping hand
Holy Land
hot dog stand
no man's land
reprimand
Rio Grande
rubber band
secondhand
sleight of hand
understand

chain of command
fantasyland
law of the land
misunderstand

supply and demand

ane as in lane,
see ain

19

ang

bang
clang
dang
fang
gang
hang
rang
sang
slang
sprang
Tang
twang

boomerang

chain gang
harangue
meringue
mustang

boomerang
overhang

orangoutang

ange

change
range
strange

arrange
downrange
exchange
long-range
shortchange

interchange

prearrange
rearrange

ank

bank
blank
clank
crank
dank
drank
frank
plank
prank
rank
sank
shrank
spank
tank
thank
yank

blood bank
fish tank
gangplank
outrank
point-blank
think tank

data bank
draw a blank
savings bank
walk the plank

blankety-blank

military rank

anky

blanky
clanky
cranky
Frankie
hankie
lanky
swanky
Yankee

hanky-panky

anned as in
banned,
see **and**

anner

banner
manner
manor
planner
scanner
tanner

anny

Annie
Danny
granny
nanny

uncanny

ans as in swans,
see **ons**

ant 1

ant

aunt
can't
chant
grant
pant
plant
rant
scant
slant

eggplant
enchant
implant
Rembrandt
supplant
transplant

disenchant
gallivant
power plant

ant 2 as in want,
see aunt

ante as in
confidante,
see aunt

ant

antic

antic
frantic

Atlantic
gigantic
romantic

transatlantic
unromantic

ants as in pants,
see ance

any as in many,
see enny

ap

cap
chap
clap
flap
gap
lap
map
nap
rap
sap
scrap
slap
snap
strap
tap
trap
wrap

yap
zap

backslap
burlap
catnap
dunce cap
firetrap
giftwrap
hubcap
kidnap
kneecap
madcap
mishap
mousetrap
recap
road map
unwrap
wiretap

baseball cap
beat the rap
booby trap
bottle cap
gender gap
gingersnap
handicap
overlap
thinking cap
tourist trap

generation gap

ape

ape

cape
drape
gape
grape
scrape
shape
tape

agape
egg-shape
escape
go ape
landscape
red tape
reshape
shipshape

fire escape
out of shape
ticker tape

aph as in graph,
  see aff

aphed as in
  autographed,
  see aft

aphic

graphic
traffic

geographic
one-way traffic
photographic

apple

apple
chapel
grapple

appy

happy
pappy
sappy
scrappy
snappy

grandpappy
slaphappy
unhappy

make it snappy
trigger-happy

ar

are
bar
car
czar
far
jar
mar
par
scar
spar
star
tar

ajar
all-star

bazaar
bizarre
boxcar
cigar
costar
disbar
guitar
jaguar
memoir
Renoir
snack bar
so far
streetcar

cable car
candy bar
caviar
cookie jar
CPR
falling star
handlebar
movie star

movie star

near and far
registrar
reservoir
salad bar
seminar
superstar
VCR
Zanzibar

ara

Clara
Sarah

mascara
Sahara

arch

arch
March
march
parch
starch

ard 1

bard
barred
card
charred
guard
hard
jarred
lard
marred
scarred
sparred

starred
tarred
yard

armed guard
backyard
barnyard
Bernard
blowhard
bombard
Coast Guard
costarred
cue card
diehard
discard
flash card
graveyard
junkyard
lifeguard
postcard
regard
safeguard
scorecard
shipyard
vanguard

avant-garde
baseball card
battle-scarred
birthday card
bodyguard
boulevard
credit card
crossing guard
disregard

leotard
report card
Saint Bernard

Saint Bernard

ard 2 as in
reward,
see ord 1

ard 3 as in
backward,
see erd

arder as in
harder,
see arter

ardy

arty
hardy
hearty
Marty
party
smarty
tardy

foolhardy
search party

tea party

birthday party

are as in care, see **air**

area

area

Bavaria

Bulgaria

hysteria

malaria

arent

parent

apparent

grandparent

inherent

transparent

unapparent

arer

barer

error

fairer

rarer

terror

pallbearer

seafarer

torchbearer

wayfarer

holy terror

trial and error

arf 1

arf

barf

scarf

arf 2

dwarf

wharf

arge

barge

charge

large

Marge

sarge

discharge

enlarge

recharge

take charge

overcharge

ari as in safari, see **arry 2**

arious

various

Aquarius

gregarious

hilarious

precarious

vicarious

Sagittarius

arity

charity

clarity

rarity

barbarity

dexterity

disparity

hilarity

posterity

prosperity

severity

sincerity

vulgarity

insincerity

popularity

regularity

similarity

solidarity

familiarity

irregularity

peculiarity

ark

arc

ark

bark

Clark

dark

hark

lark

mark

park

shark
spark
stark

aardvark
ballpark
birthmark
bookmark
check mark
Denmark
earmark
footmark
landmark
monarch
postmark
remark
skylark
theme park
trademark

baseball park
Central Park
disembark
double-park
Joan of Arc
Noah's ark
question mark

arm 1

arm
charm
farm
harm

alarm

disarm
firearm

arm in arm
false alarm
fire alarm
lucky charm
underarm

arm 2 as in warm, see orm 1

arn

barn
darn
yarn

aron

Aaron
baron
barren
heron
Karen
Sharon

arred as in barred, see ard 1

arrot

bear it
carat
carrot
dare it
ferret

merit
parrot
scare it
share it
swear it
wear it

demerit
inherit
prepare it
repair it
disinherit

arrow

arrow
marrow
narrow
pharaoh
sparrow

bolero
bone marrow
Camaro
dinero
sombrero

sombrero

wheelbarrow

bow and arrow
caballero
straight and narrow

Rio de Janeiro

arry 1 as in carry,
  see ary

arry 2

sari
sorry
starry

Ferrari
safari

calamari

art 1

art
cart
chart
dart
heart
mart
part
smart
start
tart

apart
depart
eye chart
false start

folk art
go cart
golf cart
head start
impart
jump-start
Kmart
Mozart
outsmart
Pop Tart
restart
street-smart
sweetheart
upstart

à la carte
applecart
change of heart
counterpart
fall apart
heart-to-heart
lonely heart
martial art
minimart
Purple Heart
running start
shopping cart

shopping
cart

work of art

art 2 as in wart,
  see ort

arter

ardor
barter
charter
garter
harder
martyr
smarter
starter
Tartar
tarter

self-starter
slow starter

arty as in party,
  see ardy

arve

carve
Marv
starve

ary

airy
Barry
berry
bury
Carrie
carry

cherry
dairy
fairy
ferry
Gary
hairy
Harry
Larry
marry
Mary
merry
prairie
scary
tarry
Terry
vary
very
wary

canary
contrary
library
primary
raspberry
remarry
Rosemary
strawberry
tooth fairy

adversary
arbitrary
aviary
cemetery
commentary

dictionary

culinary
customary
dictionary
dietary
dignitary
dromedary
February
fragmentary
honorary
January
legendary
literary
mercenary
military
missionary
momentary
monastery
mortuary
necessary
ordinary
planetary
sanctuary
sanitary
secondary
secretary
sedentary
solitary
stationary
stationery
temporary
visionary
voluntary

contemporary

disciplinary
extraordinary
hereditary
imaginary
itinerary
obituary
precautionary
preliminary
sugarplum fairy
unnecessary
vocabulary

revolutionary

as as in has,
see **azz**

asco

fiasco
Tabasco

ase 1 as in case,
see **ace**

ase 2 as in phase,
see **aze**

ased as in chased,
see **aste**

ash 1

ash
bash
brash
cache
cash

clash
crash
dash
flash
gash
gnash
hash
lash
mash
rash
sash
slash
smash
splash
stash
thrash
trash

backlash
eyelash
mishmash
mustache
news flash
whiplash

balderdash
corned beef hash
diaper rash
succotash

ash 2 as in wash,
see **osh**

ashy
flashy

splashy
trashy

asion
Asian

abrasion
Caucasian
equation
Eurasian
evasion
invasion
occasion
persuasion

ask
ask
bask
cask
flask
mask
task

asket   mask
basket
casket
gasket

asm
chasm
spasm

sarcasm
enthusiasm

ason
basin
chasten
hasten
Jason
mason

asp
clasp
gasp
grasp
rasp

ass
ass
bass
brass
class
crass
gas
glass
grass
lass
mass
pass
sass

amass
bypass
first class
harass
hourglass
impasse
spyglass

surpass
tear gas
trespass

boarding pass
bonny lass
laughing gas
looking glass
middle-class
out of gas
sassafras
smooth as glass

head of the class
snake in the grass

magnifying glass

assed as in
  passed,
  see ast

assy
brassy
chassis
classy
glassy
grassy
sassy

Tallahassee

ast
blast
cast
caste
fast

gassed
last
mast
passed
past
sassed
vast

aghast
amassed
at last
bombast
broadcast
contrast
downcast
forecast
full blast
gymnast
halfmast
harassed
miscast
newscast

newscast

outcast
outclassed
outlast

sandblast
steadfast
surpassed
typecast

all-star cast
flabbergast
overcast
telecast
unsurpassed

enthusiast
iconoclast

aste
aced
baste
braced
chased
chaste
faced
graced
haste
laced
paced
paste
placed
raced
spaced
taste
traced
waist
waste

bad taste

29

defaced
disgraced
displaced
distaste
embraced
erased
fast-paced
good taste
misplaced
red-faced
replaced
retraced
straitlaced
toothpaste
two-faced
unlaced

aftertaste
baby-faced
cut-and-paste
freckle-faced
haste makes waste
interlaced
interspaced

hazardous waste

asten as in
   chasten,
   see **ason**

aster

blaster
faster
master

pastor
plaster
vaster

bandmaster
broadcaster
disaster
forecaster
headmaster
newscaster
postmaster
sandblaster
schoolmaster
scoutmaster

alabaster

astic

drastic
plastic
spastic

bombastic
elastic
fantastic
gymnastic
sarcastic
scholastic

ecclesiastic
enthusiastic
interscholastic

asty

hasty
tasty

at 1

at
bat
brat
cat
chat
fat
flat
gnat
hat
mat
pat
rat
sat
spat
splat
that
vat

fat cat

chitchat
combat
dingbat
doormat
fat cat
format
hardhat
muskrat
nonfat
pack rat
place mat
tomcat
wildcat
wombat

acrobat
alley cat
army brat
baby fat
baby-sat
bureaucrat
copycat
cowboy hat
democrat
diplomat
dirty rat
fraidy cat
habitat
Laundromat
pussycat
smell a rat
thermostat
this and that
tit for tat
welcome mat

aristocrat
blind as a bat
calico cat

at 2 as in swat,
see ot

atch 1

batch
catch
hatch
latch
match

patch
scratch
snatch
thatch

arm patch
attach
detach
dispatch
knee patch
mismatch
unlatch

boxing match
cabbage patch
mix and match
reattach

atch 2 as in
watch,
see otch

atchy

catchy
patchy
scratchy

Apache

ate

ate
bait
crate
date
eight
fate

freight
gait
gate
grate
great
hate
Kate
late
mate
plate
rate
skate
slate
state
straight
strait
trait
wait
weight

await
birthrate
blind date
cellmate
cheapskate
checkmate
classmate
Colgate
create
debate
deflate
donate
elate
equate

estate
first-rate
frustrate
gyrate
helpmate
ice skate
inflate
ingrate
inmate
innate
locate
mandate
migrate
narrate
ornate
playmate
primate
prom date
pulsate
rebate
relate
rotate
sedate
stagnate
stalemate
tailgate
translate
update
vacate
vibrate

activate
advocate
aggravate

agitate
allocate
amputate
animate
calculate
candidate
captivate
celebrate
chief of state
circulate
complicate
concentrate
confiscate
contemplate
cultivate
decorate
dedicate
delegate
demonstrate
detonate
devastate
deviate
dislocate
dominate
double-date
duplicate
educate
elevate
emigrate
escalate
estimate
excavate
fascinate

fluctuate
formulate
fumigate
generate
Golden Gate
graduate
gravitate
heavyweight
hesitate
hibernate
hyphenate
illustrate
imitate
immigrate
indicate
infiltrate
instigate
integrate
irrigate
irritate
isolate
legislate
liberate
liquidate
lubricate
medicate
meditate
motivate
mutilate
nauseate
navigate
nominate
operate

out-of-date
overate
overrate
overstate
overweight
paperweight
penetrate
percolate
populate
punctuate
radiate
real estate
regulate
roller skate

roller skate

second-rate
segregate
separate
situate
speculate
stimulate
strangulate
suffocate

terminate
tolerate
underrate
underweight
up-to-date
vaccinate
validate
vindicate
violate

abbreviate
accelerate
accommodate
accumulate
alienate
alleviate
annihilate
anticipate
appreciate
asphyxiate
assassinate
associate
at any rate
carbohydrate
communicate
congratulate
contaminate
cooperate
coordinate
deliberate
discriminate
elaborate
eliminate
emancipate

evacuate
evaluate
evaporate
exaggerate
exasperate
exhilarate
exterminate
hallucinate
humiliate
illuminate
impersonate
initiate
inoculate
insinuate
interrogate
intimidate
intoxicate
investigate
invigorate
manipulate
officiate
participate
procrastinate
recuperate
reiterate
retaliate
reverberate

ater 1 as in later,
  see ader

ater 2 as in water,
  see otter

ath

bath
math
path
wrath

birdbath
steam bath
warpath

aftermath
bubble bath

bubble bath

psychopath

ather 1

gather
lather
rather

ather 2

bother
father
godfather
grandfather
no bother

atial as in spatial, see acial

atic

attic
static

asthmatic
dramatic
ecstatic
erratic
fanatic
traumatic

acrobatic
Adriatic
aromatic
Asiatic
autocratic
automatic
bureaucratic
charismatic
democratic
diplomatic
Instamatic
mathematic
problematic
symptomatic
systematic

aristocratic
melodramatic
psychosomatic

idiosyncratic

semiautomatic

atin

fatten
flatten
Latin
satin

Manhattan
pig Latin

ation

nation
station

citation
creation

Dalmatian

Dalmatian
dictation
donation
duration
elation
fire station
fixation
flirtation
formation
foundation
frustration
inflation
location
migration
ovation
plantation
probation
quotation

34

relation
rotation
starvation
summation
taxation
vacation
vibration

adaptation
admiration
aggravation
agitation
animation
application
aviation
calculation
cancellation
celebration
circulation
combination
complication
concentration
confirmation
congregation
consolation
conversation
corporation
declaration
decoration
dedication
dehydration
demonstration
desperation
destination

devastation
duplication
elevation
expectation
explanation
exploration
fabrication
fascination
generation
graduation
hesitation
illustration
imitation
immigration
inflammation
information
innovation
inspiration
integration
irritation
isolation
legislation
liberation
limitation
medication
meditation

moderation
motivation
mutilation
nomination
obligation
observation
occupation
operation
perspiration
population
preparation
presentation
preservation
punctuation
radiation
recreation
registration
regulation
relaxation
reputation
reservation
resignation
revelation
segregation
separation
situation
speculation
stimulation
transportation
variation
violation

abbreviation
acceleration

meditation

35

anticipation
appreciation
assassination
civilization
communication
consideration
cooperation
coordination
determination
discrimination
elimination
evaluation
exasperation
extermination
hallucination
humiliation
imagination
impersonation
initiation
interpretation
interrogation
intimidation
intoxication
investigation
justification
manipulation
multiplication
notification
organization
participation
procrastination
pronunciation
qualification

realization
recommendation
retaliation
sophistication
verification

atious as in
   flirtatious,
   see **acious**

ator as in narrator,
   see **ader**

atten as in
   flatten,
   see **atin**

atter

batter
bladder
chatter
clatter
fatter
flatter
gladder
ladder
latter
madder
matter
platter
sadder
scatter
shatter
splatter

tatter
gallbladder
gray matter
Mad Hatter
no matter

hook and ladder
pitter-patter

attery

battery
flattery

attle

battle
cattle
paddle
prattle
rattle
saddle
straddle
tattle

dog paddle
Seattle
sidesaddle
skedaddle

atty

batty
bratty
caddie
catty
chatty
daddy

faddy
fatty
patty
ratty

granddaddy
rice paddy

Cincinnati

aud as in fraud,
see **awed**

aught as in
taught,
see **ot**

aughter as in
daughter,
see **otter**

aughty as in
naughty,
see **ody**

aul as in haul,
see **all**

auled as in
hauled,
see **alled**

ault as in fault,
see **alt**

aulter as in
vaulter,
see **alter**

aults as in faults,
see **alts**

aunch

conch
haunch
launch
paunch
staunch

aunder as in
launder,
see **onder**

aunt

aunt
daunt
flaunt
gaunt
haunt
jaunt
taunt
want

bouffant
Vermont

confidante
debutante
dilettante
nonchalant
restaurant

bouffant

aur as in dinosaur,
see **ore**

ause

cause
clause
claws
flaws
gauze
jaws
laws
pause
paws
straws
vase

applause
because
jigsaws
lost cause
outlaws
seesaws

Santa Claus

Wizard of Oz

aust as in exhaust,
see **ost 2**

aut as in taut,
see **ot**

avage

ravage
savage

ave

brave

cave
crave
gave
grave
knave
pave
rave
save
shave

shave

slave
waive
wave

behave
brainwave
engrave
forgave
heat wave
shockwave

aftershave
galley slave
microwave

misbehave
rant and rave
tidal wave

avel
gavel
gravel
travel

unravel

aver
braver
favor
flavor
savor
shaver
waiver
waver

disfavor
flag-waver
lifesaver
time-saver

avery
Avery
bravery
savory
slavery

unsavory

avity
cavity
gravity

depravity

law of gravity

avor as in favor,
 see aver

avy
gravy
navy
wavy

aw
ah
awe
blah
claw
draw
flaw
gnaw
hah
jaw
law
ma
pa
paw
raw
saw
spa
straw
thaw

ga-ga
grandma
grandpa

ha ha
hoopla
hurrah
jigsaw
last straw
outdraw
outlaw
seesaw
southpaw
Utah
withdraw

Arkansas
hem and haw
la-de-da
Mardi Gras
Omaha
Panama
Wichita

awed

awed
broad
Claude
clawed
clod
flawed
fraud
gnawed
God
mod
nod
odd
pawed

plod
pod
prod
quad
rod
sawed
squad
Todd
trod
wad

abroad
applaud
Cape Cod
facade
hot rod
outlawed
pea pod
seesawed
slipshod
spit-wad
tightwad
tripod
vice squad

act of God
cattle prod
firing squad
fishing rod
goldenrod
hemmed and hawed
land of Nod
lightning rod
promenade

riot squad

awful

awful
lawful
waffle

falafel
unlawful

awk as in hawk,
   see OCK

awks as in hawks,
   see OX

awky

cocky
gawky
hockey
jockey
rocky
stocky

disc jockey

disc jockey

ice hockey
Milwaukee
Jabberwocky

teriyaki
walkie-talkie

awl as in crawl,
  see all
awled as in
  crawled,
  see alled
awler as in
  brawler,
  see aller
awly as in
  crawly,
  see olly

awn

con
dawn
don
drawn
fawn
gone
John
lawn
on
pawn
Ron
spawn
swan
yawn

Antoine
baton

bonbon
Cézanne
chiffon
coupon

leprechaun

doggone
Don Juan
ex-con
Iran
long gone
pecan
python
run-on
Saigon
salon
Szechwan
Taiwan
Tucson
upon
withdrawn
wonton
Yukon

Yvonne

Amazon
Audubon
Avalon
Babylon
crack of dawn
decathlon
Genghis Khan
hanger-on
hexagon
leprechaun
liaison
marathon
Mazatlán
octagon
off and on
overdrawn
paragon
Parmesan
pentagon
pro and con
silicon
talkathon
woebegone

phenomenon
Saskatchewan

awned as in
  dawned,
  see ond
awns as in lawns,
  see ons

40

awny

bonny
brawny
Connie
Johnny
scrawny
tawny

aws as in claws,
see ause

ax

acts
ax
backs
cracks
facts
fax
jacks
lacks
lax
packs
plaques
quacks
racks
sacks
sax
shacks
slacks
smacks
snacks
stacks
tax

tracks
wax
yaks

attacks
attracts
climax
contacts
distracts
drawbacks
earwax
haystacks
ice packs
kayaks
lilacs
reacts
relax
subtracts
thumbtacks
unpacks
wisecracks

artifacts
Cadillacs
candle wax
Cracker Jacks
heart attacks
income tax
interacts
jumping jacks
maniacs
overacts
railroad tracks

overreacts

axi

taxi
waxy

ay

bay
bray
clay
day
fray
gay
gray
hay
hey
lay
may
nay
neigh
pay
play
pray
prey
ray
say
slay
sleigh
spray
stay
stray
sway
they
tray
way

weigh

away
ballet

ballet

birthday
blue jay
bouquet
café
croquet
decay
delay
display
essay
forte
gangway
halfway
hallway
headway
highway
ice tray
Norway
obey

okay
one-way
railway
relay
repay
role-play
runway
someway
stairway
stingray
subway
survey
Taipei
today
weekday
x-ray

by the way
day by day
disobey
everyday
faraway
holiday
matinee
Milky Way
night and day
play-by-play
protégé
PTA
right-of-way
runaway
San Jose
Santa Fe
stowaway

throwaway
tooth decay
underway
USA
yesterday

any which way
April Fools' Day
day after day
far and away
happy birthday
out of the way
rub the wrong way
Saint Patrick's Day
vitamin A

ayed as in played,
see ade 1

ayer

grayer
layer
mayor
player

betrayer
conveyor
soothsayer
surveyor
taxpayer

ays as in days,
see aze

aze

bays

blaze
craze
days
daze
faze
gaze
glaze
graze
haze
laze
maze
nays
pays
phase
phrase
plays
praise
prays
raise
rays
slays
sprays
stays
strays
sways
trays
ways
weighs

ablaze
always
amaze
ballets
betrays

birthdays
blue jays
bouquets
cafés
decays
delays
displays
essays
hallways
obeys
okays
outweighs
portrays
railways
repays
rephrase
school days
sideways
stargaze
subways
surveys
trailblaze
x-rays

disobeys
gamma rays
holidays
mayonnaise
nowadays
paraphrase
runaways

azon

blazon

brazen
raisin

emblazon

azy

crazy
daisy
hazy
lazy

stir-crazy
upsy-daisy

azz

as
has
jazz
razz

pizzazz
topaz

Alcatraz
razzmatazz

azzy

jazzy
snazzy

e

e as in be,
see **ee**

ea as in flea,
see **ee**

each

beach
bleach
each
leech
peach
preach
reach
screech
speech
teach

free speech
impeach
outreach

figure of speech

eacher

bleacher
creature
feature
preacher
screecher
teacher

creature

ead 1 as in plead,
see **eed**

ead 2 as in bread,
see **ed**

eader 1 as in leader,
see **eeder**

eader 2 as in deader,
see **etter**

eady as in ready,
see **etty**

eager

eager
meager
Little Leaguer
overeager

eagle as in beagle,
see **egal**

eague

league

big league
blitzkrieg
colleague
fatigue
intrigue
Little League

eak 1 as in weak,
see **eek**

eak 2 as in break,
see **ake**

eaker

beaker
peeker
sneaker
speaker
weaker

loudspeaker

eaky

creaky
freaky
geeky
leaky
sneaky
squeaky

eal as in real,
see **eel**

ealed as in healed,
see **ield**

eally

freely
really
wheelie

ideally
Swahili

ealous

jealous
tell us
zealous

expel us

overzealous

eam as in dream,
see eem

eamy

creamy
dreamy
Mimi
preemie
steamy
sashimi

ean as in bean,
see een

eap as in leap,
see eep

eaper as in cheaper,
see eeper

ear 1 as in pear,
see air

ear 2 as in year,
see eer

earch as in search,
see urch

earer

clearer
dearer
mirror
nearer
severer
sincerer
interferer

earful

cheerful
earful
fearful
tearful

earl as in pearl,
see url

early as in pearly,
see urly

earn as in learn,
see urn

earse as in hearse,
see erse

earth as in earth,
see irth

eary as in weary,
see eery

eas as in fleas,
see eeze

ease 1 as in please,
see eeze

ease 2

cease
crease
fleece
geese
grease
Greece
lease
niece
peace
piece

apiece
caprice
Clarisse
Cochise
decease
decrease
hairpiece
increase
Matisse
Maurice
obese
police
release
timepiece
wild geese

world peace

centerpiece
elbow grease
Golden Fleece
masterpiece

masterpiece

piece by piece
press release
time-release

all in one piece
gaggle of geese
secret police

justice of the peace

eason

reason
season
treason

out of season
stands to reason

east

beast

ceased
creased
east
feast
greased
least
pieced
priest
yeast

deceased
decreased
Far East
increased
Near East
policed
released

Middle East
wildebeest

last but not least

beauty and the beast

easure

measure
pleasure
treasure

displeasure
tape measure

easy

breezy
cheesy
easy

queasy
sneezy

Parcheesi
uneasy
Zambezi

eat 1 as in beat,
   see eet

eat 2 as in great,
   see ate

eat 3 as in sweat,
   see et

eaten

beaten
cretin
eaten
neaten
sweeten

browbeaten
moth-eaten

moth-eaten

weatherbeaten

eater as in heater,
see **eeder**

eath 1

breath
death

bad breath
Macbeth

kiss of death
out of breath
scared to death
starve to death

Elizabeth
tickled to death

eath 2

Keith
teeth
wreath

beneath
bequeath
false teeth

underneath

eather

feather
Heather
leather
tether
weather
whether

fair-weather
together

altogether
get-together
tar and feather

birds of a feather
light as a feather
under the weather

eature as in
creature,
see **eacher**

eaty as in meaty,
see **eedy**

eave

eve
grieve
heave
leave
sleeve
Steve
weave
we've

achieve
believe
conceive
deceive
naive
perceive
pet peeve
receive

relieve
retrieve
shirtsleeve
sick leave

Christmas Eve
make believe
Tel Aviv

Adam and Eve

eaver

beaver

cleaver
fever
weaver

beaver

achiever
believer
hay fever
meat cleaver
receiver
spring fever

basket weaver
eager beaver
nonbeliever
scarlet fever

golden retriever
overachiever

47

underachiever

ebble

pebble
rebel
treble

eck

check
Czech
deck
fleck
heck
neck
peck
speck
trek
wreck

Aztec
high tech
paycheck
Quebec
raincheck
roughneck
shipwreck
spot-check
Star Trek

bottleneck
discotheque
double-check
hit the deck
hunt and peck
leatherneck

neck and neck
rubberneck
turtleneck

pain in the neck

ecked as in
checked,
see ect

eckle

freckle
heckle
Jekyll

ecks as in decks,
see ex

ecord

checkered
record

ect

checked
decked
flecked
sect
trekked
wrecked

affect
collect
connect
correct
defect
detect

direct
dissect
effect
eject
elect
erect
expect
infect
inject
insect
inspect
neglect
object
perfect
project
prospect
protect
reflect
reject
respect
select
shipwrecked
subject
suspect

architect
disconnect
disinfect
disrespect
double-checked
incorrect
indirect
intellect
intersect

recollect
reelect
self-respect
sound effect

cause and effect

ection

section

affection
collection
complexion
conception
connection
correction
cross-section
dejection
direction
ejection
election
infection
inflection
injection
inspection
objection
perfection
protection
reflection
rejection
selection

imperfection
interjection
intersection

recollection
resurrection

house of correction
sense of direction

ective

defective
detective
effective
elective
objective
perspective
reflective
selective
subjective

ineffective
retrospective

overprotective

ector

Hector
nectar
specter

collector
connector
defector
detector
director
inspector
projector
protector
reflector

ects as in insects,
see ex

ed

bed
bled
bread
bred
dead
dread
Ed
fed
fled
head
lead
led
read
red
said
shed
shred
sled
sped
spread
Ted
thread
tread
wed

ahead
bald head
behead
biped

bald head

49

blockhead
bloodshed
bobsled
bonehead
bunk bed
Club Med
coed
deathbed
drop dead
egghead
forehead
French bread
hardhead
homestead
ill-bred
inbred
instead
misread
moped
proofread
purebred
redhead
sickbed
spoonfed
spearhead
unsaid
unwed
well-bred
well-fed
widespread

arrowhead
bottlefed
city-bred

figurehead
gingerbread
Grateful Dead
infrared
knucklehead
letterhead
newlywed
overfed
overhead
sleepyhead
straight ahead
Sudafed
thoroughbred
underfed
waterbed

early to bed
full speed ahead
hole in the head
out of your head

edal as in pedal,
see **eddle**

edder as in
shredder,
see **etter**

eddle
Gretel
kettle
medal
meddle
metal
pedal

peddle
petal
settle

backpedal
gold medal
rose petal
teakettle
unsettle

heavy metal

Hansel and Gretel

ede as in precede,
see **eed**

edge
dredge
edge
hedge
ledge
pledge
veg
wedge

allege
on edge

edic
comedic

orthopedic

edicate
dedicate
medicate

edo

Frito
neat-o
veto

bandito
Benito
burrito
Toledo
torpedo
tuxedo

incognito

ee

be
bee
fee
flea
flee
free
gee
glee
he
key
knee
me
pea
plea
sea
see
she
ski
spree

tea
tee
three
tree
we

agree
carefree
CD
deep-sea
degree
emcee
home free
ID
MD
Marie
monkey
off-key
peewee
queen bee
RV
sightsee
sweet pea
tax-free
tee hee
tepee

absentee
bumblebee
caffeine-free
chimpanzee
Christmas tree
disagree
DVD

employee
fancy free
guarantee
jamboree
nominee

oversee
pardon me
pedigree
PhD
referee
refugee
Rosemarie
shopping spree
spelling bee
sugar-free
Tennessee
VIP
water ski
worry-free

college degree
family tree
fiddle-de-dee
land of the free

under lock and key
Washington, DC

eech as in speech, see each

eed

bead
bleed
breed

creed
deed
feed
freed
greed
heed
knead
kneed
lead
need
plead
read
reed
seed
skied
speed
steed
treed
tweed
weed

agreed
concede
exceed
force-feed
full speed
impede
indeed
lip-read
mislead
nosebleed
precede
proceed
proofread

recede
seaweed
speed-read
stampede
succeed

centipede
disagreed
guaranteed
overfeed
refereed
supersede
tumbleweed
up to speed

eeder

beater
bleeder
cedar
cheater
eater
feeder
heater
leader
liter
meter
neater
Peter
reader
speeder
sweeter
teeter
weeder

anteater

bandleader
born leader
cheerleader
fire eater
gang leader
impeder
mind-reader
proofreader
repeater
ringleader
Saint Peter
two-seater

centimeter
kilometer
meter reader
overeater
parking meter
trick-or-treater

eedle

beetle
needle
wheedle

eedy

beady
greedy
meaty
needy
seedy
speedy
sweetie
treaty

weedy

entreaty

graffiti

peace treaty

Tahiti

eef as in beef,
   see ief

eek

beak

bleak

cheek

creak

creek

freak

geek

Greek

leak

meek

peak

peek

pique

reek

seek

shriek

sleek

sneak

speak

squeak

streak

tweak

weak

week

antique

boutique

critique

midweek

misspeak

mystique

oblique

physique

pip-squeak

technique

unique

cheek-to-cheek

Chesapeake

hide-and-seek

so to speak

tongue in cheek

eeker as in peeker,
   see eaker

eel

deal

eel

feel

heal

heel

keel

kneel

meal

peel

real

reel

seal

squeal

steal

steel

teal

veal

wheel

zeal

appeal

bastille

big deal

cartwheel

cartwheel

chenille

conceal

congeal

fair deal

for real

genteel

high heel

ideal

misdeal

mobile

newsreel

oatmeal

53

ordeal
piecemeal
reveal
unreal

bookmobile
Ferris wheel
glockenspiel
no big deal
Oldsmobile

automobile

eeled as in peeled,
see ield

eem

beam
cream
deem
dream
gleam
ream
scheme
scream
seam
seem
steam
stream
team
teem
theme

bloodstream
daydream
downstream

drill team
esteem
extreme
ice cream
mainstream
moonbeam
pipe dream
redeem
regime
sunbeam
supreme
whipped cream

color scheme
double-team
let off steam
self-esteem
sour cream

een

bean
clean
dean
gene
glean
green
jean
keen
lean
mean
queen
scene
screen
seen

queen

sheen
teen

Bactine
between
caffeine
canteen
chlorine
Colleen
convene
cuisine
Darlene
dry clean
eighteen
Eugene
fifteen
fourteen
green bean
hygiene
Irene
Kathleen
machine
marine
Marlene
Maxine
mob scene
obscene
preteen
prom queen
protein
ravine
routine
sardine
serene

e

sixteen
smokescreen
sunscreen
thirteen
unseen
vaccine

evergreen
fairy queen
gasoline
go-between
guillotine
Halloween
intervene
jelly bean
Josephine
kerosene
lean and mean
limousine
magazine
Maybelline
mezzanine
movie screen
nectarine
nicotine
quarantine
serpentine
seventeen
squeaky clean
submarine
sweet sixteen
tambourine
tangerine
trampoline

Vaseline

eep

beep
bleep
cheap
creep
deep
heap
jeep
keep
leap
peep
reap
seep
sheep
sleep
steep
sweep
weep

asleep
Bo Peep
junk heap
knee-deep
skin-deep

beauty sleep
oversleep

eeper

beeper
cheaper
creeper
deeper

keeper
reaper
sleeper
steeper
sweeper
weeper

housekeeper
timekeeper

eepy

creepy
sleepy

tepee
weepy

sleepy

eer

beer
cheer
clear
dear
deer
ear
fear
gear
hear
here
jeer
leer

mere
near
peer
pier
rear
sheer
smear
sneer
spear
sphere
steer
tear
tier
veer
year

adhere
all clear
appear
career
cashier
cashmere
frontier
leap year
pierced ear
premier
reindeer
root beer
severe
Shakespeare
sincere
unclear

atmosphere

auctioneer
buccaneer
cavalier
chandelier
crystal clear
disappear
engineer
far and near
free and clear
hemisphere
insincere
interfere
loud and clear
Mouseketeer
musketeer
mutineer
never fear
overhear
Paul Revere
persevere
pioneer
racketeer
reappear
souvenir
stratosphere
volunteer

eery

cheery
dearie
dreary
eerie
leery

query
teary
theory
weary

hara-kiri

ees as in bees,
   see **eeze**

eese as in geese,
   see **ease 2**

eet

beat
beet
bleat
cheat
eat
feat
feet
fleet
greet
heat
meat
meet
neat
Pete
pleat
seat
sheet
sleet
street
suite
sweet

treat
tweet
wheat

athlete
backseat
browbeat
cold feet
compete
complete
conceit
concrete
deadbeat
deceit
defeat
delete
discreet
discrete
elite
excrete
flat feet
heartbeat
mistreat
off-beat
petite
receipt
repeat
retreat
secrete
upbeat
Wall Street

bittersweet
incomplete

indiscreet
overeat
parakeet
short and sweet
shredded wheat
stocking feet
trick or treat
two left feet

red as a beet
Sesame Street

eeter as in
sweeter,
see **eeder**

eethe
breathe
seethe
teethe

eeve as in sleeve,
see **eave**

eeze
bees
breeze
cheese
ease
fees
fleas
flees
frees
freeze
keys

knees
peas
pleas
please
seas
sees
seize
skis
sneeze

sprees
teas
tease
these
trees
wheeze

agrees
big cheese
Chinese
cream cheese
deep freeze
degrees
disease
displease
foresees
high seas
Louise
monkeys

sneeze

57

sea breeze
sweet peas
tepees
trapeze
TVs

ABCs
Androcles
antifreeze
bumblebees
chickadees
chimpanzees
cottage cheese
disagrees
dungarees
guarantees
Hercules
ill at ease
jamborees
Japanese
nominees
overseas
oversees
pedigrees
pretty please
referees
shopping sprees
Siamese
Socrates
water skis

eezer

Caesar
freezer

geezer
squeezer
tweezer

eezy as in breezy, see easy

ef

chef
clef
deaf
Jeff
ref

eft

deft
left
theft

eg

beg
egg
Greg
keg
leg
Meg
peg

nest egg
renege
Winnipeg

egal

beagle
eagle

legal
regal

bald eagle

bald eagle

illegal

egion

legion
region

collegian
Norwegian

eigh as in sleigh, see ay

eight as in weight, see ate

eighty as in weighty, see ady

eir as in their, see air

eist as in heist,
see iced

eit as in conceit,
see eet

eive as in receive,
see eave

el as in hotel,
see ell

elch

belch
squelch
welch

eld

held
jelled
meld
quelled
shelled
spelled
weld
yelled

beheld
compelled
excelled
expelled
handheld
misspelled
propelled
rebelled

repelled
upheld
withheld

unparalleled

elf

elf
self
shelf

bookshelf
herself
himself
itself
myself
yourself

ell

bell
belle
cell
dwell
fell
gel
hell
jell
Nell
sell
shell
smell
spell
swell
tell
well
yell

Adele
bombshell
compel
doorbell
dumbbell
eggshell
excel
expel
farewell
gazelle
hotel
inkwell
jail cell
lapel
Maxwell
misspell
motel
Noel
nutshell
pastel
propel
Raquel
rebel
repel
retell
schoolbell
sleighbell
unwell

carousel
clientele
dinner bell
Isabel
magic spell

NFL
oil well
parallel
personnel
Raphael
show and tell
Tinker Bell
very well
William Tell
wishing well

clear as a bell
mademoiselle

ella

Della

fortune-teller

Ella
fella
Stella

umbrella

a cappella
Cinderella
Isabella
mozzarella

ellar as in stellar, see **eller**

elle as in belle, see **ell**

elled as in spelled, see **eld**

eller

cellar
dweller
feller
seller
speller
stellar
teller
yeller

cave dweller
propeller
storm cellar

fortune-teller
interstellar
Rockefeller

ello as in cello, see **ellow**

ellow

bellow
cello
fellow
hello
Jell-O

mellow
yellow

Longfellow
marshmallow

elly

belly
deli
jelly
Kelly
Nellie
Shelley
smelly

New Delhi
potbelly

elp

help
kelp
yelp

elt

belt
Celt
dealt
felt
knelt
melt
pelt
svelte
welt

heartfelt
seat belt

elter
shelter
smelter
swelter

helter-skelter

elve
delve
shelve
twelve

em
gem
hem
stem
them

AM
condemn
FM
PM

ember
ember
member

December
gang member
November
remember
September

emble
tremble

assemble
resemble

eme as in theme, see eem

empt
dreamt
tempt

attempt
contempt
exempt

en
Ben
den
hen
men
pen
ten
than
then
when
yen

again
amen
bullpen
Cheyenne
hang ten
pigpen
playpen

Adrienne
lion's den

mother hen

mother hen

now and then
poison pen

ena
Gina
Tina

arena
cantina
Christina
hyena
marina
subpoena

Argentina
ballerina
Pasadena

ence as in fence, see ense

ench
bench
clench
drench
French

61

quench
stench
trench
wrench

park bench
unclench

monkey wrench

encher as in
quencher,
see **enture**

encil

pencil
stencil

utensil

end

bend
blend
end
friend
lend
mend
penned
send
spend
tend
trend

amend
ascend
attend
best friend

boyfriend
dead end
defend
depend
descend
extend
girlfriend
intend
offend
pretend
suspend
transcend
unbend
upend
wit's end

apprehend
bitter end
comprehend
dividend
end-to-end
man's best friend
overspend
recommend

fair-weather friend

ender

blender
fender
gender
lender
render
sender
slender

splendor
tender
vendor

bartender
contender
defender
goaltender

goaltender

offender
pretender
surrender
suspender

endor as in
splendor,
see **ender**

ene as in gene,
see **een**

ength

length
strength

enny

any
Benny
Denny
Jenny
Kenny
Lenny
many
penny

ense

cents
dense
dents
fence
gents
scents
sense
tense
tents
vents

commence
condense
defense
dispense
expense
good sense
immense
incense
intense
make sense
nonsense

offense
percents
presents
pretense
resents
sixth sense
suspense

common sense
compliments
consequence
evidence
false pretense
no-nonsense
represents
self-defense

dollars and cents

ension as in

tension,
see ention

ensity

density

immensity
intensity

ensive

pensive

defensive
expensive
extensive
intensive
offensive

apprehensive
comprehensive
inexpensive

labor-intensive

ent

bent
cent
dent
gent
Lent
meant
rent
scent
sent
spent
tent
vent
went

air vent
cement
consent
content
descent
dissent
event
extent
for rent
frequent
indent
intent
invent
lament

misspent
percent
present
prevent
repent
resent
torment
well-spent

came and went
circus tent
compliment
discontent
evident
heaven sent
implement
malcontent
represent
underwent

blessed event
experiment
misrepresent

ental

dental
gentle
lentil
mental
rental

judgmental
parental

accidental
continental

departmental
detrimental
elemental
fundamental
governmental
incidental
instrumental
monumental
ornamental
sentimental
temperamental
transcendental

coincidental
environmental
experimental

experiment

enter

center
enter
mentor

dissenter
inventor
off center

presenter
reenter
tormentor

civic center
do not enter
front and center
shopping center

ential

credential
essential
potential
torrential

confidential
deferential
influential
preferential
presidential
residential

ention

mention
pension
tension

attention
convention
detention
dimension
dissension
extension
intention
invention

pretension
prevention
suspension

apprehension
comprehension
hypertension
inattention
intervention
not to mention
three dimension

misapprehension
ounce of prevention

honorable mention

entive

attentive
incentive
inventive
preventive

ently

gently

contently
intently

consequently
evidently
incidentally

entor as in mentor,
see enter

ents as in cents,
see ense

enture

censure
denture
quencher
venture

adventure
fist clencher
joint venture
thirst quencher

ep

pep
prep
schlep
step
strep
yep

bicep
doorstep
sidestep

overstep

epped as in
stepped,
see ept

ept

crept
kept
pepped
slept
stepped

swept
wept

accept
concept
except
inept
rainswept
sidestepped
windswept

intercept
overslept
overstepped

eption

conception
deception
exception
perception
reception

depth perception
interception
misconception

er

blur
burr
err
fir
fur
gr-r-r
her
per

purr
sir
slur
spur
stir
were

astir
Ben Hur
concur
confer
defer
demur
deter
infer
occur
prefer
yes, sir

emperor
him and her

erb as in verb,
see **urb**

erce as in coerce,
see **erse**

erd

bird
blurred
erred
heard
herd
purred
slurred

spurred
stirred
third
word

absurd
backward
Big Bird
blackbird
buzzword
code word
concurred
conferred
crossword
deferred
deterred
forward
inferred
jailbird
lovebird
occurred
one-third
password
preferred
referred
songbird
swearword
transferred
unheard
watchword

afterward
early bird
hummingbird

ladybird
massacred
mockingbird
overheard
reoccurred
self-assured
solemn word
word for word

four-letter word
free as a bird

ere 1 as in sphere,
see **eer**

ere 2 as in there,
see **air**

erer as in sincerer,
see **earer**

erge

merge
purge
splurge
surge
urge
verge

converge
diverge
emerge
submerge

ergent

urgent

detergent
divergent
emergent
insurgent

eria

Syria

Algeria
bacteria
diphtheria
Nigeria
Siberia

cafeteria

erious

serious

delirious
mysterious

erish

bearish
cherish
garish
perish

erit as in merit,
  see arrot
erity as in
  sincerity,
  see arity

erk

clerk

irk
jerk
Kirk
lurk
perk
quirk
shirk
smirk
Turk
work

berserk
brain work
clockwork
footwork
framework
groundwork
guesswork
homework
housework
legwork
network
patchwork
schoolwork
teamwork
woodwork

dirty work
handiwork
out of work
overwork

erky

jerky
murky

perky
quirky
turkey

beef jerky
cold turkey

Albuquerque

erm

firm
germ
perm
squirm
term
worm

affirm
bookworm
confirm
earthworm
glowworm
long-term
midterm
silkworm

pachyderm
wiggle worm

ern as in stern,
  see urn

ernal

colonel
journal
kernel

eternal
external
fraternal
internal
maternal
nocturnal
paternal

ero 1

hero
Nero
zero

ero 2 as in
sombrero,
see arrow

erred as in
transferred,
see erd

error as in terror,
see arer

erry as in cherry,
see ary

erse

curse
hearse
nurse
purse
terse
verse
worse

adverse
coerce
commerce
converse
disperse
diverse
immerse
inverse
rehearse
reverse
submerse
transverse

intersperse
reimburse
universe

ersed as in
conversed,
see irst

ersion

Persian
version

nurse

aversion
coercion
conversion
diversion
excursion
immersion
submersion

ersity

adversity
diversity

university

erson

person
worsen

layperson
spokesperson

ert

Bert
blurt
curt
dirt
flirt
hurt
pert
shirt
skirt
spurt
squirt

alert
assert

avert
convert
covert
desert
dessert
divert
exert
Frankfurt
insert
invert
nightshirt
overt
pay dirt
redshirt
stuffed shirt
subvert
unhurt

extrovert
hula skirt
introvert
miniskirt
smog alert
undershirt

overexert

erter

herder
murder
squirter

absurder
converter
deserter

frankfurter

erve

curve
nerve
serve
swerve
verve

conserve
deserve
hors d'oeuvre
observe
preserve
reserve
self-serve
unnerve

brown-and-serve

ery as in very,
    see ary

escent

crescent

fluorescent
incessant

adolescent
convalescent
effervescent
incandescent
iridescent

esh

flesh

fresh
mesh

enmesh
gooseflesh
refresh

Bangladesh
in the flesh

esident

hesitant
president
resident

esque

desk

burlesque
grotesque

picaresque
picturesque

ess

Bess
bless
chess
dress
guess
less
mess
press
stress
Tess
yes

access
address
bench-press
caress
confess
depress
digress
distress
duress
excess
express
finesse
impress
Loch Ness
oppress
outguess
possess
profess
progress
recess
regress
repress
success
suppress
undress
unless

air express
fancy dress
full-court press
more or less
nonetheless
overdress
printing press

repossess
second-guess
SOS

change of address
nevertheless
pony express

pony express

anybody's guess
freedom of the press
Gettysburg Address

essed as in
  blessed,
  see **est**

esser as in lesser,
  see **essor**

essful
stressful

distressful
successful

ession
freshen
session

aggression
concession
confession
depression
discretion
expression
impression
jam session
obsession
oppression
possession
procession
profession
progression
rap session
recession
refreshen
repression
succession
suppression

indiscretion
self-expression
summer session

essive
aggressive
excessive
expressive
impressive

70

obsessive
oppressive
possessive
progressive

essor

dresser
guesser
lesser
yes, sir

aggressor
assessor
compressor
confessor
hairdresser
oppressor
possessor
processor
professor

professor

successor

fancy dresser
food processor
predecessor
second-guesser
word processor

essy

dressy
Jessie
messy

est

best
blessed
breast
chest
crest
dressed
guessed
guest
jest
messed
nest
pest
pressed
quest
rest
stressed
test
vest
west
zest

addressed
arrest
bird nest
blood test
caressed
Celeste
confessed
conquest
contest
crow's nest
depressed
detest
digressed
distressed
expressed
finessed
fun fest
hope chest
impressed
invest
life vest
next best
obsessed
oppressed
outguessed
possessed
professed
progressed
protest
recessed
repressed
request
screen test

suggest
suppressed
undressed
Wild West

beauty rest
day of rest
decongest
false arrest
hornet's nest
last request
level best
manifest
overdressed
second best
treasure chest
unimpressed

bulletproof vest
medicine chest
permanent-pressed
under arrest

ester

Chester
Esther
fester
jester
Lester
pester
tester

ancestor
court jester
investor

protestor
semester

polyester

estion

question

congestion
digestion
suggestion

decongestion
indigestion
pop the question

out of the question

estor as in

investor,
see ester

et

bet
debt
fret
get
jet
met
net
pet
set
sweat
threat
vet
wet
whet
yet

abet
all set
all wet
brunette
cadet
cold sweat
coquette
Corvette
dragnet
dudette
duet
forget
Jeanette
jet set
no sweat
not yet

court jester

72

Paulette
quartet
regret
reset
sunset
Tibet
upset

alphabet
Antoinette
bassinet
bayonet
Bernadette
better yet
cigarette
clarinet
dripping wet
Juliet
majorette
minuet
out of debt
pirouette
safety net
silhouette
Soviet
suffragette
teacher's pet

mosquito net
national debt
Russian roulette

etal as in metal,
  see **eddle**

etch

etch
fetch
retch
sketch
stretch
wretch

homestretch

ete as in athlete,
  see **eet**

eter as in meter,
  see **eeder**

ether as in
  together,
  see **eather**

etic

athletic
cosmetic
frenetic
genetic
magnetic
pathetic
phonetic
poetic
synthetic

anesthetic
diabetic
dietetic
energetic

sympathetic

apologetic

ette as in brunette,
  see **et**

etter

better
cheddar
deader
debtor
letter
redder
shredder
sweater
wetter

fan letter
forgetter
go-getter
jet setter
love letter
newsletter
trendsetter

doubleheader
paper shredder

etti as in confetti,
  see **etty**

ettle as in kettle,
  see **eddle**

etto

ghetto

73

meadow
falsetto
Gepetto
libretto
stiletto

etty

Betty
Eddie
Freddie
heady
petty
ready
steady
sweaty
Teddy

already
confetti
go steady
machete
spaghetti
unsteady

rough and ready

eur as in
chauffeur,
see ure

evel

bevel
devil
level
revel

daredevil
dishevel

even

Devon
heaven
Kevin
seven

eleven
thank heaven

ever

clever
ever

spaghetti

lever
never
sever
Trevor

endeavor
forever
however
whatever
whenever
wherever
whichever
whoever

ew

blew
blue
boo
brew
chew
clue
crew
cue
dew
do
drew
due
ewe
few
flew
flu
glue
gnu
goo

grew
hue
knew
mew
moo
new
pew
pooh
rue
screw
shoe
slew
stew
sue
threw
through
to
too
true
two
view
who
woo
you
zoo

ado
ah-choo
anew
bamboo
boo-boo
boohoo
brand-new
breakthrough

canoe
cashew
choo-choo
construe
corkscrew
cuckoo
curfew
debut
dog-doo
drive-through
goo-goo
hairdo
horseshoe
how-to
into
IQ
kazoo
kung fu
miscue
misdo
muumuu
on cue
on view
outdo
outgrew
past due
Peru
PU
pursue
redo
renew
review
revue

says who?
see-through
shampoo
snafu
subdue
taboo
tattoo
thank you
true blue
tutu

kung fu

undo
unscrew
unto
untrue
voodoo
who's who
withdrew
world-view

yoo-hoo

avenue
ballyhoo
barbecue
bird's-eye view
black-and-blue
book review
buckaroo
bugaboo
caribou
cockatoo
countersue
curlicue
I love you
impromptu
interview
Irish stew
jujitsu
kangaroo
Malibu
misconstrue
navy blue
no can do
Oahu
overdo
overdue
peek-a-boo
point of view
postage due
quite a few
rendezvous
residue
revenue

stinkaroo
Super Glue
switcheroo
through and through
Timbuktu
toodle-oo
tried and true
two by two
Waterloo
well-to-do
whoop-de-do

catch-22
hullabaloo
out of the blue
red, white, and blue
skeleton crew
Winnie the Pooh

cock-a-doodle-doo
panoramic view

ewd as in shrewd,
see **ude**

ewed as in
brewed,
see **ude**

ews as in chews,
see **use 2**

ewy
buoy
chewy
dewy

gooey
phooey
screwy

chop suey
mildewy

ex
checks
decks
ex
flecks
flex
hex
necks
pecks
sex
treks
vex
wrecks

affects
annex
apex
collects
complex
connects
corrects
defects
detects
directs
duplex
effects
ejects
elects

erects
expects
index
infects
injects
insects
inspects
Kleenex
neglects
objects
perfects
perplex
projects
prospects
protects
reflects
reflex
rejects
respects

selects
subjects
suspects

architects
birth defects
dialects
disconnects
double-checks
intersects
reelects
rubbernecks
sound effects

exed as in vexed,
see ext

ext
flexed
hexed

next
text
vexed

annexed
context
indexed
perplexed

ey 1 as in monkey,
see ee

ey 2 as in they,
see ay

eyor as in
conveyor,
see ayer

eys as in keys,
see eeze

reelects

i

i as in alibi,
  see y

iable

liable
pliable
viable

reliable

justifiable
undeniable
unreliable

ial as in trial,
  see ile 1

iance

clients
giants
science

alliance
appliance
defiance
reliance

iant

Bryant
client
giant
pliant

defiant
reliant

self-reliant

ib

bib
crib
fib
glib
nib
rib

ad lib
prime rib
sparerib

women's lib

ibble

dribble

giant

kibble
nibble
quibble
scribble
Sibyl

ibe

bribe
gibe
scribe
tribe

describe
imbibe
inscribe
prescribe
subscribe
transcribe

diatribe

ibit

ad-lib it
exhibit
inhibit
prohibit

flibbertigibbet

ic as in picnic,
  see ick

ice 1

dice
ice
lice

mice
nice
price
rice
slice
spice
splice
twice
vice

advice
concise
device
entice
no dice
precise
sale price
suffice
think twice

merchandise
paradise
sacrifice
three blind mice

at any price
fool's paradise
legal advice
self-sacrifice
sugar and spice

ice 2 as in police,
   see ease 2

iced

diced

heist
iced
priced
sliced
spiced

enticed
high-priced
sufficed

overpriced
poltergeist
sacrificed

ich as in rich,
   see itch

icial

initial
judicial
official

artificial
beneficial
prejudicial
superficial
unofficial

ician as in
   musician,
   see ition

icient

deficient
efficient
omniscient

sufficient
inefficient
insufficient
self-sufficient

icious

vicious

ambitious
auspicious
delicious
fictitious
judicious
malicious
nutritious
suspicious

repetitious
superstitious

icit

kiss it
miss it

dismiss it
elicit
explicit
illicit
implicit
is this it?
solicit

icity

duplicity
ethnicity

79

publicity
simplicity
toxicity

authenticity
domesticity
eccentricity
elasticity
electricity

electricity

ick

brick
chick
click
flick
kick
lick
nick
pick
prick
quick
sick
slick
stick

thick
tick
trick

airsick
beatnik
broomstick
card trick
ChapStick
chopstick
drumstick
handpick
heartsick
homesick
lipstick
lovesick
nitpick
picnic
Saint Nick
seasick
sidekick
slapstick
toothpick
yardstick

candlestick
dirty trick
heretic
lunatic
Moby Dick
nervous tic

icked as in licked, see ict

icken

chicken
quicken
sicken
stricken
thicken

grief-stricken
spring chicken

panic-stricken
rubber chicken

icker

bicker
clicker
flicker
kicker
liquor
picker
quicker
sicker
slicker
sticker
thicker
ticker
wicker

nitpicker
picnicker

city slicker

icket

cricket
picket

thicket
ticket
wicket

ickle

fickle
nickel
pickle
sickle
tickle
trickle

bicycle
dill pickle
icicle
Popsicle
tricycle
vehicle

pumpernickel

hammer and sickle

ickly

prickly
quickly
sickly
thickly
tickly

icks

bricks
chicks
clicks
fix
flicks

kicks
licks
mix
nicks
nix
picks
pricks
six
sticks
ticks
tricks
wicks

cake mix
chopsticks
conflicts
drumsticks
evicts
lipsticks
nitpicks
picnics
pinpricks
predicts
quick fix
restricts
toothpicks
transfix

bag of tricks
contradicts
fiddlesticks
pick-up-sticks
politics
ton of bricks

icky

icky
Mickey
Nicky
picky
quickie
sticky
tricky
Vicki

icle as in vehicle,
 see ickle

ics as in politics,
 see icks

ict

clicked
flicked
kicked
licked
nicked
picked
pricked
slicked
strict
ticked
tricked

afflict
conflict
convict
evict
handpicked

Popsicle

81

inflict
nitpicked
picnicked
predict
restrict

contradict
derelict

iction

diction
fiction
friction

addiction
conviction
eviction
nonfiction
prediction
restriction

benediction
contradiction
drug addiction
jurisdiction
science fiction

ictor

stricter
tricked 'er
victor

constrictor
predictor

contradictor

icts as in conflicts,
see icks

icy

icy
pricey
spicy

nicey-nicey

id

bid
did
grid
hid
id
kid
lid
rid
Sid
skid
slid
squid

amid
eyelid
forbid
hybrid
Madrid
outbid
outdid
redid
whiz kid

arachnid

overdid
pyramid

idal as in tidal,
see idle

idden

bidden
hidden

bedridden
forbidden

overridden

idder as in
bidder,
see itter

iddle

brittle
diddle
fiddle
griddle
little
middle
piddle
riddle
twiddle
whittle

acquittal
belittle
committal
hospital
transmittal

82

Chicken Little
noncommittal
peanut brittle
second fiddle

little by little

iddy as in giddy,
see itty

ide
bride

bride

chide
cried
died
dried
dyed
eyed
fried
glide
guide
hide

lied
pride
pried
ride
shied
side
sighed
slide
snide
spied
stride
tide
tied
tried
vied
wide

applied
aside
bedside
beside
bright-eyed
chloride
cockeyed
collide
confide
cross-eyed
decide
deep-fried
defied
denied
divide
fireside
implied

inside
joyride
landslide
misguide
outside
provide
relied
replied
reside
riptide
roadside
subside
supplied
tongue-tied
untied
worldwide

clarified
coincide
dignified
eagle-eyed
far and wide
glorified
horrified
horseback ride
justified
magnified
modified
multiplied
notified
occupied
pacified
petrified
qualified

83

satisfied
side by side
slip and slide
teary-eyed
terrified
verified

disqualified

firefighter

dissatisfied
exemplified
here comes the bride
identified
insecticide
Jekyll and Hyde
personified
preoccupied
unsatisfied

ider

biter

brighter
cider
fighter
glider
lighter
rider
slighter
spider
tighter
whiter
wider
writer

crime fighter
divider
firefighter
ghostwriter
hang glider
highlighter
insider
moonlighter
nail biter
outsider
provider
songwriter
typewriter

idge

bridge
fridge
ridge

abridge
drawbridge

idious

hideous
fastidious
insidious

idity

acidity
cupidity
humidity
morbidity
stupidity
timidity
validity

idle

bridal
bridle
idle
idol

nail biter

tidal
title
vital

entitle
recital
subtitle

homicidal

idy

flighty
Friday
Heidi
ID
mighty
nightie
tidy

almighty
untidy

Aphrodite
high and mighty

ie as in pie,
    see y

iece as in piece,
    see **ease 2**

ied as in lied,
    see **ide**

ief

beef
brief
chief
grief
leaf
reef

thief

thief

belief
corned beef
debrief
fire chief
good grief
motif
relief
roast beef

cloverleaf
disbelief
handkerchief

commander-in-chief

ield

field
healed
peeled
reeled
sealed
shield
yield

appealed
concealed

four-wheeled
high-heeled
mine field
revealed
windshield

ier as in pier,
    see **eer**

ies as in lies,
    see **ize**

iet

buy it
diet
eye it
quiet
riot
try it

iety

piety

anxiety
propriety
society
variety

notoriety

ieve as in grieve,
    see **eave**

iever as in
    believer,
    see **eaver**

ife

knife
life
strife
wife

housewife
jackknife
nightlife
wildlife

husband and wife
larger-than-life

iff

cliff
if
miff
sniff
stiff
tiff
whiff

midriff
scared stiff

iffed as in sniffed, see ift

iffy

iffy
jiffy
spiffy

ific

horrific

Pacific
prolific
specific
terrific

scientific

ift

drift
gift

gift

lift
miffed
rift
shift
sift
sniffed
swift
thrift
whiffed

airlift
face-lift
makeshift
night shift

shoplift
ski lift
snowdrift
spendthrift
uplift

ifty

fifty
nifty
shifty
thrifty

ig

big
dig
fig
gig
jig
pig
rig
swig
twig
wig

bigwig
oil rig
shindig

guinea pig
thingamajig

igger

bigger
digger
rigor

snigger
trigger
vigor

ditchdigger
gold digger
hair trigger

iggle

giggle
jiggle
squiggle
wiggle

iggly

giggly
jiggly
squiggly
wiggly

igh as in high, see y

ighs as in sighs, see ize

ight

bite
blight
bright
cite
Dwight
fight
flight

fright
height
kite
knight
light
might
night
plight
quite
right
rite
sight
site
slight
spite
sprite
tight
trite
white
write

airtight
all-night
all right
birthright
bullfight
catfight
daylight
delight
excite
eyesight
finite
firelight
fistfight

flashlight
foresight
forthright
frostbite
gang fight
good night
green light
handwrite
headlight
highlight
hindsight
ignite
incite
indict
insight
invite
limelight
midnight
moonlight
night-light
not quite
outright
playwright
polite
prizefight
recite
red light
searchlight
skintight
snakebite
Snow White
spotlight
stage fright

87

starlight
stoplight
sunlight
termite
tonight
twilight
unite
upright
uptight
white knight

appetite
black and white
civil right
copyright
day and night
dynamite
Fahrenheit
gesundheit
impolite
neon light
neophyte
out-of-sight
overbite
overnight
oversight
parasite
pillow fight
reunite
satellite
socialite

meteorite
opening night

out like a light

ighten

brighten
frighten
heighten
lighten
tighten
whiten

enlighten

ighter as in
  fighter,
  see **ider**

ighty as in
  flighty,
  see **idy**

ign as in sign,
  see **ine 1**

igned as in
  signed,
  see **ind 1**

hiker

igor as in vigor,
  see **igger**

igue as in intrigue,
  see **eague**

ike

bike
hike
like
mic
pike
psych
spike
strike
tyke

alike
dislike
hitchhike
lifelike
unlike
warlike

childlike
hunger strike
ladylike
look-alike
motorbike

iker

biker
hiker
striker

hitchhiker

ild

child
dialed
filed
mild
piled
riled
smiled
styled
tiled
wild

brainchild
exiled
godchild
hogwild
misdialed
misfiled
moonchild
stepchild
stockpiled

ile 1

aisle
dial
file
I'll
isle
mile
Nile
pile
rile

smile
style
tile
trial
vile
while

argyle
awhile
exile
freestyle
high style
lifestyle
meanwhile
nail file
profile
reptile
senile
stockpile
turnstile
woodpile
worthwhile

crocodile
domicile
family style
infantile
juvenile
out of style
rank and file
reconcile
single file

after a while
bibliophile

fingernail file
once in a while

ile 2 as in automobile, see eel

iled as in filed, see ild

ilian as in reptilian, see illion

ility

ability
agility
civility
facility
futility
hostility
humility
mobility
nobility
senility
stability
tranquillity
utility

capability
credibility
disability
durability
flexibility
gullibility

inability
liability
possibility
probability
sensibility
versatility

acceptability
adaptability
amiability
availability
compatibility
dependability
impossibility
responsibility

ilk

bilk
ilk
milk
silk

buttermilk
malted milk

ill

bill
chill
dill
drill
fill
frill
gill
grill
hill

ill
Jill
kill
mill
nil
Phil
pill
shrill
sill
skill
spill

still
thrill
till
trill
will

anthill
Brazil
downhill
dullsville
fire drill
free will
fulfill
goodwill

ill will
instill
oil spill
refill
standstill
treadmill
until
uphill
vaudeville
windmill

chlorophyll
daffodil
dollar bill
game of skill

spill

Jack and Jill
overkill
whippoorwill
windowsill

Buffalo Bill
Capitol Hill
king of the hill
run-of-the-mill

illa

villa

Attila
chinchilla

gorilla
guerilla
Manila
Priscilla
vanilla

ille
as in
bastille,
see **eel**

illed
billed
build
chilled
drilled
filled
frilled
grilled
guild
killed
milled
skilled
spilled
stilled
thrilled
tilled
trilled
willed

fulfilled
rebuild
strong-willed
unskilled

gorilla

overbuild
unfulfilled

iller
chiller
filler
killer
pillar
thriller

pain killer

caterpillar
chiller-diller

illion
billion
million
trillion
zillion

Brazilian
civilian
cotillion
pavilion
reptilian
Sicilian

illow
pillow
willow

Amarillo
armadillo
pussy willow
weeping willow

illy
Billy
chili
chilly
filly
frilly
hilly
lily
Millie
shrilly
silly

water lily
willy-nilly

ilt
built
guilt
hilt
jilt
kilt
lilt
quilt
spilt
stilt
tilt

91

wilt

im

brim
dim
grim
him
hymn
Jim
Kim
limb
prim
rim
skim
slim
swim
Tim
trim
whim

antonym
homonym
pseudonym
sink or swim
synonym

imble

cymbal
nimble
symbol
thimble

imbo

limbo

ime

chime
climb
crime
dime
grime
I'm
lime
mime
prime
rhyme
slime
thyme
time

bedtime
big-time
daytime
enzyme
lifetime
meantime
nighttime
old-time
part-time
pastime
peacetime
prime time
showtime
small-time
sometime
springtime
sublime

wartime

anytime
curtain time
dinnertime
every time
Father Time
maritime
mountain climb
one more time
overtime
pantomime
party time
summertime

all in good time
nursery rhyme
one at a time
partners in crime

once in a lifetime
once upon a time

immer

dimmer
glimmer
grimmer
shimmer
simmer
slimmer
swimmer

swimmer

trimmer

imp

blimp
chimp
crimp
imp
limp
primp
shrimp
skimp
wimp

imple

dimple
pimple
simple

impy

shrimpy
skimpy
wimpy

in

been
bin
chin
din
fin
grin
in
inn
kin
pin

shin
sin
skin
spin
thin
tin
twin
win

again
begin
Berlin
break-in
captain
cave-in
Corryn
drive-in
hairpin
has-been
pigskin
sheepskin
shoo-in
snakeskin
stand-in
tailspin
trash bin
unpin
within

bobby pin
bowling pin
discipline
double chin
Gunga Din

mandolin
next of kin
play to win
Rin Tin Tin
rolling pin
safety pin
thick and thin
violin

fraternal twin
guilty as sin
Rumpelstiltskin
self-discipline

Huckleberry Finn
identical twin
time and time again

ina 1 as in
   ballerina,
   see ena

ina 2

China
Dinah

angina

North Carolina
South Carolina

ince

blintze
chintz
hints
mince
mints

prince
prints
rinse
since
sprints
tints
wince

blueprints
convince
footprints
imprints
misprints

inch

cinch
clinch
finch
flinch
inch
lynch
pinch

inch by inch

inct

blinked
clinked
inked
kinked
linked
winked

distinct
extinct

hoodwinked
instinct
precinct
succinct

ind 1

bind
blind
dined
find
fined
grind
kind
lined
mind
mined
pined
rind
signed
whined
wind

assigned
behind
combined
confined
declined
defined
designed
entwined
headlined
outlined
refined
remind

resigned
snow-blind
streamlined
unkind
unwind

change of mind
colorblind
humankind
intertwined
lemon rind
mastermind
never mind
one-track mind
peace of mind
underlined
undermined
unrefined

boggle the mind
one of a kind

ind 2 as in wind, see inned

indle

dwindle
kindle
spindle
swindle

ine 1

dine
fine
line

mine
nine
pine
shine
shrine
sign
spine
swine
twine
vine
whine
wine

airline
alpine
assign
baseline
beeline
benign
canine
chow line
clothesline
cloud nine
coal mine
coastline
combine
confine
cosign
deadline
decline
define
design
divine
Einstein

entwine
feline
goal line
gold mine
grapevine
guideline
hairline
headline
hemline
hot line
incline
lifeline
neckline
outline
outshine
peace sign

peace sign

pipeline
punch line
recline
refine
resign
shoeshine
sideline

skyline
stop sign
streamline
sunshine

borderline
checkout line
clinging vine
danger sign
dollar sign
draw the line
drop a line
first in line
Frankenstein
intertwine
iodine
out of line
Palestine
picket line
porcupine
rain or shine
rise and shine
storyline
toe the line
traffic fine
underline
undermine
valentine
warning sign

ine 2 as in routine,
   see een

ined as in dined,
   see ind 1

iner

diner
miner
minor
shiner
whiner

airliner
coal miner
designer
eyeliner
headliner
jetliner
one-liner
recliner
shoeshiner

Asia Minor
forty-niner
hair designer

ing

bring
cling
ding
fling
king
ping
ring
sing
sling
spring
sting
string

swing
thing
wing
wring
zing

bee sting
Beijing
class ring
drawstring
earring
first-string
offspring
plaything
porch swing
shoestring
Sing Sing
something
wingding

anything
bathtub ring
boxing ring
diamond ring
ding-a-ling
everything
rite of spring
static cling
teething ring

puppet on a string

inge

binge
cringe

fringe
hinge
singe
tinge
twinge

infringe
syringe

inger 1

finger
linger
ringer
singer
stinger
zinger

bee stinger
folk singer
gunslinger
humdinger
mud slinger
wingdinger

inger 2

binger
ginger
injure

ingle

jingle
mingle
shingle
single
tingle

commingle
Kriss Kringle

ingo

bingo
dingo
gringo
lingo
Ringo

flamingo

flamingo

ingy 1

clingy
dinghy
springy
zingy

ingy 2

dingy
fringy
stingy

ini

beanie
genie

Jeanie
meany
teeny
wienie

bikini
Houdini
linguine
martini
zucchini

eeny meeny
fettuccine
teeny weeny
tortellini

inister

minister
sinister

administer
prime minister

inity

trinity

affinity
divinity
infinity
vicinity

femininity
masculinity

ink

blink
brink

clink
drink
fink
ink
kink
link
mink
pink
rink
shrink
sink
slink
stink
think
wink
zinc

cuff link
hoodwink
hot pink
lip sync
rethink
soft drink

missing link
on the blink
pen and ink
rinky-dink
roller rink
tickled pink

drink

inked as in

blinked,
see inct

97

inkle

crinkle
sprinkle
twinkle
wrinkle

periwinkle
Rip Van Winkle

inky

blinky
dinky
pinkie
slinky
stinky
Twinkie

Helsinki

rinky-dinky

inned

grinned
pinned
sinned
skinned
thinned
wind

downwind
tailwind
thick-skinned
whirlwind
woodwind

bag of wind

disciplined

inner

dinner
grinner
inner
sinner
spinner
thinner
winner

beginner
Berliner
prizewinner

inny

any
Ginny
many
mini
Minnie
ninny
skinny
tinny
whinny

New Guinea

ino 1

rhino

albino

ino 2

Reno

bambino

casino
Latino

Angeleno
cappuccino
Filipino
palomino

int

flint
glint
hint
lint
mint
print
splint
sprint
squint
stint
tint

blueprint
fine print
footprint
imprint
misprint
newsprint
shin splint
spearmint

fingerprint
peppermint
US Mint

inter

printer

splinter
sprinter
winter

midwinter

ints as in hints,
  see **ince**

inus
dryness
Linus
minus
shyness
sinus
slyness
spryness

Your Highness

plus or minus

iny
shiny
spiny
tiny
whiny

ion
Brian
lion
Ryan

Hawaiian

O'Brien
Orion
sea lion

dandelion

ip
blip
chip
clip
dip
drip
flip
grip
gyp
hip
lip
nip
pip
quip
rip
ship
sip
skip
slip
snip
strip
tip
trip
whip
zip

bean dip
catnip
courtship
drag strip
equip
fat lip

field trip
friendship
guilt trip
hardship
hot tip
kinship
Q-tip
round trip
spaceship
unzip

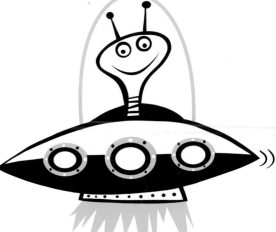

spaceship

battleship
censorship
chips and dip
comic strip
crack the whip
double-dip
ego trip
fellowship

fingertip
Gaza Strip
internship
leadership
membership
ownership
paper clip
penmanship
pirate ship
poker chip
salesmanship
scholarship
skinny-dip
sportsmanship
Sunset Strip

apprenticeship
bargaining chip
championship
chocolate chip
citizenship
companionship
dictatorship
Freudian slip
good sportsmanship
guardianship
one-upmanship
postnasal drip
potato chip
stiff upper lip

ipe

gripe
hype

pipe
ripe
stripe
swipe
type
wipe

bagpipe
peace pipe
pinstripe
pitch pipe
sideswipe
tailpipe
unripe
windpipe

guttersnipe
overripe
prototype

media hype
stereotype

iper

diaper
griper
hyper
piper
sniper
viper
wiper

bagpiper
pied piper
sandpiper

ipped

chipped
clipped
crypt
dipped
dripped
flipped
gypped
nipped
quipped
ripped
script
shipped
sipped
skipped
slipped
snipped
stripped
tipped
tripped
whipped
zipped

equipped
postscript
tight-lipped
transcript

manuscript
nondescript

ipper

chipper
clipper

dipper
dripper
flipper
shipper
sipper
skipper
slipper
tipper
tripper
zipper

Big Dipper
glass slipper

ipple

cripple
ripple
triple

ippy

dippy
drippy
hippie
lippy
nippy
Skippy
snippy
yippee
zippy

Mississippi

ipsy

gypsy
tipsy

ipt as in script,
see **ipped**

iption

conniption
description
Egyptian
inscription
prescription
subscription

ique as in unique,
see **eek**

ir as in stir,
see **er**

ird as in third,
see **erd**

ire

choir
dire
fire
hire
sire
spire
squire
tire
wire

acquire
admire
afire
aspire

hippie

attire
backfire
barbed wire
bonfire
campfire
cease-fire
church choir
conspire
crossfire
desire
entire
expire
flat tire
haywire
hot-wire
inquire
inspire
live wire
on fire
perspire

require
retire
sapphire
satire
spitfire
surefire
transpire

perspire

101

umpire
vampire

ball of fire
overtire
rapid-fire

irk as in smirk,
see **erk**

irl as in twirl,
see **url**

irly as in swirly,
see **urly**

irm as in firm,
see **erm**

irred as in stirred,
see **erd**

irst
burst
cursed
first
nursed
thirst
worst

cloudburst
coerced
conversed
dispersed
feet-first
headfirst
immersed

knockwurst
outburst
rehearsed
reversed
sunburst
well-versed

die of thirst
ladies first
reimbursed
unrehearsed

irt as in skirt,
see **ert**

irth
birth
earth
girth
mirth
worth

childbirth

cloudburst

net worth
rebirth
self-worth
unearth

irty
dirty
flirty
Gertie
squirty
thirty

is 1 as in this,
see **iss**

is 2 as in his,
see **iz**

isco
Crisco
disco
Frisco

Nabisco

San Francisco

ise 1 as in paradise,
see **ice 1**

ise 2 as in rise,
see **ize**

iser as in wiser,
see **izer**

ish
dish

102

fish
squish
swish
wish

cold fish
death wish
goldfish

jellyfish

ision

vision

collision
decision
division
envision
incision
precision
provision
revision

double vision
indecision
split decision
supervision
television
tunnel vision

landmark decision

isk

brisk
disc
disk
frisk

risk
whisk

high risk
slipped disk
tsk tsk

asterisk
floppy disk

isky

frisky
risky
whiskey

ism

prism
quiz 'em
schism

baptism
fascism
racism
realism
truism

activism
atheism
barbarism
chauvinism
communism
criticism
cynicism
egotism
heroism
hypnotism

idealism
journalism
magnetism
mannerism
mysticism
optimism
organism
pacifism
pessimism
plagiarism
skepticism
socialism
symbolism
terrorism
vandalism
witticism

antagonism
cannibalism
capitalism
commercialism
favoritism
patriotism
romanticism
volunteerism

colloquialism
industrialism
materialism
professionalism
sensationalism
spiritualism

individualism
vegetarianism

isor as in visor,
see izer

isp

crisp
lisp
wisp

isper

crisper
lisper
whisper

iss

bliss
hiss
kiss
miss
sis
Swiss
this

amiss
dismiss
near miss

hit or miss

issed as in kissed,
see ist

ission as in
mission,
see ition

issive

missive

admissive
permissive
submissive

issue

issue
kiss you
miss you
tissue

scar tissue

issy

hissy
kissy
missy
prissy
sissy

ist

cyst
fist
gist
hissed
kissed
list
missed
mist
twist
wrist

assist

blacklist
checklist
consist
dismissed
enlist
exist
gymnast
insist
persist
price list
resist
tongue twist

coexist
reminisced
shopping list

enthusiast

istance

distance

assistance
consistence
existence
insistence
long-distance
persistence
resistance

istence as in
existence,
see istance

ister

blister

Mister
sister
twister

stepsister
transistor

istic

mystic

artistic
holistic
linguistic
simplistic
statistic

altruistic
fatalistic
futuristic
optimistic
realistic

animalistic
antagonistic
characteristic
idealistic
opportunistic
ritualistic
unrealistic
vital statistic

istle

bristle
gristle
missile
thistle

whistle
dismissal

istory

blistery
history
mystery

it

bit
fit
flit
grit
hit
it
kit
knit
lit
mitt
pit
quit
sit
skit
slit
spit
split
wit
zit

acquit
admit
armpit
close-knit
cockpit

commit
helmet
legit
mess kit
misfit
moonlit
nitwit
omit
outfit
outwit
permit
pinch-hit
smash hit
snake pit
submit
sunlit
switch-hit
tar pit
tight fit
tool kit
transmit
unfit

advocate
baby-sit
benefit
bit by bit
counterfeit
estimate
first-aid kit
graduate
hypocrite
perfect fit
separate

throw a fit
banana split

banana split

bottomless pit
conniption fit
deliberate
lickety-split

ita

cheetah
pita
Rita

fajita
Juanita

señorita

Santa Anita

ital as in vital, see idle

itch

ditch
glitch
hitch
itch
niche

pitch
rich
snitch
stitch
switch
twitch
which
witch

bewitch
enrich
light switch
unhitch

fever pitch
master switch
strike it rich

ite 1 as in bite, see ight

ite 2 as in petite, see eet

iter as in writer, see ider

ith

myth
smith
with

blacksmith
gunsmith
herewith
locksmith

ither

dither
hither
slither
wither
zither

itic

critic

arthritic

analytic
movie critic
parasitic

itical

critical

political

analytical
hypocritical

ition

mission

addition
admission
ambition
audition
beautician
commission
condition
edition
ignition
magician

musician

musician

nutrition
optician
permission
petition
physician
position
rendition
submission
suspicion
technician
tradition
transition
transmission
tuition

abolition
acquisition

air-condition
ammunition
apparition
coalition
competition
composition
definition
demolition
dietician
disposition
electrician
exhibition
expedition
imposition
inhibition
inquisition
intermission
intuition
malnutrition
obstetrician
politician
premonition
preposition
prohibition
proposition
recognition
repetition
superstition

decomposition
mathematician
out of commission
pediatrician

itious as in ambitious, see **icious**

itis

arthritis
bronchitis
delight us
despite us
excite us
gastritis
invite us

laryngitis
reunite us
tonsillitis

appendicitis

ito as in bandito, see **edo**

its

bits
blitz
fits
flits
grits
hits
its
kits
knits
mitts
pits
quits

sits
skits
slits
spits
splits
spritz
wits
zits

admits
armpits
cockpits
commits
misfits
nitwits
outfits
outwits
permits
tar pits
tidbits
transmits

baby-sits
counterfeits
hypocrites
on the fritz

banana splits
hominy grits

ittal as in acquittal,
see **iddle**

itten

bitten

kitten
mitten
smitten
written

frostbitten
Great Britain
handwritten
typewritten
unwritten

itter

bidder
bitter
critter
fritter
glitter
hitter
kidder
knitter
litter
quitter
sitter
spitter
titter
twitter

consider
low bidder

baby-sitter
kitty litter
reconsider

ittery

glittery

jittery
skittery

ittle as in little,
see **iddle**

itty

biddy
bitty
city
ditty
flitty
giddy
gritty
kiddie
kitty
pity
pretty
witty

committee
self-pity

inner city
itty-bitty
nitty-gritty
Salt Lake City

itz as in blitz,
see **its**

itzy

ditzy
glitzy
Mitzi
ritzy

itsy-bitsy

iva

Godiva
saliva

ival

rival

archrival
arrival
revival
survival

ive 1

dive
drive
five
hive
I've
jive
live
strive
thrive

alive
archive
arrive
beehive
connive
contrive
crash-dive
deprive
high dive
high five

nosedive
revive
skydive
survive
take five
test drive

deep-sea dive
nine-to-five

ive 2

give
live
sieve

forgive
outlive
relive

ivel

civil
drivel
shrivel
snivel
swivel

uncivil

iven

driven
given
striven

forgiven
God-given

power-driven

iver 1

diver
driver

cabdriver
conniver
screwdriver
skydiver
slave driver
survivor

racecar driver

racecar
driver

iver 2

giver
liver
quiver
river
shiver
sliver

chopped liver
deliver
downriver
forgive her

ivity

activity

109

captivity
festivity
nativity

creativity
objectivity
productivity
relativity
sensitivity

insensitivity

radioactivity

ix as in fix,
    see icks

iz

fizz
frizz
his
is
Liz
Ms.
quiz
'tis
whiz

as is
gee whiz
pop quiz
showbiz

izard

blizzard
gizzard
lizard

wizard

ize

buys
cries
dies
dries
dyes
eyes
flies
fries
guise
guys
highs
lies
pies
prize
rise
shies
sighs
size
skies
spies
thighs
ties
tries
vise
wise

advise
applies
arise
baptize
capsize

chastise
clockwise
comprise
defies
denies
despise
devise
disguise
door prize
drip-dries
first prize
franchise
French fries
high-rise
implies
king-size
Levi's
likewise
mud pies
neckties

neckties

outcries
pigsties
relies
replies

revise	glorifies	plagiarize
snake eyes	goo-goo eyes	publicize
sunrise	gratifies	qualifies
supplies	harmonize	ratifies
surprise	horrifies	realize
unties	hypnotize	recognize
unwise	idolize	satirize
wise guys	improvise	satisfies
advertise	jeopardize	scrutinize
agonize	justifies	sensitize
alibis	legalize	signifies
analyze	lullabies	simplifies
authorize	magnifies	socialize
beautifies	memorize	specialize
booby prize	mesmerize	specifies
burglarize	mobilize	stabilize
butterflies	modernize	sterilize
certifies	modifies	stupefies
civilize	mortifies	summarize
clarifies	multiplies	supervise
colonize	mystifies	sympathize
compromise	neutralize	take the prize
criticize	Nobel Prize	tantalize
dragonflies	notifies	televise
dramatize	occupies	tenderize
eagle eyes	organize	terrifies
emphasize	ostracize	terrorize
energize	otherwise	theorize
enterprise	pacifies	tranquilize
exercise	paralyze	traumatize
family ties	pasteurize	unifies
fantasize	patronize	utilize
fertilize	penalize	verbalize

verifies
victimize
vitalize
vocalize

alphabetize
antagonize
apologize
capitalize
categorize
characterize
commercialize
demoralize
demystifies
deodorize
disqualifies
dissatisfies
economize
exemplifies
familiarize
family ties
idealize

identifies
intensifies
little white lies
monopolize
nationalize
personifies
popularize
preoccupies
reorganize
revitalize
romanticize
solidifies
take by surprise
visualize

izer

geyser
miser
riser
visor
wiser

advisor
incisor

advertiser
atomizer
energizer
exerciser
fertilizer
improviser
organizer
supervisor
vaporizer

deodorizer

izz as in frizz,
   see iz
izzard as in
   blizzard,
   see izard

izzle

chisel
drizzle
fizzle
sizzle

izzy

busy
dizzy
fizzy
frizzy
is he?
tizzy

miser

O

O 1

beau
blow
bow
crow
doe
dough
flow
foe
go
glow
grow
Joe
know
low
mow

sew
show
slow
snow
so
stow
though
throw
toe
tow
whoa
woe

aglow
ago
although
below
death row
game show
golf pro
gung ho
heave-ho

no-no
no-show
outgrow
pueblo
rainbow
scarecrow
sideshow
skid row
so-so
talk show
tiptoe
yo-yo

Alamo
apropos
blow by blow
buffalo
calico
cookie dough
cupid's bow
do-si-do
dynamo
ebb and flow
even though
fashion show
fatal blow
friend or foe
heel-and-toe
high and low
Idaho

mow

no
oh
owe
pro
row

hello
info
John Doe
low blow
no-go

Ivanhoe
Jacques Cousteau
long ago
Mary Jo
Mexico
mistletoe
Navajo
Oreo
overflow
piccolo
picture show
radio

radio

ratio
right to know
rodeo
Romeo
Sloppy Joe
sourdough
status quo
stereo
stop and go
studio
talent show
tale of woe
tic-tac-toe
tippytoe
to and fro

Tokyo
touch and go
TV show
undertow
video
yes and no

Geronimo
get-up-and-go
New Mexico
pay as you go
Pinocchio
pistachio
portfolio
ready, set, go

O **2** as in do,
  see ew

oach

broach
coach
poach
roach

approach
cockroach
reproach
stagecoach

oad **1** as in toad,
  see ode

oad **2** as in broad,
  see awed

oaf
loaf
oaf

oak as in soak,
  see oke

oaks as in cloaks,
  see okes

oal as in coal,
  see ole

oam as in foam,
  see ome **1**

oan as in loan,
  see one **1**

oar as in soar,
  see ore

oard as in board,
  see ord **1**

oarder as in boarder,
  see order

oared as in roared,
  see ord **1**

oarse as in coarse,
  see orse

oast as in coast,
  see ost **1**

oat as in coat,
see **ote**

oax as in coax,
see **okes**

ob

blob
bob
daub
glob
gob
job
knob
lob
mob
rob
slob

slob

snob
sob

swab
throb

con job
corncob
doorknob
heartthrob
hobnob
snow job

cotton swab
inside job
shish kebab

corn on the cob
thingamabob

obber

clobber
robber
slobber
sobber

grave robber
macabre

obble

bauble
bobble
gobble
hobble
squabble
wobble

obbler

cobbler

gobbler
hobbler
squabbler
wobbler

cherry cobbler

obby

Bobby
hobby
knobby
lobby
snobby

obe

globe
Job
lobe
probe
robe

bathrobe
disrobe
earlobe
space probe
wardrobe

oble

global
Mobile
mobile
noble

Chernobyl
immobile

115

ocal

focal
local
vocal
yokel

bifocal

ocious

atrocious
ferocious
precocious

supercalifragilistic-
 expialidotious

ocity

atrocity
ferocity
monstrosity
velocity

animosity
curiosity
generosity
reciprocity

ock

Bach
block
chalk
clock
crock
doc
dock

flock
frock
gawk
hawk
Jacques
jock
knock
lock
mock
rock
shock
smock
sock
squawk
stock
talk
walk
wok

back talk
Bangkok
beanstalk
boardwalk
cell block
crosswalk
deadlock
fast-talk
girl talk
gridlock
hard rock
headlock
Hitchcock
jaywalk
jive talk

knock knock
livestock
Mohawk
o'clock
outtalk
padlock
peacock
pep talk
punk rock
roadblock
shamrock
shell shock
Sherlock
sidewalk
sleepwalk
small talk
space walk
sunblock
sweet talk
ticktock
unlock
woodblock

aftershock
alarm clock

alarm clock

auction block
baby talk
butcher block
chopping block
cuckoo clock
culture shock
double talk
laughingstock
mental block
nature walk
out of stock
poppycock
round-the-clock
stumbling block
tomahawk
"What's up, Doc?"
writer's block

ocker

blocker
knocker
locker
rocker
shocker
soccer
talker
walker

fast talker
footlocker
jaywalker
night stalker
sleepwalker

ocket

docket
locket
pocket
rocket
socket

light socket
pickpocket
skyrocket

Davy Crockett

ocks as in rocks,
see ox

ockey as in
hockey,
see awky

ocky as in rocky,
see awky

oco

cocoa
loco

ocracy

autocracy
bureaucracy
democracy
hypocrisy

aristocracy

od as in nod,
see awed

oda as in soda,
see ota

oddle

bottle
coddle
dawdle
model
throttle
toddle
waddle

Aristotle

ode

bowed
code
crowed
flowed
glowed
goad
load
mode
mowed
ode
owed
road
rode
rowed
showed
slowed
snowed
stowed
strode

toad
towed

abode
carload
crossroad
decode
dress code
erode
explode
freeload
implode
Morse code
railroad
tiptoed
truckload
unload
workload
zip code

à la mode
electrode
episode
hit the road
overflowed
overload
penal code
pigeon-toed

area code

odge

dodge
lodge

dislodge

hodgepodge

odious

odious

commodious
melodious

ody

Audi
bawdy
body
Dotty
gaudy
haughty
knotty
naughty
potty
Saudi
Scottie
shoddy
snotty
spotty

embody
homebody
karate
nobody
somebody

antibody
anybody
busybody
student body

everybody
heavenly body

oe 1 as in doe,
 see o 1

oe 2 as in shoe,
 see ew

oes 1 as in shoes,
 see use 2

oes 2 as in goes,
 see ose 2

off

coif
cough
off
scoff
trough

blast off
brush-off
cutoff
kickoff
liftoff
payoff
play-off
rip-off
show-off
trade-off
well-off

on and off
Stroganoff

often

coffin

blast off

118

often
soften

og
bog
clog
dog
flog
fog
frog
grog
hog
jog
log

bulldog
bullfrog
groundhog
hound dog
leapfrog
prologue
road hog

ship's log
top dog
watchdog

catalog
chili dog
dialogue
monologue
synagogue
travelogue
underdog

oggle
boggle
goggle
joggle
ogle

boondoggle

oggy
doggie
foggy
froggy
groggy
smoggy
soggy

ogical
logical

illogical

astrological
biological
chronological

geological
mythological
psychological

ography
biography
demography
geography
photography

bibliography
choreography
oceanography

autobiography

ogue 1
brogue
rogue
vogue

ogue 2 as in
dialogue,
see og

oic
stoic

heroic

oice
choice
Joyce
voice

first choice
no choice

watchdog

119

one voice
rejoice
Rolls-Royce
turquoise

oid

Floyd
Freud
Lloyd
toyed
void

annoyed
avoid
destroyed
devoid
employed
enjoyed
tabloid

asteroid
celluloid
null and void
overjoyed
paranoid
Polaroid
self-employed
unemployed

oil

boil
broil
coil
foil
loyal

oil
royal
soil
spoil
toil

disloyal
gargoyle
hard-boil
recoil
tinfoil
turmoil

oin

coin
groin
join
loin

Des Moines
purloin
rejoin
sirloin

flip a coin
tenderloin

oing as in going,
see owing

oint

joint
point

appoint
ballpoint
checkpoint

high point
pinpoint
viewpoint
West Point

disappoint
focal point
needlepoint
out of joint
starting point

oir as in memoir,
see ar

oise as in noise,
see oys

oke

broke
choke
Coke
croak
folk
joke
oak
poke
smoke
soak
spoke
stoke
stroke
woke
yolk

awoke
cowpoke

dead broke

dead broke

egg yolk
heatstroke
kinfolk
provoke
slowpoke
sunstroke

artichoke
cloud of smoke
Diet Coke
go for broke
holy smoke
okey-doke
poison oak

oken

broken
oaken

spoken
token

awoken
heartbroken
Hoboken
housebroken
love token
misspoken
outspoken
plainspoken
soft-spoken
unbroken
unspoken

oker

broker
choker
joker
poker
smoker

pawnbroker
provoker
stockbroker

mediocre

okes

chokes
cloaks
coax
Cokes
croaks
folks

hoax
jokes
oaks
pokes
smokes
spokes
stokes
strokes
yolks

provokes

artichokes

Diet Cokes

ol 1 as in alcohol,
  see all

ol 2 as in control,
  see ole

ola

cola
Lola

Crayola
Loyola
payola
viola

ayatollah
Coca-Cola
gladiola
Pepsi-Cola

olar

bowler

molar
polar
roller
solar
stroller

controller
high roller
patroller
steamroller

old

bold
bowled

bowled

cold
doled
fold
gold
hold
mold
old
polled
rolled
scold

sold
strolled
told

age-old
behold
billfold
blindfold
cajoled
catch cold
choke hold
consoled
controlled
enfold
enrolled
extolled
foothold
household
ice-cold
out cold
paroled
patrolled
retold
steamrolled
stronghold
threshold
toehold
unfold
untold
withhold

common cold
days of old
good as gold

heart of gold
hot and cold
pigeonholed
pot of gold
rock-and-rolled
self-controlled
solid gold
stranglehold
uncontrolled

out in the cold

older

bolder
boulder
colder
older
shoulder
smolder

cold shoulder
pot holder
shareholder

ole

bowl
coal
dole
foal
goal
hole
Joel
knoll
Lowell
mole

pole
poll
role
roll
scroll
sole
soul
stole
stroll
toll
troll
whole

cajole
charcoal
console
control
Creole
drumroll
egg roll
enroll
extol
fishbowl
flagpole
foxhole
keyhole
loophole
manhole
mud hole
North Pole
parole
patrol
payroll
peephole

porthole
pothole
Rose Bowl
steamroll
tadpole
unroll

buttonhole
camisole
casserole
cruise control
cubbyhole
fishing pole
heart and soul
Old King Cole
pigeonhole
rock and roll
self-control

manhole

starring role
sugar bowl
swimming hole
toilet bowl
Tootsie Roll
totem pole

ace in the hole
body and soul
Hollywood Bowl
out of control
remote control

oled as in cajoled,
see old

olen

colon
Nolan
stolen
swollen

semicolon

olic

colic
frolic

hydraulic
symbolic

chocoholic
diabolic
foodaholic
fun and frolic
sleepaholic
workaholic

olish

polish
smallish
tallish

abolish
demolish

apple-polish
spit-and-polish

olk as in yolk,
see oke

olks as in folks,
see okes

oll 1 as in roll,
see ole

oll 2 as in doll,
see all

ollar as in dollar,
see aller

oller as in roller,
see olar

olley as in trolley,
see olly

ollow as in
follow,
see allow 2

olly

Ali

collie
crawly
dolly
folly
golly
holly
jolly
Molly
Polly
trolley
volley
Wally

by golly
finale
Svengali
tamale

creepy-crawly
grand finale
hot tamale
melancholy

olo

polo
solo

ologist

biologist
ecologist
geologist
psychologist
zoologist

archaeologist

dermatologist
sociologist

ology

anthology
apology
astrology
biology
chronology
ecology
geology
mythology
pathology
psychology
technology
zoology

archaeologist

archaeology
criminology
dermatology
sociology
terminology

meteorology

olster

bolster
holster
oldster
pollster

olt

bolt
colt
dolt
jolt

deadbolt
revolt

lightning bolt

olve

solve

dissolve
evolve
involve
resolve
revolve

oly

goalie
holey

holy
slowly
solely
wholly

parolee
unholy

guacamole
ravioli
roly-poly

om

balm
bomb
calm
Guam
mom
palm
prom
psalm
qualm
tom

A-bomb
dive-bomb
embalm
fire bomb
pompom
sitcom
time bomb
tom-tom
wigwam

intercom
Peeping Tom

supermom
Vietnam

oma

coma

aroma
diploma

Oklahoma

omb 1 as in comb,
see ome 1

omb 2 as in
tomb,
see oom

ome 1

chrome
comb
dome
foam
gnome
home
poem
roam
Rome

Stockholm
syndrome

Astrodome
broken home
foster home
home sweet home
honeycomb

125

metronome
mobile home

palindrome
shaving foam
Superdome

ome 2 as in come,
see **um**

ometer

barometer
kilometer
odometer
speedometer
thermometer

omic

comic

atomic

astronomic
economic
stand-up comic

omination

domination
nomination
abomination

denomination

ommy

mommy
swami
Tommy

pastrami
tsunami

origami

omp

chomp
clomp
romp
stomp
swamp
tromp
whomp

on 1 as in con,
see **awn**

on 2 as in ton,
see **un**

ona

Jonah
Mona

kimono

Arizona
Barcelona

oncho

honcho

poncho

ond

blond
bond
conned
dawned
donned
fawned
fond
pawned
pond
wand
yawned

beyond
doggoned
fishpond
James Bond
respond

correspond

magic wand

vagabond

onder

blonder
condor
fonder
launder
ponder
squander
wander
yonder

onds as in bonds,
see ons

one 1

blown
bone
clone
cone
drone
flown
groan
grown
hone
Joan
known
loan
lone
moan
own
phone
prone
sewn
shone
shown
stone
throne
thrown
tone
zone

alone
backbone
birthstone

cell phone
cologne
condone
cyclone
dethrone
dial tone
disown
end zone
full-blown
full-grown
grindstone
headphone
headstone
homegrown
hormone
jawbone
milestone
outshone
ozone
pay phone
pinecone
postpone
Ramon
rhinestone
sno-cone
T-bone
time zone
tombstone
trombone
unknown
war zone
well-known
windblown

wishbone
baritone
buffer zone
chaperon
cobblestone
combat zone
crazy bone
doggie bone
funny bone
ice cream cone
microphone
moan and groan
monotone
overgrown
rolling stone
saxophone

saxophone

stepping-stone
telephone
twilight zone
xylophone
Yellowstone

127

accident-prone

one 2 as in gone, see awn

one 3 as in done, see un

one 4 as in minestrone, see ony

oney as in money, see unny

ong

dong
gong
long
song
strong
thong
throng
wrong

along
belong
ding-dong
folk song
headlong
headstrong
Hong Kong
King Kong
lifelong
love song
oblong

Ping-Pong
prolong
sarong
so long
swan song

all along
dinner gong
get along
hop-a-long
right or wrong
sing-along
tagalong

oni as in macaroni, see ony

onia

Sonia

ammonia
begonia
Bologna
pneumonia

onial

colonial

ceremonial
matrimonial
testimonial

onic

chronic
phonic
sonic
tonic

bionic
demonic
harmonic
ironic
moronic
Platonic
symphonic

catatonic
electronic
Panasonic
supersonic
telephonic

stereophonic

onica

Hanukkah

harmonica
Veronica

Santa Monica

onical

chronicle
conical
monocle

ironical

onish

admonish
astonish

onk

bonk
honk

konk
zonk

only

lonely
only

one and only
sad and lonely

onna

Donna
Ghana
gonna
sauna
wanna

Chicana
iguana
mañana
piranha

piranha

prima donna
Tijuana

Americana
flora and fauna

onned as in
conned,
see **ond**

onomy

astronomy
autonomy
economy

onor

goner
honor
yawner

dishonor

ons

blonds
bonds
bronze
cons
dawns
dons
fawns
Hans
lawns
pawns
ponds
swans
wands
yawns

batons
ex-cons

icons
long johns
morons
neutrons
pecans
pythons
responds

Amazons
corresponds
leprechauns
marathons
paragons
pros and cons
vagabonds

ont as in front,
see **unt**

onto

pronto
Tonto

Toronto

ony

bony
crony
phony
pony
Sony
stony
Tony

baloney
Shoshone

abalone
alimony
ceremony
macaroni
matrimony
minestrone
pepperoni
rigatoni
sanctimony
testimony

phony-baloney

OO as in zoo,
   see **ew**

ooch

mooch
pooch
smooch

ood 1 as in food,
   see **ude**

ood 2 as in blood,
   see **ud**

ood 3

could
good
hood
should
stood
wood
would

childhood
deadwood
driftwood
falsehood
no-good
redwood
sainthood

brotherhood
fatherhood
Hollywood
likelihood
livelihood
motherhood
neighborhood
pretty good
Robin Hood
sisterhood
understood

misunderstood
Red Riding Hood
so far, so good

finger-licking good

oodle

brutal
doodle
feudal
futile
noodle
poodle
strudel

apple strudel

Yankee Doodle

oody

beauty
bootie
booty
cootie
cutie
duty
fruity
Judy
moody
snooty
Trudy

off duty

bathing beauty
double-duty
heavy duty
Howdy Doody
Sleeping Beauty
tutti-frutti

ooed as in
   shampooed,
   see **ude**

ooey as in gooey,
   see **ewy**

oof 1

goof
poof
proof
roof

spoof
aloof
childproof
fireproof
foolproof
soundproof

oof 2

hoof
roof
woof

oofy

goofy
poofy
spoofy

ook 1 as in

spook,
see uke

ook 2

book
brook
cook
crook
hook
look
nook
rook
shook
took

checkbook

fishhook
handbook
mistook
notebook
outlook
scrapbook
textbook
unhook

Captain Cook
comic book

comic book

dirty look
donnybrook
overlook

gobbledygook

ookie

bookie

cookie
hooky
rookie

ool

cool
drool
fool
fuel
ghoul
mule
pool
rule
school
spool
stool
tool
yule

barstool
car pool
cesspool
gag rule
high school
home rule
mob rule
module
preschool
tidepool
toadstool
whirlpool

April fool
as a rule
golden rule

131

Liverpool
minuscule
molecule
overrule
ridicule
Sunday school
supercool
swimming pool

nobody's fool
nursery school

majority rule

ooler

cooler
crueler
drooler
jeweler
ruler

car pooler
preschooler

oom

bloom
boom
broom
doom
fume
gloom
groom
loom
plume
room
tomb

whom
womb
zoom

assume
bathroom
bridegroom
classroom
consume
costume
courtroom
entomb
exhume
heirloom
homeroom
leg room
mushroom
perfume
presume
restroom

baby boom
bride and groom
elbow room
gloom and doom
locker room
love in bloom
powder room
smoke-filled room
sonic boom

oomer as in
   groomer,
   see umor

oomy

gloomy
roomy

perfumy

oon

croon
dune
goon
June
loon
moon
noon
prune
soon
spoon
strewn
swoon
tune

baboon
balloon
bassoon
buffoon
cartoon
cocoon
commune
fine tune
full moon
harpoon
high noon
immune
lagoon

lampoon
maroon
monsoon
Neptune
platoon
pontoon
raccoon
Rangoon
saloon
spittoon
too soon
twelve noon
tycoon
typhoon

afternoon
Cameroon
Daniel Boone
honeymoon
loony tune
macaroon
opportune
out of tune
pretty soon
trial balloon

hot-air balloon
man in the moon

ooner

crooner
lunar
schooner
sooner
tuner

honeymooner

oop

bloop
coop
coupe
droop
dupe
goop
group
hoop
loop
poop
scoop
sloop
snoop
soup
stoop
swoop

hot-air balloon

troop
troupe
whoop

in-group
peer group
regroup
scout troop

alley oop
chicken soup
hula hoop
inside scoop
nincompoop
pressure group

ooper

blooper
drooper
pooper
scooper
snooper
stupor
super
trooper
trouper

state trooper

paratrooper
party pooper
pooper-scooper
super-duper

oopy

droopy

133

goopy
snoopy
soupy
whoopee

oor 1 as in poor,
see **ure**

oor 2 as in door,
see **ore**

oos as in tattoos,
see **use 2**

oose 1 as in
choose,
see **use 2**

oose 2 as in
moose,
see **use 1**

oost as in roost,
see **uced**

ooster

booster
rooster

oot 1 as in hoot,
see **ute**

oot 2

foot
put
root
soot

afoot
barefoot
Big Foot
hotfoot
input
kaput
output
shotput

pussyfoot
tenderfoot
underfoot

ooter as in
scooter,
see **uter**

ooth

booth
couth
Ruth
sleuth
tooth
truth
youth

Babe Ruth
half-truth
phone booth
sweet tooth
uncouth
untruth

kissing booth
naked truth
snaggletooth

voting booth
fountain of youth
moment of truth

ootie as in cootie,
see **oody**

ooty as in snooty,
see **oody**

ooze as in snooze,
see **use 2**

op

bop
chop
clop
cop
crop
drop
flop
hop
lop
mop
plop
pop
prop
shop
slop
stop
swap
top

Aesop
bebop

bellhop
big top
blacktop
box top
bus stop
cough drop
doorstop
eavesdrop
flattop
flip-flop
gumdrop
hilltop
hip-hop
kerplop
name-drop
nonstop
pawnshop
pit stop
pork chop
raindrop
rooftop
shortstop
sock hop
teardrop
tiptop
treetop
truck stop
workshop

barbershop
belly flop
body shop
coffee shop
curly top

lemon drop
lollipop
mom and pop
mountaintop
party-hop
traffic-stop
window shop

cream of the crop
karate chop

ope

cope
dope
grope
hope
lope
mope
nope
pope
rope
scope
slope

soap
taupe

elope
jump rope
no hope
tightrope
towrope

antelope
bar of soap
cantaloupe
envelope
horoscope
microscope
periscope
stethoscope
telescope

opey

dopey
Hopi
mopey
soapy

opia

utopia

cornucopia
Ethiopia

opic

topic
tropic
subtopic

belly flop

135

microscopic
telescopic

opper

chopper
copper
dropper
pauper
popper
proper
shopper
stopper
topper
whopper

clodhopper
eavesdropper
eyedropper
eyepopper
grasshopper
heartstopper
improper
name-dropper
sharecropper
showstopper
woodchopper

teenybopper
window-shopper

oppy

choppy
copy
floppy
poppy

sloppy
jalopy
serape
carbon copy

option

option
adoption

opy as in copy,
see oppy

or as in for,
see ore

ora

aura
Dora
Nora

angora
fedora
menorah
señora

oral

choral
coral
floral
laurel
moral
oral
quarrel
amoral

immoral
pastoral

orce as in force,
see orse

orch

porch
scorch
torch

ord 1

board
bored
chord
cord
floored
Ford
gourd
hoard
lord
poured
roared
scored
snored
soared
stored
sword
ward
warred

abhorred
aboard
adored
afford

award
backboard
billboard
blackboard
cardboard
chalkboard
dashboard
discord
explored
fjord
ignored
keyboard
landlord
outscored
record
restored
reward
rip cord
scoreboard
skateboard
slumlord
surfboard
toward
washboard

all aboard
boogieboard
checkerboard
diving board
drawing board
harpsichord
overboard
room and board
smorgasbord

sounding board
spinal cord
tape-record
unexplored

across the board
bulletin board
stiff as a board

ord 2 as in word,
see erd

order

boarder
border
courter
hoarder
mortar
order
porter
quarter
shorter

cavorter
court order
exporter
gag order
importer
recorder
reporter
supporter
transporter

flight recorder
law and order
made-to-order

out of order
tape recorder

ore

boar
bore
chore
core
corps
door
drawer
floor
for
four
gore
lore
more
nor
oar
or
poor
pore
pour

pour

137

roar
score
shore
snore
soar
sore
store
swore
tore
war
wore
your

abhor
adore
ashore
before
cold sore
cold war
condor
decor
downpour
drugstore
encore
explore
eyesore
folklore
galore
hard-core
hoped-for
ignore
indoor
mentor
next-door

no more
outdoor
outscore
Peace Corps
postwar
rapport
restore
seashore
señor
ten-four
therefore
trapdoor
uproar

all ashore
antiwar
anymore
apple core
Baltimore
blood and gore
carnivore
civil war
corridor

dinosaur
door-to-door
Ecuador
evermore
furthermore

Marine Corps
matador
metaphor
nevermore
por favor
reservoir
rich or poor
saddle sore
ship-to-shore
Singapore
sophomore
Theodore
troubadour
tug of war
two-by-four
underscore

forevermore
titanosaur

ored as in bored,
see **ord** 1

orge
forge
George
gorge
engorge
Valley Forge

orial
oriole
censorial
memorial

dinosaur

pictorial
tutorial

dictatorial
editorial
territorial

oric

caloric
euphoric
historic

prehistoric
sophomoric

orify

glorify
horrify

orious

glorious

laborious
notorious
uproarious
victorious

ority

authority
majority
minority
priority
seniority
sorority

inferiority
moral majority

silent majority
superiority

orium

emporium

auditorium
crematorium
moratorium

ork 1

cork
dork
fork
pork
stork

New York
pitchfork

ork 2 as in work, see erk

orm 1

dorm
form
norm
storm
swarm
warm

barnstorm
brainstorm
conform
deform
duststorm

free-form
inform
lukewarm
perform
platform
reform
snowstorm
transform

coed dorm
misinform
thunderstorm
uniform

orm 2 as in worm, see erm

ormal

formal
normal

abnormal
informal

semiformal

ormer

former
warmer

barnstormer
benchwarmer
chairwarmer
conformer
informer
performer
reformer

139

transformer

orn

born
corn
horn
morn
mourn
scorn
sworn
thorn
torn
warn
worn

acorn
adorn
airborne
bullhorn
first-born
foghorn
forewarn
forlorn
greenhorn
inborn
lovelorn
newborn
outworn
popcorn
reborn
shoehorn
timeworn
unborn
well-worn

Capricorn
ear of corn
foreign-born
Matterhorn
native-born
unicorn
weatherworn

orning

morning
mourning
warning

flood warning
good morning

tornado warning

orse

coarse
course
force
hoarse
horse

popcorn

source

air force
brute force
clotheshorse
crash course
dark horse
divorce
endorse
enforce
golf course
main course
of course
racehorse
remorse
resource
task force
workforce

charley horse
driving force
reinforce
rocking horse
show of force

collision course
matter of course
obstacle course

ort

court
fort
forte
port
quart

short
snort
sort
sport
thwart
wart

airport
bad sport
cavort
cohort
contort
deport
distort
escort
export
good sport
import
Newport

rocking horse

night court
passport
report
resort
seaport
spoilsport

support
transport

child support
heliport
last resort
Supreme Court
tennis court
traffic court
worrywart

orter as in shorter,
see **order**

orth
fourth
north

come forth

back and forth
July Fourth

so on and so forth

ortify
fortify
mortify

ortion
portion

contortion
distortion
proportion

orty
forty
shorty

sporty
warty

ory
glory
gory
Laurie
quarry
story

love story
Old Glory
rock quarry

allegory
bedtime story
category
hunky-dory
laboratory
lavatory
mandatory
morning glory
purgatory
territory

conservatory
derogatory
explanatory
obligatory
reformatory

os 1 as in cosmos,
see **ose 1**

os 2 as in videos,
see **ose 2**

141

osal

disposal
proposal

ose 1

close
dose
gross

cosmos
engross
morose
up close
verbose

adios
comatose
diagnose
grandiose

ose 2

beaux
blows
bows
chose
close
clothes
crows
doze
flows
foes
froze
glows
goes

grows
hose
knows
lows
mows
nose
owes
pose
pros
prose
rose
rows
sews
shows
slows
snows
those
throws
toes
tows
woes

bozos
bulldoze
dispose
enclose
expose
fire hose
impose
low blows
no-nos
no-shows
oppose
propose

pug nose
rainbows
scarecrows
sideshows
suppose
tiptoes
yo-yos

buffaloes
bungalows
Cheerios
come to blows
decompose
dominoes
dynamos
Eskimos
heaven knows
nose-to-nose
Oreos
overflows
panty hose
radios
rodeos
runny nose
stereos
twinkle toes
videos

anything goes
open and close
overexpose

osh

gosh
josh

nosh
posh
quash
slosh
squash
wash

brainwash
carwash
hogwash
mouthwash
my gosh
whitewash

osion

corrosion
erosion
explosion
implosion

osity as in
curiosity,
see ocity

osive

corrosive
erosive
explosive

OSS 1 as in gross,
see ose 1

OSS 2

boss
cross

floss
gloss
loss
moss
Ross
sauce
toss

across
crisscross
hot sauce

hot sauce

lip gloss
Red Cross
ring toss
soy sauce

applesauce
at a loss
dental floss

double-cross
hearing loss

memory loss
profit and loss
sign of the cross

ossed 1 as in
grossed,
see ost 1

ossed as in
bossed,
see ost 2

ossum

awesome
blossom
possum

opossum
play possum

ossy

Aussie
bossy
glossy
mossy
posse
saucy

ost 1

boast
coast
ghost
grossed

143

host
most
post
roast
toast

toast

almost
bedpost
engrossed
goalpost
guidepost
outgrossed
outpost
pot roast
signpost
topmost
utmost

coast-to-coast
diagnosed
hitching post

innermost
parcel post
trading post
whipping post

ost 2

bossed
cost
crossed
flossed
frost
glossed
lost
tossed

crisscrossed
defrost
exhaust
low-cost

double-crossed
holocaust

at any cost

oster

foster
roster

defroster
impostor

osure

closure

composure
enclosure

exposure

osy

cozy
mosey
nosy
Rosie
rosy

ot

blot
bought
brought
caught
clot
cot
dot
fought
got
hot
jot
knot
lot
not
ought
plot
pot
rot
Scot
shot
slot
snot
sought

spot
squat
swat
taught
taut
thought
tot
trot
what
yacht

big shot
blind spot
bloodshot
boycott
cannot
cheap shot
crackpot
distraught
dogtrot
flowerpot
forgot
gunshot
hot shot
inkblot
jackpot
long shot
mascot
mug shot
red-hot
robot
self-taught
slingshot
snapshot

somewhat
so what?
store-bought
teapot
tight spot
whatnot

afterthought
apricot
astronaut

astronaut

beauty spot
boiling hot
booster shot
Camelot
coffeepot

diddly-squat
food for thought
hit the spot
hot to trot
Lancelot
melting pot
not so hot
on the dot
on the spot
parking lot
polka dot
thanks a lot
tie the knot

forget-me-not
like it or not

ota

quota
soda

iota
pagoda
ricotta
Toyota

Minnesota
North Dakota
South Dakota

otch

blotch
botch
notch
Scotch

swatch
watch

birdwatch
hopscotch
stopwatch
topnotch
weight-watch
wristwatch

ote

bloat
boat
coat
dote
float
gloat
goat
moat
note
oat
quote
throat
tote
vote
wrote

afloat
cutthroat
devote
dreamboat
footnote
keynote
lifeboat
love note

misquote
outvote

promote
raincoat
remote
rewrote
rowboat
scapegoat
sore throat
steamboat
turncoat

anecdote
antidote
miss the boat
overcoat
petticoat
right to vote
rock the boat
root beer float
sugarcoat

one man, one vote

oth 1

both
growth
oath

regrowth

overgrowth
under oath

oth 2

broth

cloth
froth
moth
sloth

chicken broth
three-toed sloth

other

brother
mother
other
smother

another
each other
godmother
grandmother
none other
Oh, brother!
stepmother

one another

fairy godmother

otic

aquatic
chaotic
exotic
hypnotic
melodic
narcotic
neurotic
psychotic
quixotic

idiotic
patriotic

antibiotic

otion

lotion
motion
notion
ocean
potion

commotion
devotion
emotion
love potion
promotion
slow motion

locomotion
magic potion

otional

devotional
emotional
promotional

unemotional

otten

cotton
gotten
rotten

forgotten
spoiled rotten

otter

broader
daughter
fodder
hotter
odder
otter
plotter
potter
prodder
slaughter
tauter
totter
trotter
water

bathwater
dishwater
floodwater

fly swatter

fly swatter
globetrotter
hot rodder
manslaughter
stepdaughter

alma mater
bread and water
holy water
teeter-totter
underwater
walk on water

ottery

lottery
pottery
watery

ottle as in bottle, see oddle

otto

auto
grotto
lotto
motto

otty as in knotty, see ody

ou as in you, see ew

ouble

bubble
double

rubble
stubble
trouble

car trouble

car trouble

see double
soap bubble

double trouble
on the double

ouch

couch
crouch
grouch
ouch
pouch
slouch
vouch

oud

bowed
cloud
crowd

loud
plowed
proud

shroud

vowed
wowed

allowed
aloud
in-crowd
kowtowed
meowed
outloud
rain cloud
war cloud

bushy-browed
overcrowd
thundercloud

ouder as in
   louder,
   see **owder**

ough 1 as in
   rough,
   see **uff**

ough 2 as in
   cough,
   see **off**

ough 3 as in
   through,
   see **ew**

ough 4 as in
   dough,
   see **o 1**

ougher as in
   tougher,
   see **uffer**

ought as in
   bought,
   see **ot**

ould as in would,
   see **ood 3**

oulder as in
   boulder,
   see **older**

ounce

bounce
counts
flounce

mounts
ounce
pounce
trounce

accounts
amounts
announce
discounts
pronounce
renounce

bank accounts
mispronounce
ounce for
   ounce

ound

bound
browned
clowned
crowned
downed
drowned
found
frowned
ground
hound
mound
pound
round
sound
wound

abound

aground
around
astound
background
bloodhound

bloodhound

campground
chowhound
compound
dog pound
dumbfound
earthbound
foreground
greyhound
inbound
newfound
outbound
playground
profound
rebound
renowned
snowbound

spellbound
surround
year-round

all around
battleground
fool around
homeward bound
honorbound
lost and found
musclebound
neutral ground
outward bound
pitcher's mound
round and round
runaround
solid ground
underground

merry-go-round
up and around

happy hunting
   ground

ount

count
mount

account
amount
discount
head count

bank account
paramount
tantamount

ounts as in
  accounts,
  see **ounce**

oup as in soup,
  see **oop**

our 1
cower
flour
flower
hour
our
power
scour
shower
sour
tower

devour
empower
horsepower
lunch hour
Mayflower
noon hour
rain shower
rush hour
wallflower
wildflower
willpower

cauliflower
dinner hour
Eiffel Tower

overpower
superpower
sweet and sour
veto power

ivory tower

our 2 as in tour,
  see **ure**

our 3 as in four,
  see **ore**

oured as in
  devoured,
  see **owered**

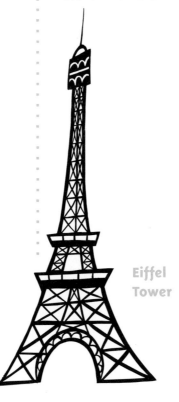

Eiffel
Tower

ourn as in
  adjourn,
  see **urn**

ourse as in
  course,
  see **orse**

ouse
blouse
douse
house
louse
mouse
spouse

birdhouse
church mouse
clubhouse
courthouse
doghouse
firehouse
full house
lighthouse
madhouse
outhouse
penthouse
powerhouse
roughhouse
warehouse
White House

cat and mouse
haunted house

house-to-house
Mickey Mouse
on the house

oust

doused
joust
oust
roust

out

bout
clout
doubt
drought
out
pout
rout
route
scout
shout
snout
spout
sprout
stout
trout

about
blackout
blowout
Boy Scout
campout
cookout
devout

dropout
dugout
fade-out
fallout
far out
Girl Scout
handout
hangout
holdout
knockout
lookout
no doubt
pass out
psych-out
sauerkraut
shoot-out
sold-out
stakeout
standout
take-out
throughout
tryout
without
workout

beyond doubt
Brussels sprout
do without
down and out
falling-out
go without
in and out
inside out
knockabout

odd man out
roundabout
runabout
talent scout

day in, day out
knock-down-
    drag-out
over and out
up and about

outer as in
   stouter,
   see owder

outh 1

mouth
south

big mouth
Deep South
loudmouth

blabbermouth
hand-to-mouth
word of mouth

outh 2 as in
   youth,
   see ooth

ove 1

clove
cove
dove
drove

grove
mauve
stove
wove

alcove
by jove

ove 2

dove
glove
love
of
shove

above
self-love
sort of

boxing glove
puppy love
turtledove

brotherly love
labor of love
tunnel of love

none of the above

ove 3

groove
move
prove
you've

approve
disprove
false move

improve
remove

disapprove
on the move

over

clover
over
rover

bowl over
changeover
hangover
Land Rover
layover
leftover
once-over
pushover
sleep over
spillover
turnover
warmed-over

Cliffs of Dover
four-leaf clover

ow 1

bough
bow
brow
chow
cow
how
now

ow
plow
pow
row
sow
vow
wow

allow
bowwow
eyebrow
know-how
kowtow
luau
meow
Moscow
powwow
snowplow
somehow

anyhow
cat's meow
here and now
holy cow
solemn vow
take a bow

OW 2 as in blow,
see O 1

owder

chowder
doubter
louder
pouter

powder
prouder
shouter
stouter

clam chowder
gun powder

owed 1 as in
snowed,
see **ode**

owed 2 as in
vowed,
see **oud**

owel as in towel,
see **owl**

ower as in power,
see **our 1**

owered

coward
cowered
flowered
Howard
powered
scoured
showered
soured
towered

devoured
empowered

overpowered

owing

blowing
crowing
flowing
glowing
going
growing
knowing
mowing
rowing
sewing
showing
snowing
throwing
towing

all-knowing
churchgoing
free-flowing
mind-blowing
ongoing
outgoing
tiptoeing

easygoing
overflowing
partygoing

owl

bowel
foul
growl
howl
owl

rowing

prowl
scowl
towel
vowel

on the prowl
wise old owl

owledge

college
knowledge

acknowledge

own 1 as in flown,
see **one 1**

own 2

brown
clown
crown
down
drown
frown

153

gown
noun
town

ballgown
breakdown
countdown
crackdown
crosstown
downtown
face-down
ghost town
hoedown
hometown
knockdown
letdown
lowdown
meltdown
nightgown
pronoun
put-down
renown
slowdown
small-town
splashdown
sundown
touchdown

broken-down
cap and gown
Chinatown
circus clown
hand-me-down
out-of-town

trickle-down
up and down
upside down
wedding gown

owned as in
  drowned,
  see ound

ows as in blows,
  see ose 2

owy
blowy
Chloe
doughy
Joey
showy
snowy

ox
blocks
box

circus clown

clocks
docks
flocks
fox
gawks
hawks
jocks
knocks
locks
mocks
ox
pox
rocks
shocks
smocks
socks
sox
squawks
stocks
talks
walks
woks

cashbox
crosswalks
deadlocks
detox
Fort Knox
jaywalks
knee socks
lunchbox
mailbox
Mohawks
outfox

peacocks
Reeboks
roadblocks
sandbox
shamrocks
sleepwalks
soap box
sweat socks
ticktocks
toy box
unlocks
Xerox

aftershocks
chatterbox
chickenpox
Goldilocks
music box
orthodox
paradox
shadowbox
stumbling blocks
tomahawks

jack-in-the-box
Pandora's box
unorthodox

oxy

boxy
foxy
proxy

oy

boy
buoy
coy
joy
ploy
Roy
soy
toy
Troy

ahoy
annoy
destroy
employ
enjoy
killjoy
life buoy
oh boy

corduroy
Illinois
overjoy
pride and joy
real McCoy

oyal as in royal, see oil

oyed as in employed, see oid

oys

boys

joys
noise
ploys
poise
toys

annoys
cowboys
decoys
destroys
enjoys
killjoys
turquoise

Tinkertoys
traffic noise

oze as in doze, see ose 2

ozen

chosen
frozen

frozen

155

u

u as in flu,
see ew

ub

club
cub
dub
flub
grub
hub
pub
rub
scrub
shrub
snub
stub
sub
tub

backrub
bathtub
fan club
hot tub
hubbub
nightclub

billy club
lion cub
ticket stub

ubber

blubber
rubber
scrubber

foam rubber
landlubber

money grubber

ubble as in
bubble,
see ouble

ubby

chubby
grubby
hubby
nubby
stubby

ube

cube
lube
tube

boob tube

boob tube

Danube
ice cube
test tube

uce as in truce,
see use 1

uced

boost
juiced
roost
spruced

deduced
produced
reduced
vamoosed

introduced
reproduced

uch as in much,
see utch

uck

buck
chuck
cluck
duck
luck
muck
pluck
puck
struck
stuck
suck

truck
yuck

amok
awestruck
dumbstruck
fire truck
good luck
lame duck
lovestruck
moonstruck
mukluk
potluck
stagestruck
starstruck
tough luck
tow truck
woodchuck

Donald Duck

duck

hockey puck
horror-struck
Lady Luck

out of luck
pass the buck
sitting duck
thunderstruck

beginner's luck

ucked as in
plucked,
see uct

ucker
clucker
pucker
sucker
trucker

bloodsucker

uckle
buckle
chuckle
knuckle

pinochle
swashbuckle
white-knuckle

honeysuckle

ucks
bucks
clucks
crux
ducks
flux
plucks

pucks
shucks
sucks
trucks
tux

aw, shucks
deluxe
dump trucks

ucky
Chuckie
ducky
lucky
mucky
plucky
yucky

Kentucky
unlucky

rubber ducky

happy-go-lucky

uct
bucked
chucked
clucked
ducked
duct
plucked
sucked
trucked
tucked

abduct

157

conduct
construct
deduct
destruct
instruct
obstruct
tear duct

aqueduct
reconstruct
self-destruct

uction

suction

abduction
construction
deduction
destruction
instruction
obstruction
production
reduction

introduction
reconstruction
reproduction

uctive

constructive
destructive
instructive
productive

reproductive
self-destructive

unproductive
counterproductive

uctor

abductor
conductor
instructor

ud

blood
bud
crud
dud
flood
mud
scud
spud
thud

blue blood
flash flood
Milk Dud
rosebud
taste bud

creeping crud
flesh and blood

stick in the mud

uda

Buddha
Gouda
Judah

Bermuda

barracuda

udder as in
rudder,
see utter

uddle

cuddle

cuddle

huddle
muddle
puddle
scuttle
shuttle
subtle

befuddle
mud puddle
space shuttle

uddy

bloody

buddy
cruddy
muddy
nutty
putty
study

good buddy
peanutty

fuddy-duddy
nature study
Silly Putty
understudy

ude

booed
brewed
brood
chewed
crewed
crude
cued
dude
feud
food
glued
hued
mewed
mood
mooed
nude
poohed
prude
rude

rued
shrewd
spewed
stewed
sued
viewed
wooed

allude
boo-hooed
conclude
construed
delude
dog food
elude
exclude
exude
fast food
include
intrude
protrude
pursued
renewed
reviewed
Saint Jude
seafood
seclude
shampooed
soul food
subdued
tattooed
unglued

altitude

aptitude
attitude
baby food
ballyhooed
barbecued
family feud
gratitude
interlude
interviewed
in the mood
latitude
longitude
misconstrued
multitude
rendezvoused
solitude

udent

prudent
student

udge

budge
drudge
fudge
grudge
judge
nudge
sludge
smudge
trudge

hot fudge
misjudge

prejudge

ue as in blue,
  see ew

ued as in glued,
  see ude

uel
cruel
dual
duel
fuel
gruel
jewel

jewel

renewal

ues as in blues,
  see use 2

uff
bluff
buff
cuff

fluff
gruff
huff
muff
puff
rough
scruff
scuff
snuff
stuff
tough

cream puff
enough
handcuff
kid stuff
rebuff

blindman's bluff
fair enough
huff and puff
overstuff
powder puff
rough and tough
sure enough

uffer
bluffer
buffer
gruffer
rougher
suffer
tougher

stocking stuffer

uffle
duffel
muffle
ruffle
scuffle
shuffle
snuffle
truffle

dust ruffle

uffy
fluffy
huffy
puffy
stuffy
toughie

ug
bug

bug

chug
drug
dug
glug
hug

jug
lug
mug
plug
pug
rug
shrug
slug
smug
snug
thug
tug
ugh

bear hug
bedbug
beer mug
earplug
fireplug
humbug
unplug

chugalug
doodlebug
jitterbug
ladybug
litterbug
wonder drug

uge
huge
rouge
Scrooge
stooge

deluge
refuge
Baton Rouge
subterfuge

uggle
juggle
smuggle
snuggle
struggle

uggler
juggler
smuggler
snuggler
struggler

uild as in build, see **illed**

uise as in bruise, see **use 2**

uiser as in cruiser, see **user**

uit as in suit, see **ute**

uke
duke
fluke
kook
Luke
nuke

puke
spook
rebuke
antinuke
goobledygook

ule as in rule, see **ool**

ulge
bulge
divulge
indulge
overindulge

ulk
bulk
hulk
skulk
sulk

ull 1
cull
dull
gull
hull
lull
null
skull

annul
numskull
seagull

161

ull 2

bull
full
pull
wool

chock-full
pit bull
push-pull
steel wool

Istanbul
Sitting Bull

ully

bully
fully
pulley
woolly

wild and woolly

ulp

gulp
pulp

ulsive

compulsive
impulsive
repulsive

ult

cult

adult
consult

exult
insult
occult
result
tumult

catapult
difficult
young adult

ulture

culture
vulture

agriculture
counterculture
horticulture

uly

coolly
cruelly
drooly
newly
stoolie
truly

unruly

um

bum
chum
come
crumb
drum
dumb
from

glum

glum

gum
hum
mum
numb
plum
rum
scum
slum
some
strum
sum
thumb
yum

beach bum
become
eardrum
green thumb
ho-hum

humdrum
outcome
succumb
Tom Thumb
yum-yum

bubble gum
chewing gum
cookie crumb
deaf and dumb
overcome
rule of thumb

chrysanthemum
fee-fie-fo-fum

umb as in
crumb,
see **um**

umber 1
lumber
number
slumber

cucumber
outnumber

umber 2 as in
plumber,
see **ummer**

umble
bumble
crumble
fumble

grumble
humble
jumble
mumble
rumble
stumble

stumble

tumble

rough-and-tumble

umbling
bumbling
fumbling
grumbling
humbling
jumbling
mumbling
rumbling
stumbling
tumbling

ume as in assume,
see **oom**

umer as in
consumer,
see **umor**

ummer
bummer
drummer
dumber
hummer
plumber
strummer
summer

latecomer
midsummer
newcomer
nose-thumber

up-and-comer

Indian summer

ummy
chummy
crummy
dummy
gummy
mummy
rummy
scummy
tummy
yummy

gin rummy

umor

bloomer
groomer
humor
rumor
tumor

consumer
costumer
good humor
late bloomer

baby boomer

umorous

humorous
numerous

ump

bump
chump
clump
dump
grump
hump
jump
lump
plump
pump
rump
slump
stump
thump

trump
ump

broad jump
goose bump
ski jump
speed bump
trash dump
tree stump

city dump
stomach pump
sugar lump
triple jump

umpkin

bumpkin
pumpkin

pumpkin

umption

gumption

assumption
consumption
presumption

umpy

bumpy
clumpy
dumpy
frumpy
grumpy
jumpy
lumpy
stumpy

un

bun
done
fun
gun
hon
Hun
none
nun
one
pun
run
shun
son
spun
stun
sun
ton
won

all done
begun
blowgun

dog run
grandson
hired gun
home run
homespun
no one
outdone
outrun
redone
rerun
shotgun
someone
top gun
trial run
undone
well done

Air Force One
all or none
anyone
everyone
hit-and-run
hole in one
honeybun
hot dog bun
jump the gun
native son
9-1-1
number one
one by one
overdone
underdone

fun in the sun

hamburger bun
over and done
prodigal son

Attila the Hun

unch

brunch
bunch
crunch
hunch
lunch
munch
punch
scrunch

fruit punch
school lunch
whole bunch

honeybunch
out to lunch
pleased as punch

unction

function
junction

conjunction
dysfunction
malfunction

und

fund
gunned
punned

shunned
stunned
sunned

refund
trust fund
cummerbund

cummerbund

under

blunder
plunder
thunder
under
wonder

boy wonder
down under
no wonder

blood and thunder
loot and plunder

une as in tune,
see **oon**

ung

clung
flung
hung
lung
rung
sprung
stung

stung

sung
swung
tongue
wrung
young

among
far-flung
forked tongue
high-strung
unsung

egg foo yung
iron lung
mother tongue

slip of the tongue

unge

lunge
plunge
sponge

unger

hunger
younger

fishmonger
warmonger

rumormonger

ungle

bungle
jungle

concrete jungle

union

union

communion
reunion

unity

unity

community
immunity
impunity

opportunity

equal opportunity

diplomatic immunity

unk

bunk
chunk
clunk
drunk
dunk
flunk
funk
hunk
junk
monk
plunk
punk
shrunk
skunk
slunk
spunk
stunk
sunk
trunk

chipmunk
kerplunk
preshrunk
slam dunk

unken

drunken
Duncan

166

shrunken
sunken

unker
bunker
clunker
drunker
hunker
punker

slam-dunker

Archie Bunker

unky
chunky
clunky
funky
junky
monkey
punky
spunky

grease monkey

junk-food junky

unned as in
punned,
see und

unnel
funnel
tunnel

unner
gunner

punner
runner
stunner

front-runner
roadrunner
tail gunner

unny
bunny
funny
honey
money
runny
sonny
sunny

Bugs Bunny
hush money

Easter bunny
even money

unt
blunt
brunt
bunt
front
grunt
hunt
punt
runt
stunt

confront
forefront

homefront
manhunt
witch hunt

elephant
treasure hunt

unter
hunter
punter

headhunter
manhunter

unts
bunts
dunce
fronts
grunts
hunts
months
once
punts
runts
stunts

at once
witch hunts

all at once

up
cup
pup
up

backup

167

blow up

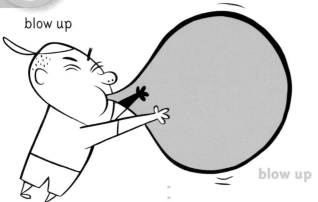

blow up

breakup
buildup
checkup
close-up
crackup
cutup
dress up
foul-up
grown-up
hang-up
hiccup
lineup
makeup
mix-up
pickup
roundup
setup
shut up
stickup
teacup
throw up
toss-up
touch-up

washed-up
all shook up
buckle up
buttercup
coffee cup
cover-up
cuddle up
giddy-up
paper cup
pick-me-up
runner up
7-Up

uper as in super,
see **ooper**

upid
cupid
stupid

upiter
Jupiter
stupider

uple
pupil
scruple
quadruple

upped as in
hiccupped,
see **upt**

upper
supper
hiccupper
picker-upper

uppy
guppy
puppy
yuppie

upt
cupped
upped

abrupt
bankrupt
corrupt
disrupt
erupt
hiccupped
interrupt

uption
corruption

disruption
eruption
interruption

ur as in fur,
   see er

urable
curable
durable

endurable
incurable
securable

ural
mural
plural
rural

intramural

urance
assurance
endurance
insurance

reassurance
self-assurance

urb
blurb
curb
herb
verb

adverb

disturb
news blurb
perturb
proverb
suburb
superb

do not disturb

urch
birch
church
lurch
perch
search

research
soul-search

urder as in
   murder,
   see erter

urdle
curdle
fertile
girdle
hurdle
hurtle
turtle

urdy
birdy
nerdy
sturdy

wordy

hurdy-gurdy

ure
boor
cure
lure
poor
pure
sure
tour
your
you're

amour
assure
brochure
chauffeur
contour
demure
detour
endure
ensure
for sure
impure

turtle

insure
liqueur
masseur
mature
obscure
secure
unsure
velour

amateur
aperture
connoisseur
curvature
immature
insecure
manicure
overture
pedicure
premature
reassure
saboteur

urf
serf
Smurf
surf
turf

urge as in surge,
see **erge**

urgency
urgency

emergency

insurgency

urgent as in
insurgent,
see **ergent**

urious
curious
furious

injurious
luxurious

urity
purity
surety

impurity
maturity
obscurity
security

immaturity
insecurity

urk as in lurk,
see **erk**

url
curl
earl
girl
hurl
pearl
squirrel
swirl
twirl

whirl
awhirl
dream girl
unfurl

cover girl

mother-of-pearl

urly
burly
curly

curly

early
pearly
Shirley
surly
swirly
twirly

hurly-burly

urn
burn

churn
earn
fern
learn
stern
turn
urn
yearn

adjourn
concern
downturn
heartburn
intern
Jules Verne
nocturne
return
slow burn
sojourn
sunburn
upturn
U-turn

live and learn
out of turn
overturn
tax return
toss and turn

urp

burp
chirp
slurp
usurp

Wyatt Earp

urr as in burr,
   see **er**

urred as in
   occurred,
   see **erd**

urry

blurry
curry
flurry
furry
hurry
scurry
worry

Missouri

not to worry

urse as in nurse,
   see **erse**

ursed as in
   nursed,
   see **irst**

urst as in burst,
   see **irst**

urt as in blurt,
   see **ert**

urtle as in turtle,
   see **urdle**

ury

fury
jury

grand jury
Missouri

us

bus
cuss

furry

fuss
muss
plus
pus
thus
us

discuss
nonplus
school bus

Gloomy Gus
make a fuss

no fuss, no muss

usable

bruisable
usable

excusable
reusable
unusable

inexcusable

use 1

Bruce
deuce
goose
juice
loose
moose
mousse
noose
spruce
truce
use
Zeus

abuse
caboose
chartreuse
deduce
excuse
footloose
hang loose
induce
masseuse
misuse
mongoose

no use
papoose
produce
recluse
reduce
refuse
vamoose

child abuse
Dr. Seuss
hangman's noose
introduce
Mother Goose
no excuse
on the loose
out of use
reproduce
silly goose
what's the use?

chocolate mousse

use 2

blues
boos
bruise
chews
choose
clues
cruise
dues
fuse
glues
hues
lose

mews
moos
muse
news
ooze
ruse
screws
shoes

shoes

snooze
stews
sues
use
views
whose
zoos

abuse
accuse
amuse
bad news
boo-boos
boohoos
canoes

cashews
confuse
construes
corkscrews
cuckoos
curfews
defuse
effuse
enthuse
excuse
gumshoes
infuse
kazoos
miscues
misuse
muumuus
peruse
pursues
refuse
reviews
shampoos
short fuse
subdues
taboos
tattoos

avenues
baby shoes
barbecues
blow a fuse
born to lose
buckaroos
high-heeled
  shoes

interviews
kangaroos
pick and choose
revenues
win or lose

rhythm and blues

user

bruiser
chooser
cruiser
doozer
loser
muser
snoozer
user

abuser
accuser
bad loser
nonuser

barbecues

child abuser
two-time loser

ush 1

blush
brush
crush
flush
gush
hush
lush
mush
plush
rush
shush
slush

bum's rush
cheek blush
gold rush
hairbrush
hush-hush
toothbrush

ush 2

bush
push
whoosh

ambush
rosebush

ushy

bushy
cushy

173

gushy
pushy

usion

fusion

collusion
conclusion
confusion
delusion
exclusion
illusion
inclusion
intrusion
protrusion
seclusion
transfusion

blood transfusion
disillusion

optical illusion

usive

abusive
conclusive
conducive
elusive
exclusive
illusive
intrusive
obtrusive
reclusive
seclusive

inconclusive

unobtrusive

usk

brusque
dusk
husk
musk
tusk

uss 1

puss
schuss

octopus

octopus

Oedipus
platypus
sourpuss

uss 2 as in fuss,
see **us**

ussed as in
discussed,
see **ust**

ussion

Russian

concussion
discussion
percussion

repercussion

ust

bussed
bust
crust
cussed
dust
fussed
gust
just
mussed
must
rust
thrust
trust

adjust
brain trust
coal dust
combust
crop dust
discussed
disgust
distrust
drug bust
entrust
gold dust

mistrust
nonplussed
pie crust
robust
sawdust
stardust
tongue thrust
unjust

bite the dust
wanderlust

usted

busted
dusted
rusted
trusted

disgusted
mistrusted

uster

cluster
duster
fluster
luster
muster

blockbuster
crimebuster
lackluster

filibuster

ustle

bustle

hustle
muscle
mussel
Russell
rustle
tussle

hustle and bustle

usty

crusty
dusty
gusty
musty
rusty
trustee

ut 1

but
butt
cut
glut
gut
hut
jut
mutt
nut
putt
rut
shut
smut
strut
what
catgut

chestnut
clear-cut
haircut
King Tut
precut
rebut
shortcut
somewhat
so what
uncut

coconut
halibut
in a rut
Lilliput
scuttlebutt
undercut
uppercut

cigarette butt
emerald cut
open and shut

ut 2 as in put, see oot 2

utch

clutch
crutch
Dutch
hutch
much
such
touch

not much

175

retouch
soft touch

final touch
Midas touch
overmuch
pretty much
rabbit hutch

rabbit hutch

such and such

ute
beaut
boot
brute
Butte
chute
coot
cute
flute
fruit
hoot
loot
lute
moot

mute
newt
root
route
scoot
shoot
snoot
suit
toot

acute
astute
Beirut
commute
compute
deaf mute
dilute
dispute
en route
grapefruit
lawsuit
minute
outshoot
pollute
pursuit
recruit
refute
repute
salute
space suit
square root
tribute
uproot
zoot suit

absolute
attribute
birthday suit
constitute
destitute
execute
hot pursuit
ill repute
institute
monkey suit
overshoot
parachute
persecute
prosecute
resolute
substitute
troubleshoot

electrocute
forbidden fruit

Trivial Pursuit

uter
cuter
looter
neuter
pewter
rooter
scooter
shooter
suitor
tutor

commuter

computer
peashooter
polluter
recruiter
sharpshooter

motor scooter
persecutor
prosecutor
troubleshooter

uth as in truth,
see **ooth**

ution

pollution
solution

absolution
air pollution
constitution
contribution
destitution
dissolution
distribution
evolution
execution
institution
persecution
prosecution
resolution
retribution
revolution
substitution

electrocution

utor as in tutor,
see **uter**

utt as in mutt,
see **ut 1**

utter

butter
clutter
cutter
flutter
gutter
mutter
putter
rudder
shudder
shutter
sputter
stutter
udder
utter

rain gutter
woodcutter

bread and butter
cookie cutter
paper cutter
peanut butter

uttle as in scuttle,
see **uddle**

utty as in nutty,
see **uddy**

uture

future
moocher
suture

ux as in flux,
see **ucks**

uy as in guy,
see **y**

uys as in buys,
see **ize**

uzz

buzz
does
fuzz
was

abuzz

uzzle

guzzle
muzzle
nuzzle
puzzle

y

y

buy
by
bye
cry
die
dry
dye
eye
fly
fry
guy
hi
high
I
lie
my
pie

pry
rye
shy
sigh
sky
sly
spry
spy

spy

sty
thigh
tie
try
why
wry

ally
apply
black tie
blow-dry
bonzai
bow tie
bull's-eye
bye-bye
comply
deep-fry

defy
deny
drip-dry
firefly
French fry
good-bye
gun-shy
hi-fi
hog-tie
horsefly
imply
July
magpie
Masai
mud pie
nearby
necktie
outcry
pigsty
Popeye
rabbi
rely
reply
sci-fi
Shanghai
shut-eye
sky-high
small fry
standby
supply
tongue-tie
untie
war cry

pie

wise guy

alibi
amplify
apple pie
battle cry
beautify
beddy-bye
butterfly
camera-shy
certify
clarify
classify
crucify
cutie pie
dignify
do or die
dragonfly
evil eye
eye to eye
falsify
FBI
fortify
glorify
gratify
high and dry
horrify
hushaby
justify
lullaby
magnify
modify
mortify
multiply

mummify
mystify
notify
nullify
occupy
pacify
Paraguay
passerby
petrify
pizza pie
private eye
purify
qualify
ratify
rectify
rockaby
samurai
satisfy
signify
simplify
specify
stupefy
terrify
testify
tsetse fly
underlie
unify
Uruguay
verify
you and I

demystify
disqualify
dissatisfy

electrify
Eskimo Pie
exemplify
Fourth of July
identify
intensify
little white lie
personify
preoccupy
solidify

ycle as in bicycle,
   see ickle
ye as in bye,
   see y
yle as in style,
   see ile 1
ym as in synonym,
   see im
yme as in rhyme,
   see ime
ype as in type,
   see ipe

mummify

179

index

agitate/ate
agitation/ation
agitator/ader
aglow/o 1
ago/o 1
agonize/ize
agree/ee
agreed/eed
agrees/eeze
agriculture/ulture
aground/ound
ah/aw
ah-choo/ew
ahead/ed
ahoy/oy
aid/ade 1
aide/ade 1
ail/ale 1
aim/aim
air/air
airborne/orn
aircraft/aft
airfare/air
airlift/ift
airline/ine 1
airliner/iner
airmail/ale 1
airplane/ain
airport/ort
airsick/ick
airtight/ight
airy/ary
aisle/ile 1
ajar/ar
akimbo/imbo
Al/al
Alabama/ama 2
alabaster/aster
Alamo/o 1
alarm/arm 1
albino/ino 1
Albuquerque/erky
Alcatraz/azz

alcohol/all
alcove/ove 1
ale/ale 1
alert/ert
Algeria/eria
Ali/olly
alibi/y
alibis/ize
alienate/ate
alike/ike
alimony/ony
alive/ive 1
all/all
allege/edge
allegory/ory
alleviate/ate
alley/alley
alliance/iance
alligator/ader
allocate/ate
allow/ow 1
allowed/oud
allude/ude
ally/y
alma mater/otter
almanac/ack
almighty/idy
almost/ost 1
aloe/allow 1
alone/one 1
along/ong
aloof/oof 1
aloud/oud
alphabet/et
alphabetize/ize
alpine/ine 1
already/etty
altar/alter
alter/alter
although/o 1
altitude/ude
altogether/eather
altruistic/istic

always/aze
am/am
AM/em
Amarillo/illow
amass/ass
amassed/ast
amateur/ure
amaze/aze
Amazon/awn
Amazons/ons
ambition/ition
ambitious/icious
ambush/ush 2
amen/en
amend/end
Americana/onna
amiability/ility
amid/id
amiss/iss
ammonia/onia
ammunition/ition
amnesiac/ack
amok/uck
among/ung
amoral/oral
amount/ount
amounts/ounce
amour/ure
amp/amp
amplify/y
amputate/ate
Amsterdam/am
amuse/use 2
an/an 1
anagram/am
analytic/itic
analytical/itical
analyze/ize
ancestor/ester
and/and
Androcles/eeze
anecdote/ote
anesthetic/etic

anew/ew
Angeleno/ino 2
angina/ina 2
angora/ora
animalistic/istic
animate/ate
animation/ation
animator/ader
animosity/ocity
Anna/ana 1
Anne/an 1
annex/ex
annexed/ext
Annie/anny
annihilate/ate
announce/ounce
annoy/oy
annoyed/oid
annoys/oys
annul/ull 1
another/other
ant/ant 1
antagonism/ism
antagonistic/istic
antagonize/ize
anteater/eeder
antelope/ope
anthill/ill
anthology/ology
antibiotic/otic
antibody/ody
antic/antic
anticipate/ate
anticipation/ation
antidote/ote
antifreeze/eeze
antinuke/uke
antique/eek
antiwar/ore
Antoine/awn
Antoinette/et
antonym/im
ants/ance

anxiety/iety
any/enny, inny
anybody/ody
anyhow/ow 1
anymore/ore
anyone/un
anyplace/ace
anything/ing
anytime/ime
anywhere/air
Apache/atchy
apart/art 1
ape/ape
aperture/ure
apex/ex
Aphrodite/idy
apiece/ease 2
Apollo/allow 2
apologetic/etic
apologize/ize
apology/ology
appall/all
appalled/alled
apparent/arent
apparition/ition
appeal/eel
appealed/ield
appear/eer
appendicitis/itis
appetite/ight
applaud/awed
applause/ause
apple/apple
applecart/art 1
applesauce/oss 2
appliance/iance
application/ation
applied/ide
applies/ize
apply/y
appoint/oint
appreciate/ate
appreciation/ation

apprehend/end
apprehension/ention
apprehensive/ensive
apprenticeship/ip
approach/oach
approve/ove 3
apricot/ot
apropos/o 1
aptitude/ude
Aquarius/arious
aquatic/otic
aqueduct/uct
arachnid/id
arbitrary/ary
arc/ark
arcade/ade 1
arch/arch
archaeologist/ologist
archaeology/ology
Archie Bunker/unker
architect/ect
architects/ex
archive/ive 1
archrival/ival
ardor/arter
are/ar
area/area
arena/ena
arf/arf 1
Argentina/ena
argyle/ile 1
arise/ize
aristocracy/ocracy
aristocrat/at 1
aristocratic/atic
Aristotle/oddle
Arizona/ona
ark/ark
Arkansas/aw
arm/arm 1
armada/ada
armadillo/illow
armband/and

armpit/it
armpits/its
aroma/oma
aromatic/atic
around/ound
arrange/ange
arrest/est
arrival/ival
arrive/ive 1
arrow/arrow
arrowhead/ed
art/art 1
arthritic/itic
arthritis/itis
artichoke/oke
artichokes/okes
artifact/act
artifacts/ax
artificial/icial
artistic/istic
arty/ardy
as/azz
ascend/end
ascertain/ain
ash/ash 1
ashore/ore
Asian/asion
Asiatic/atic
aside/ide
ask/ask
asleep/eep
asphalt/alt
asphyxiate/ate
aspire/ire
ass/ass
assassinate/ate
assassination/ation
assassinator/ader
assault/alt
assaulter/alter
assaults/alts
assemble/emble
assert/ert

assessor/essor
assign/ine 1
assigned/ind 1
assist/ist
assistance/istance
associate/ate
assume/oom
assumption/umption
assurance/urance
assure/ure
asterisk/isk
asteroid/oid
asthmatic/atic
astir/er
astonish/onish
astound/ound
Astrodome/ome 1
astrological/ogical
astrology/ology
astronaut/ot
astronomic/omic
astronomy/onomy
astute/ute
at/at 1
ate/ate
atheism/ism
athlete/eet
athletic/etic
Atlantic/antic
atmosphere/eer
atomic/omic
atomizer/izer
atrocious/ocious
atrocity/ocity
attach/atch 1
attack/ack
attacked/act
attacks/ax
attempt/empt
attend/end
attention/ention
attentive/entive
attic/atic

Attila/illa
attire/ire
attitude/ude
attract/act
attraction/action
attractive/active
attracts/ax
attribute/ute
auctioneer/eer
audacious/acious
audacity/acity
Audi/ody
audition/ition
auditorium/orium
Audubon/awn
aunt/ant 1, aunt
aunts/ance
aura/ora
auspicious/icious
Aussie/ossy
authenticity/icity
authority/ority
authorize/ize
auto/otto
autobiography/ography
autocracy/ocracy
autocratic/atic
autograph/aff
autographed/aft
automatic/atic
automobile/eel
autonomy/onomy
availability/ility
Avalon/awn
avant-garde/ard 1
avenue/ew
avenues/use 2
aversion/ersion
avert/ert
Avery/avery
aviary/ary
aviation/ation

aviator/ader
avoid/oid
await/ate
awake/ake
award/ord 1
aware/air
away/ay
awe/aw
awed/awed
awesome/ossum
awestruck/uck
awful/awful
awhile/ile 1
awhirl/url
awoke/oke
awoken/oken
ax/ax
ayatollah/ola
Aztec/eck

babble/abble
Babe Ruth/ooth
baboon/oon
baby/aby
baby-faced/aste
Babylon/awn
baby-sat/at 1
baby-sit/it
baby-sits/its
baby-sitter/itter
Bach/ock
back/ack
backache/ake
backboard/ord 1
backbone/one 1
backed/act
backfire/ire
background/ound
backhand/and
backlash/ash 1
backpack/ack

backpacked/act
backpedal/eddle
backrub/ub
backs/ax
backseat/eet
backslap/ap
backstab/ab 1
backstabber/abber
backstage/age 1
backtrack/ack
backup/up
backward/erd
backyard/ard 1
bacteria/eria
Bactine/een
bad/ad 1
bag/ag
baggy/aggy
bagpipe/ipe
bagpiper/iper
bail/ale 1
bait/ate
bake/ake
bald/alled
balderdash/ash 1
Bali/alley
ball/all
ballerina/ena
ballet/ay
ballets/aze
ballgown/own 2
balloon/oon
ballpark/ark
ballpoint/oint
ballyhoo/ew
ballyhooed/ude
balm/alm, om
baloney/ony
Baltimore/ore
bambino/ino 2
bamboo/ew
ban/an 1
banana/ana 1

band/and
Band-Aid/ade 1
bandanna/ana 1
bandito/edo
bandleader/eeder
bandmaster/aster
bandstand/and
bang/ang
Bangkok/ock
Bangladesh/esh
bank/ank
bankrupt/upt
banned/and
banner/anner
baptism/ism
baptize/ize
bar/ar
barbarism/ism
barbarity/arity
barbecue/ew
barbecued/ude
barbecues/use 2
barbershop/op
Barcelona/ona
bard/ard 1
bare/air
barefoot/oot 2
barer/arer
barf/arf 1
barge/arge
baritone/one 1
bark/ark
barn/arn
barnstorm/orm 1
barnstormer/ormer
barnyard/ard 1
barometer/ometer
baron/aron
barracuda/uda
barrage/age 2
barred/ard 1
barren/aron
barricade/ade 1

b

Barry ▸ Big Bird

Barry/ary
barstool/ool
bartender/ender
barter/arter
base/ace
baseball/all
baseline/ine 1
bash/ash 1
basin/ason
bask/ask
basket/asket
basketball/all
bass/ace, ass
bassinet/et
bassoon/oon
baste/aste
bastille/eel
bat/at 1
batch/atch 1
bath/ath
bathrobe/obe
bathroom/oom
bathtub/ub
bathwater/otter
Batman/an
baton/awn
Baton Rouge/uge
batons/ons
batter/atter
battery/attery
battle/attle
battleground/ound
battleship/ip
batty/atty
bauble/obble
Bavaria/area
bawdy/ody
bawl/all
bawled/alled
bay/ay
bayonet/et
bays/aze
bazaar/ar

be/ee
beach/each
bead/eed
beady/eedy
beagle/egal
beak/eek
beaker/eaker
beam/eem
bean/een
beanbag/ag
beanie/ini
beanstalk/ock
bear/air
bearish/erish
beast/east
beat/eet
beaten/eaten
beater/eeder
beatnik/ick
beau/o 1
beaut/ute
beautician/ition
beautifies/ize
beautify/y
beauty/oody
beaver/eaver
beaux/ose 2
bebop/op
became/aim
because/ause
become/um
bed/ed
bedbug/ug
bedpost/ost 1
bedridden/idden
bedside/ide
bedtime/ime
bee/ee
beef/ief
beefsteak/ake
beehive/ive 1
beeline/ine 1
been/in

beep/eep
beeper/eeper
beer/eer
bees/eeze
beet/eet
beetle/eedle
before/ore
beforehand/and
befuddle/uddle
beg/eg
began/an
begin/in
beginner/inner
begonia/onia
begun/un
behalf/aff
behave/ave
behead/ed
beheld/eld
behind/ind 1
behold/old
Beijing/ing
Beirut/ute
belch/elch
belief/ief
believe/eave
believer/eaver
belittle/iddle
bell/ell
belle/ell
bellhop/op
bellow/ellow
belly/elly
bellyache/ake
belong/ong
below/o 1
belt/elt
Ben/en
bench/ench
bend/end
beneath/eath 2
benediction/iction
beneficial/icial

benefit/it
Ben Hur/er
benign/ine 1
Benito/edo
Benny/enny
bent/ent
bequeath/eath 2
Berlin/in
Berliner/inner
Bermuda/uda
Bernadette/et
Bernard/ard 1
berry/ary
berserk/erk
Bert/ert
beside/ide
Bess/ess
best/est
bet/et
betrayed/ade 1
betrayer/ayer
betrays/aze
better/etter
Betty/etty
between/een
bevel/evel
beware/air
bewitch/itch
beyond/ond
bib/ib
bibliography/
   ography
bibliophile/ile 1
bicep/ep
bicker/icker
bicycle/ickle
bid/id
bidden/idden
bidder/itter
biddy/itty
bifocal/ocal
big/ig
Big Bird/erd

Big Foot/oot 2
bigger/igger
big-time/ime
bigwig/ig
bike/ike
biker/iker
bikini/ini
bilk/ilk
bill/ill
billboard/ord 1
billed/illed
billfold/old
billion/illion
billionaire/air
Billy/illy
bin/in
bind/ind 1
binge/inge
binger/inger 2
bingo/ingo
biography/ography
biological/ogical
biologist/ologist
biology/ology
bionic/onic
biped/ed
birch/urch
bird/erd
birdbath/ath
birdbrain/ain
birdcage/age 1
birdcall/all
birdwatch/otch
birdy/urdy
Birmingham/am
birth/irth
birthday/ay
birthdays/aze
birthmark/ark
birthplace/ace
birthrate/ate
birthright/ight
birthstone/one 1

bit/it
bite/ight
biter/ider
bits/its
bitten/itten
bitter/itter
bittersweet/eet
bitty/itty
bizarre/ar
blab/ab 1
blabber/abber
blabbermouth/outh 1
blabby/abby
black/ack
blackball/all
blackballed/alled
blackbird/erd
blackboard/ord 1
blackjack/ack
blacklist/ist
blackmail/ale 1
blackout/out
blacksmith/ith
blacktop/op
bladder/atter
blade/ade 1
blah/aw
Blake/ake
blame/aim
bland/and
blank/ank
blanky/anky
blare/air
blast/ast
blaster/aster
blaze/aze
blazon/azon
bleach/each
bleacher/eacher
bleak/eek
bleat/eet
bled/ed
bleed/eed

bleeder/eeder
bleep/eep
blend/end
blender/ender
bless/ess
blessed/est
blew/ew
blight/ight
blimp/imp
blind/ind 1
blindfold/old
blink/ink
blinked/inct
blinky/inky
blintze/ince
blip/ip
bliss/iss
blister/ister
blistery/istory
blitz/its
blitzkrieg/eague
blizzard/izard
bloat/ote
blob/ob
block/ock
blockade/ade 1
blockbuster/uster
blocker/ocker
blockhead/ed
blocks/ox
blond/ond
blonder/onder
blonds/ons
blood/ud
bloodhound/ound
bloodshed/ed
bloodshot/ot
bloodstain/ain
bloodstream/eem
bloodsucker/ucker
bloody/uddy
bloom/oom
bloomer/umor

bloop/oop
blooper/ooper
blossom/ossum
blot/ot
blotch/otch
blouse/ouse
blow/o 1
blowgun/un
blowhard/ard 1
blowing/owing
blown/one 1
blowout/out
blows/ose 2
blow up/up
blowy/owy
blubber/ubber
blue/ew
blue jay/ay
blue jays/aze
blueprint/int
blueprints/ince
blues/use 2
bluff/uff
bluffer/uffer
blunder/under
blunt/unt
blur/er
blurb/urb
blurred/erd
blurry/urry
blurt/ert
blush/ush 1
boar/ore
board/ord 1
boarder/order
boardwalk/ock
boast/ost 1
boat/ote
bob/ob
bobble/obble
Bobby/obby
bobsled/ed
body/ody

bodyguard/ard 1
bog/og
boggle/oggle
boil/oil
bold/old
bolder/older
bolero/arrow
Bologna/onia
bolster/olster
bolt/olt
bomb/om
bombard/ard 1
bombast/ast
bombastic/astic
bombshell/ell
bonbon/awn
bond/ond
Bond, James/ond
bonds/ons
bone/one 1
bonehead/ed
bonfire/ire
bonk/onk
bonny/awny
bon voyage/age 2
bony/ony
bonzai/y
boo/ew
boo-boo/ew
boo-boos/use 2
booed/ude
boogieboard/ord 1
boohoo/ew
boohooed/ude
boohoos/use 2
book/ook 2
bookcase/ace
bookie/ookie
bookmark/ark
bookmobile/eel
bookshelf/elf
bookworm/erm
boom/oom

boomerang/ang
boondoggle/oggle
Boone, Daniel/oon
boor/ure
boos/use 2
boost/uced
booster/ooster
boot/ute
booth/ooth
bootie/oody
booty/oody
bop/op
Bo Peep/eep
border/order
borderline/ine 1
bore/ore
bored/ord 1
born/orn
boss/oss 2
bossed/ost 2
bossy/ossy
botch/otch
both/oth 1
bother/ather 2
bottle/oddle
bottle cap/ap
bottlefed/ed
bottleneck/eck
bouffant/aunt
bough/ow 1
bought/ot
boulder/older
boulevard/ard 1
bounce/ounce
bound/ound
bouquet/ay
bouquets/aze
bout/out
boutique/eek
bow/o 1, ow 1
bowed/ode, oud
bowel/owl
bowl/ole

bowled/old
bowler/olar
bows/ose 2
bowwow/ow 1
box/ox
boxcar/ar
boxy/oxy
boy/oy
boycott/ot
boyfriend/end
boys/oys
bozos/ose 2
brace/ace
braced/aste
brag/ag
braid/ade 1
Braille/ale 1
brain/ain
brainchild/ild
brainstorm/orm 1
brainwash/osh
brainwave/ave
brake/ake
bran/an
brand/and
brand-new/ew
brash/ash 1
brass/ass
brassy/assy
brat/at 1
bratty/atty
brave/ave
braver/aver
bravery/avery
brawl/all
brawled/alled
brawler/aller
brawny/awny
bray/ay
brazen/azon
Brazil/ill
Brazilian/illion
bread/ed

break/ake
breakdown/own 2
breakthrough/ew
breakup/up
breast/est
breath/eath 1
breathe/eethe
bred/ed
breed/eed
breeze/eeze
breezy/easy
brew/ew
brewed/ude
Brian/ion
bribe/ibe
brick/ick
bricks/icks
bridal/idle
bride/ide
bridegroom/oom
bridesmaid/ade 1
bridge/idge
bridle/idle
brief/ief
briefcase/ace
bright/ight
brighten/ighten
brighter/ider
brim/im
bring/ing
brink/ink
brisk/isk
bristle/istle
brittle/iddle
broach/oach
broad/awed
broadcast/ast
broadcaster/aster
broader/otter
brochure/ure
brogue/ogue 1
broil/oil
broke/oke

broken/oken
broker/oker
bronchitis/itis
bronze/ons
brood/ude
brook/ook 2
broom/oom
broomstick/ick
broth/oth 2
brother/other
brotherhood/ood 3
brought/ot
brow/ow 1
browbeat/eet
browbeaten/eaten
brown/own 2
browned/ound
Bruce/use 1
bruisable/usable
bruise/use 2
bruiser/user
brunch/unch
brunette/et
brunt/unt
brush/ush 1
brush-off/off
brusque/usk
brutal/oodle
brutality/ality 1
brute/ute
Bryant/iant
bubble/ouble
buccaneer/eer
buck/uck
buckaroo/ew
buckaroos/use 2
bucked/uct
buckle/uckle
bucks/ucks
bud/ud
Buddha/uda
buddy/uddy
budge/udge

buff/uff
buffalo/o 1
Buffalo Bill/ill
buffaloes/ose 2
buffer/uffer
buffoon/oon
bug/ug
bugaboo/ew
build/illed
buildup/up
built/ilt
Bulgaria/area
bulge/ulge
bulk/ulk
bull/ull 2
bulldog/og
bulldoze/ose 2
bullfight/ight
bullfrog/og
bullhorn/orn
bullpen/en
bully/ully
bum/um
bumble/umble
bumblebee/ee
bumblebees/eeze
bumbling/umbling
bummer/ummer
bump/ump
bumpkin/umpkin
bumpy/umpy
bun/un
bunch/unch
bungalows/ose 2
bungle/ungle
bunk/unk
bunk bed/ed
bunker/unker
Bunker, Archie/unker
bunny/unny
bunt/unt
bunts/unts
buoy/ewy, oy

bureaucracy/ocracy
bureaucrat/at 1
bureaucratic/atic
burglarize/ize
burlap/ap
burlesque/esque
burly/urly
burn/urn
burp/urp
burr/er
burrito/edo
burst/irst
bury/ary
bus/us
bush/ush 2
bushy/ushy
bussed/ust
bust/ust
busted/usted
bustle/ustle
busy/izzy
busybody/ody
but/ut 1
butt/ut 1
Butte/ute
butter/utter
butterball/all
buttercup/up
butterflies/ize
butterfly/y
buttermilk/ilk
buttonhole/ole
buy/y
buys/ize
buzz/uzz
buzzword/erd
by/y
bye/y
bypass/ass

Ⓒ

cab/ab 1

caballero/arrow
cabby/abby
cabdriver/iver 1
cable/able
caboose/use 1
cache/ash 1
cackle/ackle
cad/ad 1
caddie/atty
cadet/et
Cadillac/ack
Cadillacs/ax
Caesar/eezer
café/ay
cafés/aze
cafeteria/eria
caffeine/een
cage/age 1
cajole/ole
cajoled/old
cake/ake
calamari/arry 2
calculate/ate
calculation/ation
calculator/ader
calf/aff
calico/o 1
call/all
called/alled
caller/aller
calm/alm, om
caloric/oric
Camaro/arrow
came/aim
camelback/ack
Camelot/ot
Cameroon/oon
camisole/ole
camouflage/age 2
camp/amp
campaign/ain
camper/amper
campfire/ire

campground/ound
can/an 1
canal/al
canary/ary
cancan/an 1
cancellation/ation
candidate/ate
candlestick/ick
cane/ain
canine/ine 1
canned/and
cannibalism/ism
cannonball/all
cannot/ot
canoe/ew
canoes/use 2
can't/ant 1
cantaloupe/ope
canteen/een
cantina/ena
cap/ap
capability/ility
capacity/acity
cape/ape
Cape Cod/awed
capitalism/ism
capitalize/ize
cappuccino/ino 2
caprice/ease 2
Capricorn/orn
capsize/ize
captain/in
captivate/ate
captivity/ivity
car/ar
carat/arrot
caravan/an 1
carbohydrate/ate
card/ard 1
cardboard/ord 1
care/air
career/eer
carefree/ee

caress/ess
caressed/est
caribou/ew
carload/ode
carnivore/ore
carousel/ell
Carrie/ary
carrot/arrot
carry/ary
cart/art 1
cartoon/oon
cartwheel/eel
carve/arve
carwash/osh
case/ace
Casey/acy
cash/ash 1
cashbox/ox
cashew/ew
cashews/use 2
cashier/eer
cashmere/eer
casino/ino 2
cask/ask
casket/asket
casserole/ole
cast/ast
caste/ast
cat/at 1
catalog/og
catalytic/itic
catamaran/an 1
catapult/ult
catatonic/onic
catch/atch 1
catch-22/ew
catchy/atchy
categorize/ize
category/ory
cater/ader
caterpillar/iller
caterwaul/all
catfight/ight

catgut/ut 1
catnap/ap
catnip/ip
cattle/attle
catty/atty
Caucasian/asion
caught/ot
cauliflower/our 1
cause/ause
cavalcade/ade 1
cavalier/eer
cave/ave
caveman/an 1
caviar/ar
cavity/avity
cavort/ort
cavorter/order
CD/ee
cease/ease 2
ceased/east
cease-fire/ire
cedar/eeder
celebrate/ate
celebration/ation
Celeste/est
cell/ell
cellar/eller
cellmate/ate
cello/ellow
cellophane/ain
cell phone/one 1
celluloid/oid
Celt/elt
cement/ent
cemetery/ary
censorial/orial
censorship/ip
censure/enture
cent/ent
center/enter
centerpiece/ease 2
centigrade/ade 1
centimeter/eeder

centipede/eed
cents/ense
ceremonial/onial
ceremony/ony
certifies/ize
certify/y
cesspool/ool
Cézanne/awn
Chad/ad 1
chain/ain
chair/air
chalk/ock
chalkboard/ord 1
champ/amp
champagne/ain
championship/ip
chance/ance
chandelier/eer
change/ange
changeover/over
chant/ant 1
chants/ance
chaotic/otic
chap/ap
chapel/apple
chaperon/one 1
characteristic/istic
characterize/ize
charade/ade 1
charcoal/ole
charge/arge
charismatic/atic
charity/arity
charm/arm 1
charred/ard 1
chart/art 1
charter/arter
chartreuse/use 1
chase/ace
chased/aste
chasm/asm
chassis/assy
chaste/aste

chasten/ason
chastise/ize
chat/at 1
chatter/atter
chatterbox/ox
chatty/atty
chauffeur/ure
chauvinism/ism
cheap/eep
cheaper/eeper
cheapskate/ate
cheat/eet
cheater/eeder
check/eck
checkbook/ook 2
checked/ect
checkerboard/ord 1
checkered/ecord
checklist/ist
checkmate/ate
checkpoint/oint
checks/ex
checkup/up
cheddar/etter
cheek/eek
cheer/eer
cheerful/earful
Cheerios/ose 2
cheerleader/eeder
cheery/eery
cheese/eeze
cheesecake/ake
cheesy/easy
cheetah/ita
chef/ef
chenille/eel
cherish/erish
Chernobyl/oble
cherry/ary
Chesapeake/eek
chess/ess
chest/est
Chester/ester

chestnut/ut 1
chew/ew
chewed/ude
chews/use 2
chewy/ewy
Cheyenne/en
Chicana/onna
chick/ick
chickadees/eeze
chicken/icken
chickenpox/ox
chicks/icks
chide/ide
chief/ief
chiffon/awn
child/ild
childbirth/irth
childhood/ood 3
childlike/ike
childproof/oof 1
chili/illy
chill/ill
chilled/illed
chiller/iller
chilly/illy
chime/ime
chimp/imp
chimpanzee/ee
chimpanzees/eeze
chin/in
China/ina 2
Chinatown/own 2
chinchilla/illa
Chinese/eeze
chintz/ince
chip/ip
chipmunk/unk
chipped/ipped
chipper/ipper
chirp/urp
chisel/izzle
chitchat/at 1
Chloe/owy

chloride/ide
chlorine/een
chlorophyll/ill
chocoholic/olic
choice/oice
choir/ire
choke/oke
choker/oker
chokes/okes
cholesterol/all
chomp/omp
choose/use 2
chooser/user
chop/op
Chopin/an 1
chopper/opper
choppy/oppy
chopstick/ick
chopsticks/icks
chop suey/ewy
choral/oral
chorale/al
chord/ord 1
chore/ore
choreography/
  ography
chose/ose 2
chosen/ozen
chow/ow 1
chowder/owder
chowhound/ound
chow mein/ain
Christina/ena
chrome/ome 1
chronic/onic
chronicle/onical
chronological/ogical
chronology/ology
chrysanthemum/um
chubby/ubby
chuck/uck
chucked/uct
Chuckie/ucky

chuckle/uckle
chug/ug
chugalug/ug
chum/um
chummy/ummy
chump/ump
chunk/unk
chunky/unky
church/urch
churchgoing/
  owing
churn/urn
chute/ute
cicada/ada
cider/ider
cigar/ar
cigarette/et
cinch/inch
Cincinnati/atty
Cinderella/ella
cinerama/ama 1,
  ama 2
circulate/ate
circulation/ation
circumstance/ance
citation/ation
cite/ight
citizenship/ip
city/itty
civil/ivel
civilian/illion
civility/ility
civilization/ation
civilize/ize
clad/ad 1
claim/aim
clam/am
clambake/ake
clammy/ammy
clamp/amp
clan/an 1
clang/ang
clank/ank

189

clanky/anky
clap/ap
Clara/ara
clarified/ide
clarifies/ize
clarify/y
clarinet/et
Clarisse/ease 2
clarity/arity
Clark/ark
clash/ash 1
clasp/asp
class/ass
classify/y
classmate/ate
classroom/oom
classy/assy
clatter/atter
Claude/awed
clause/ause
claw/aw
clawed/awed
claws/ause
clay/ay
clean/een
clear/eer
clearer/earer
cleaver/eaver
clef/ef
clench/ench
clerk/erk
clever/ever
click/ick
clicked/ict
clicker/icker
clicks/icks
client/iant
clientele/ell
clients/iance
cliff/iff
Cliffs of Dover/over
climax/ax
climb/ime

clinch/inch
cling/ing
clingy/ingy 1
clink/ink
clinked/inct
clip/ip
clipped/ipped
clipper/ipper
cloaks/okes
clobber/obber
clock/ock
clocks/ox
clockwise/ize
clockwork/erk
clod/awed
clodhopper/opper
clog/og
clomp/omp
clone/one 1
clop/op
close/ose 1, ose 2
closure/osure
clot/ot
cloth/oth 2
clothes/ose 2
clotheshorse/orse
clothesline/ine 1
cloud/oud
cloudburst/irst
clout/out
clove/ove 1
clover/over
cloverleaf/ief
clown/own 2
clowned/ound
club/ub
clubhouse/ouse
Club Med/ed
cluck/uck
clucked/uct
clucker/ucker
clucks/ucks
clue/ew

clues/use 2
clump/ump
clumpy/umpy
clung/ung
clunk/unk
clunker/unker
clunky/unky
cluster/uster
clutch/utch
clutter/utter
coach/oach
coal/ole
coalition/ition
coarse/orse
coast/ost 1
coastline/ine 1
coat/ote
coax/okes
cobbler/obbler
cobblestone/one 1
Cochise/ease 2
cockatoo/ew
cockeyed/ide
cockpit/it
cockpits/its
cockroach/oach
cocktail/ale 1
cocky/awky
cocoa/oco
coconut/ut 1
cocoon/oon
coddle/oddle
code/ode
coed/ed
coerce/erse
coerced/irst
coercion/ersion
coexist/ist
coffeepot/ot
cohort/ort
coif/off
coil/oil
coin/oin

coincide/ide
coincidental/ental
Coke/oke
Cokes/okes
cola/ola
cold/old
colder/older
Colgate/ate
colic/olic
collage/age 2
collar/aller
colleague/eague
collect/ect
collection/ection
collector/ector
collects/ex
Colleen/een
college/owledge
collegian/egion
collide/ide
collie/olly
collision/ision
colloquialism/ism
collusion/usion
cologne/one 1
colon/olen
colonel/ernal
colonial/onial
colonize/ize
colorblind/ind 1
colt/olt
coma/oma
comatose/ose 1
comb/ome 1
combat/at 1
combination/ation
combine/ine 1
combined/ind 1
combust/ust
come/um
comedic/edic
comic/omic
comma/ama 1

command/and
commence/ense
commentary/ary
commerce/erse
commercialism/ism
commercialize/ize
commingle/ingle
commission/ition
commit/it
commits/its
committal/iddle
committee/itty
commodious/odious
commotion/otion
commune/oon
communicate/ate
communication/ation
communion/union
communism/ism
community/unity
commute/ute
commuter/uter
compact/act
companionship/ip
compare/air
compatibility/ility
compel/ell
compelled/eld
compete/eet
competition/ition
complain/ain
complete/eet
complex/ex
complexion/ection
complicate/ate
complication/ation
compliment/ent
compliments/ense
comply/y
composition/ition
composure/osure
compound/ound
comprehend/end

comprehension/ention
comprehensive/ensive
compressor/essor
comprise/ize
compromise/ize
compulsive/ulsive
compute/ute
computer/uter
comrade/ad 1
con/awn
conceal/eel
concealed/ield
concede/eed
conceit/eet
conceive/eave
concentrate/ate
concentration/ation
concept/ept
conception/eption
concern/urn
concession/ession
conch/aunch
concise/ice 1
conclude/ude
conclusion/usion
conclusive/usive
concrete/eet
concur/er
concurred/erd
concussion/ussion
condemn/em
condense/ense
condition/ition
condone/one 1
condor/onder, ore
conducive/usive
conduct/uct
conductor/uctor
cone/one 1
confer/er
conferred/erd

confess/ess
confessed/est
confession/ession
confessor/essor
confetti/etty
confidante/aunt
confide/ide
confidential/ential
confidentiality/ality 1
confine/ine 1
confined/ind 1
confirm/erm
confirmation/ation
confiscate/ate
conflict/ict
conflicts/icks
conform/orm 1
conformer/ormer
confront/unt
confuse/use 2
confusion/usion
congeal/eel
congeniality/ality 1
congestion/estion
congratulate/ate
congregation/ation
conical/onical
conjunction/unction
connect/ect
connection/ection
connector/ector
connects/ex
conned/ond
Connie/awny
conniption/iption
connive/ive 1
conniver/iver 1
connoisseur/ure
conquest/est
cons/ons
consent/ent
consequence/ense
consequently/ently

conservatory/ory
conserve/erve
consider/itter
consideration/ation
cosign/ine 1
consist/ist
consistence/istance
consolation/ation
console/ole
consoled/old
conspire/ire
constitute/ute
constitution/ution
constitutionality/
   ality 1
constrictor/ictor
construct/uct
construction/uction
constructive/uctive
construe/ew
construed/ude
construes/use 2
consult/ult
consume/oom
consumer/umor
consumption/
   umption
contacts/ax
contagious/ageous
contain/ain
contaminate/ate
contemplate/ate
contemporary/ary
contempt/empt
contender/ender
content/ent
contently/ently
contest/est
context/ext
continental/ental
contort/ort
contortion/ortion
contour/ure

contraband/and
contract/act
contraction/action
contradict/ict
contradiction/iction
contradictor/ictor
contradicts/icks
contrary/ary
contrast/ast
contribution/ution
contrive/ive 1
control/ole
controlled/old
controller/olar
convalescent/escent
convene/een
convention/ention
converge/erge
conversation/ation
converse/erse
conversed/irst
conversion/ersion
convert/ert
converter/erter
conveyor/ayer
convict/ict
conviction/iction
convince/ince
cook/ook 2
cookie/ookie
cookout/out
cool/ool
cooler/ooler
coolly/uly
coop/oop
cooperate/ate
cooperation/ation
coordinate/ate
coordination/ation
coordinator/ader
coot/ute
cootie/oody
cop/op

cope/ope
copper/opper
copy/oppy
copyright/ight
coquette/et
coral/oral
cord/ord 1
corduroy/oy
core/ore
cork/ork 1
corkscrew/ew
corkscrews/use 2
corn/orn
corncob/ob
cornucopia/opia
corporation/ation
corps/ore
corral/al
correct/ect
correction/ection
corrects/ex
correspond/ond
corresponds/ons
corridor/ore
corrosion/osion
corrosive/osive
corrupt/upt
corruption/uption
Corryn/in
corsage/age 2
Corvette/et
cosmetic/etic
cosmos/ose 1
cost/ost 2
costar/ar
costarred/ard 1
costume/oom
costumer/umor
cot/ot
cotillion/illion
cotton/otten
cottontail/ale 1
couch/ouch

cough/off
could/ood 3
count/ount
countdown/own 2
counterculture/
  ulture
counterfeit/it
counterfeits/its
counterpart/art 1
counterproductive/
  uctive
countersue/ew
counts/ounce
coupe/oop
coupon/awn
courageous/ageous
course/orse
court/ort
courter/order
courthouse/ouse
courtroom/oom
courtship/ip
Cousteau, Jacques/o 1
couth/ooth
cove/ove 1
covert/ert
cow/ow 1
coward/owered
cowboys/oys
cower/our 1
cowered/owered
cowhand/and
cowpoke/oke
coy/oy
cozy/osy
CPR/ar
crab/ab 1
crabby/abby
crack/ack
crackdown/own 2
cracked/act
crackerjack/ack
crackle/ackle

crackpot/ot
cracks/ax
crackup/up
craft/aft
crafty/afty
cram/am
cramp/amp
crane/ain
crank/ank
cranky/anky
crash/ash 1
crass/ass
crate/ate
crater/ader
crave/ave
crawl/all
crawled/alled
crawly/olly
Crayola/ola
craze/aze
crazy/azy
creak/eek
creaky/eaky
cream/eem
creamy/eamy
crease/ease 2
creased/east
create/ate
creation/ation
creativity/ivity
creator/ader
creature/eacher
credential/ential
credibility/ility
creed/eed
creek/eek
creep/eep
creeper/eeper
creepy/eepy
crematorium/orium
Creole/ole
crept/ept
crescent/escent

crest/est
cretin/eaten
crew/ew
crewed/ude
crib/ib
cricket/icket
cried/ide
cries/ize
crime/ime
criminology/ology
crimp/imp
cringe/inge
crinkle/inkle
cripple/ipple
Crisco/isco
crisp/isp
crisper/isper
crisscross/oss 2
crisscrossed/ost 2
critic/itic
critical/itical
criticism/ism
criticize/ize
critique/eek
critter/itter
croak/oke
croaks/okes
crock/ock
Crockett, Davy/ocket
crocodile/ile 1
crony/ony
crook/ook 2
croon/oon
crooner/ooner
crop/op
croquet/ay
cross/oss 2
crossed/ost 2
crossfire/ire
crossroad/ode
crosstown/own 2
crosswalk/ock
crosswalks/ox

crossword/erd
crouch/ouch
crow/o 1
crowd/oud
crowed/ode
crowing/owing
crown/own 2
crowned/ound
crows/ose 2
crucify/y
crud/ud
cruddy/uddy
crude/ude
cruel/uel
crueler/ooler
cruelly/uly
cruise/use 2
cruiser/user
crumb/um
crumble/umble
crummy/ummy
crunch/unch
crusade/ade 1
crusader/ader
crush/ush 1
crust/ust
crusty/usty
crutch/utch
crux/ucks
cry/y
crypt/ipped
cub/ub
cubbyhole/ole
cube/ube
cuckoo/ew
cuckoos/use 2
cucumber/umber 1
cuddle/uddle
cue/ew
cued/ude
cuff/uff
cuisine/een
cul-de-sac/ack

culinary/ary
cull/ull 1
cult/ult
cultivate/ate
culture/ulture
cummerbund/und
cup/up
cupcake/ake
cupid/upid
cupidity/idity
cupped/upt
curable/urable
curb/urb
curdle/urdle
cure/ure
curfew/ew
curfews/use 2
curiosity/ocity
curious/urious
curl/url
curlicue/ew
curly/urly
curry/urry
curse/erse
cursed/irst
curt/ert
curtail/ale 1
curvacious/acious
curvature/ure
curve/erve
cushy/ushy
cuss/us
cussed/ust
customary/ary
cut/ut 1
cute/ute
cuter/uter
cutie/oody
cutoff/off
cutter/utter
cutthroat/ote
cutup/up
cyclone/one 1

cymbal/imble
cynicism/ism
cyst/ist
czar/ar
Czech/eck

dab/ab 1
dabble/abble
dad/ad 1
daddy/atty
daffodil/ill
daily/aily
dairy/ary
daisy/azy
dally/alley
Dalmatian/ation
dam/am
damp/amp
damper/amper
dance/ance
dandelion/ion
dang/ang
Daniel Boone/oon
dank/ank
Danny/anny
Danube/ube
dare/air
daredevil/evel
dark/ark
Darlene/een
darn/arn
dart/art 1
dash/ash 1
dashboard/ord 1
date/ate
daub/ob
daughter/otter
daunt/aunt
Davy Crockett/ocket
dawdle/oddle
dawn/awn

dawned/ond
dawns/ons
day/ay
daybreak/ake
daydream/eem
daylight/ight
days/aze
daytime/ime
daze/aze
dead/ed
deadbeat/eet
deadbolt/olt
deader/etter
deadline/ine 1
deadlock/ock
deadlocks/ox
deadpan/an 1
deadwood/ood 3
deaf/ef
deal/eel
dealt/elt
dean/een
dear/eer
Dear Abby/abby
dearer/earer
dearie/eery
death/eath 1
deathbed/ed
Death Valley/alley
debacle/ackle
debate/ate
debater/ader
debonair/air
debrief/ief
debt/et
debtor/etter
debut/ew
debutante/aunt
decade/ade 1
decaf/aff
decal/al
decathlon/awn
decay/ay

decayed/ade 1
decays/aze
decease/ease 2
deceased/east
deceit/eet
deceive/eave
December/ember
deception/eption
decide/ide
decision/ision
deck/eck
decked/ect
decks/ex
declaration/ation
declare/air
decline/ine 1
declined/ind 1
decode/ode
decompose/ose 2
decomposition/ition
decongest/est
decongestion/estion
decor/ore
decorate/ate
decoration/ation
decorator/ader
decoys/oys
decrease/ease 2
decreased/east
dedicate/ate,
    edicate
dedication/ation
deduce/use 1
deduced/uced
deduct/uct
deduction/uction
deed/eed
deem/eem
deep/eep
deeper/eeper
deep-fried/ide
deer/eer
deface/ace

defaced/aste
defame/aim
default/alt
defaults/alts
defeat/eet
defect/ect
defective/ective
defector/ector
defects/ex
defend/end
defender/ender
defense/ense
defensive/ensive
defer/er
deferential/ential
deferred/erd
defiance/iance
defiant/iant
deficient/icient
defied/ide
defies/ize
define/ine 1
defined/ind 1
definition/ition
deflate/ate
deform/orm 1
defrost/ost 2
defroster/oster
deft/eft
defuse/use 2
defy/y
degree/ee
degrees/eeze
dehydration/ation
dejection/ection
Delaware/air
delay/ay
delayed/ade 1
delays/aze
delegate/ate
delete/eet
deli/elly
deliberate/ate, it

delicious/icious
delight/ight
delirious/erious
deliver/iver 2
Della/ella
delude/ude
deluge/uge
delusion/usion
deluxe/ucks
delve/elve
demand/and
demerit/arrot
democracy/ocracy
democrat/at 1
democratic/atic
demography/
    ography
demolish/olish
demolition/ition
demonic/onic
demonstrate/ate
demonstration/ation
demonstrator/ader
demoralize/ize
demur/er
demure/ure
demystifies/ize
demystify/y
den/en
denied/ide
denies/ize
Denmark/ark
Denny/enny
denomination/
    omination
dense/ense
density/ensity
dent/ent
dental/ental
dents/ense
denture/enture
deny/y
deodorize/ize

deodorizer/izer
depart/art 1
departmental/ental
depend/end
dependability/ility
deport/ort
depravity/avity
depress/ess
depressed/est
depression/ession
deprive/ive 1
derail/ale 1
derelict/ict
dermatologist/ologist
dermatology/ology
derogatory/ory
descend/end
descent/ent
describe/ibe
description/iption
desert/ert
deserter/erter
deserve/erve
design/ine 1
designed/ind 1
designer/iner
desire/ire
desk/esque
Des Moines/oin
despair/air
desperation/ation
despise/ize
dessert/ert
destination/ation
destitute/ute
destitution/ution
destroy/oy
destroyed/oid
destroys/oys
destruct/uct
destruction/uction
destructive/uctive
detach/atch 1

detail/ale 1
detect/ect
detective/ective
detector/ector
detects/ex
detention/ention
deter/er
detergent/ergent
determination/ation
deterred/erd
detest/est
dethrone/one 1
detonate/ate
detonator/ader
detour/ure
detox/ox
detrimental/ental
deuce/use 1
devastate/ate
devastation/ation
deviate/ate
device/ice
devil/evel
devise/ize
devoid/oid
Devon/even
devote/ote
devotion/otion
devotional/otional
devour/our 1
devoured/owered
devout/out
dew/ew
dewy/ewy
dexterity/arity
diabetic/etic
diabolic/olic
diagnose/ose 1
diagnosed/ost 1
diagram/am
dial/ile 1
dialects/ex
dialed/ild

dialogue/og
Diana/ana 1
diaper/iper
diatribe/ibe
dice/ice 1
diced/iced
dictation/ation
dictator/ader
dictatorial/orial
dictatorship/ip
diction/iction
dictionary/ary
did/id
diddle/iddle
die/y
died/ide
diehard/ard 1
dies/ize
diet/iet
dietary/ary
Diet Coke/oke
Diet Cokes/okes
dietetic/etic
dietician/ition
difficult/ult
dig/ig
digestion/estion
digger/igger
dignified/ide
dignify/y
dignitary/ary
digress/ess
digressed/est
dilettante/aunt
dill/ill
dilute/ute
dim/im
dime/ime
dimension/ention
dimmer/immer
dimple/imple
din/in
Din, Gunga/in

Dinah/ina 2
dine/ine 1
dined/ind 1
diner/iner
dinero/arrow
ding/ing
ding-a-ling/ing
dingbat/at 1
dinghy/ingy 1
dingo/ingo
dingy/ingy 2
dinky/inky
dinner/inner
dinnertime/ime
dinosaur/ore
dip/ip
diphtheria/eria
diploma/oma
diplomat/at 1
diplomatic/atic
dipped/ipped
dipper/ipper
dippy/ippy
dire/ire
direct/ect
direction/ection
director/ector
directs/ex
dirt/ert
dirty/irty
disability/ility
disable/able
disagree/ee
disagreed/eed
disagrees/eeze
disappear/eer
disappoint/oint
disapprove/ove 3
disarm/arm 1
disaster/aster
disband/and
disbar/ar
disbelief/ief

disc/isk
discard/ard 1
discharge/arge
disciplinary/ary
discipline/in
disciplined/inned
disco/isco
disconnect/ect
disconnects/ex
discontent/ent
discord/ord 1
discotheque/eck
discount/ount
discounts/ounce
discreet/eet
discrete/eet
discretion/ession
discriminate/ate
discrimination/ation
discuss/us
discussed/ust
discussion/ussion
disdain/ain
disease/eeze
disembark/ark
disenchants/ance
disfavor/aver
disgrace/ace
disgraced/aste
disguise/ize
disgust/ust
disgusted/usted
dish/ish
dishevel/evel
dishonor/onor
dishpan/an 1
dishrag/ag
dishwater/otter
disillusion/usion
disinfect/ect
disinherit/arrot
disk/isk
dislike/ike

dislocate/ate
dislodge/odge
disloyal/oil
dismiss/iss
dismissal/istle
dismissed/ist
Disneyland/and
disobey/ay
disobeyed/ade 1
disobeys/aze
disown/one 1
disparity/arity
dispatch/atch 1
dispense/ense
disperse/erse
dispersed/irst
displaced/aste
display/ay
displayed/ade 1
displays/aze
displease/eeze
displeasure/easure
disposal/osal
dispose/ose 2
disposition/ition
disprove/ove 3
dispute/ute
disqualified/ide
disqualifies/ize
disqualify/y
disregard/ard 1
disrespect/ect
disrobe/obe
disrupt/upt
disruption/uption
dissatisfaction/
   action
dissatisfied/ide
dissatisfies/ize
dissatisfy/y
dissect/ect
dissension/ention
dissent/ent

dissenter/enter
dissolution/ution
dissolve/olve
distance/istance
distaste/aste
distinct/inct
distort/ort
distortion/ortion
distract/act
distraction/action
distracts/ax
distraught/ot
distress/ess
distressed/est
distressful/essful
distribution/ution
distrust/ust
disturb/urb
ditch/itch
ditchdigger/igger
dither/ither
ditty/itty
ditzy/itzy
dive/ive 1
diver/iver 1
diverge/erge
divergent/ergent
diverse/erse
diversion/ersion
diversity/ersity
divert/ert
divide/ide
dividend/end
divider/ider
divine/ine 1
divinity/inity
division/ision
divorce/orse
divulge/ulge
Dixieland/and
dizzy/izzy
do/ew
doc/ock

dock/ock
docket/ocket
docks/ox
Dr. Seuss/use 1
dodge/odge
doe/o 1
Doe, John/o 1
does/uzz
dog/og
dog-doo/ew
doggie/oggy
doggone/awn
doggoned/ond
doghouse/ouse
dogtrot/ot
dole/ole
doled/old
doll/all
dollar/aller
dolly/olly
dolt/olt
domain/ain
dome/ome 1
domesticity/icity
domicile/ile 1
dominate/ate
domination/
   omination
dominoes/ose 2
don/awn
Donald Duck/uck
donate/ate
donation/ation
done/un
dong/ong
Don Juan/awn
Donna/onna
donned/ond
donnybrook/ook 2
dons/ons
doodad/ad 1
doodle/oodle
doodlebug/ug

Doody, Howdy/oody
doom/oom
door/ore
doorbell/ell
doorknob/ob
doormat/at 1
doorstep/ep
doorstop/op
doozer/user
dope/ope
dopey/opey
Dora/ora
dork/ork 1
dorm/orm 1
dose/ose 1
dot/ot
dote/ote
Dotty/ody
double/ouble
double-check/eck
double-checked/ect
doubleheader/etter
doubt/out
doubter/owder
dough/o 1
doughy/owy
douse/ouse
doused/oust
dove/ove 1, ove 2
dovetail/ale 1
down/own 2
downcast/ast
downed/ound
downfall/all
downhill/ill
downpour/ore
downrange/ange
downriver/iver 2
downstream/eem
downtown/own 2
downturn/urn
downwind/inned
doze/ose 2

drab/ab 1
drabber/abber
drabby/abby
draft/aft
drafter/after
drafty/afty
drag/ag
draggy/aggy
dragnet/et
dragonflies/ize
dragonfly/y
drain/ain
drama/ama 1
dramatic/atic
dramatize/ize
drank/ank
drape/ape
drastic/astic
draw/aw
drawback/ack
drawbacks/ax
drawbridge/idge
drawer/ore
drawl/all
drawled/alled
drawn/awn
drawstring/ing
dread/ed
dream/eem
dreamboat/ote
dreamland/and
dreamt/empt
dreamy/eamy
dreary/eery
dredge/edge
drench/ench
dress/ess
dressed/est
dresser/essor
dressy/essy
drew/ew
dribble/ibble
dried/ide

dries/ize
drift/ift
driftwood/ood 3
drill/ill
drilled/illed
drink/ink
drip/ip
dripped/ipped
dripper/ipper
drippy/ippy
drive/ive 1
drivel/ivel
driven/iven
driver/iver 1
drizzle/izzle
dromedary/ary
drone/one 1
drool/ool
drooler/ooler
drooly/uly
droop/oop
drooper/ooper
droopy/oopy
drop/op
dropout/out
dropper/opper
drought/out
drove/ove 1
drown/own 2
drowned/ound
drudge/udge
drug/ug
drugstore/ore
drum/um
drummer/ummer
drumstick/ick
drumsticks/icks
drunk/unk
drunken/unken
drunker/unker
dry/y
dryness/inus
dual/uel

dub/ub
duck/uck
Duck, Donald/uck
ducked/uct
ducks/ucks
ducky/ucky
duct/uct
dud/ud
dude/ude
dudette/et
due/ew
duel/uel
dues/use 2
duet/et
duffel/uffle
dug/ug
dugout/out
duke/uke
dull/ull 1
dullsville/ill
dumb/um
dumbbell/ell
dumber/ummer
dumbfound/ound
dumbstruck/uck
dummy/ummy
dump/ump
dumpy/umpy
Duncan/unken
dunce/unts
dune/oon
dungarees/eeze
dunk/unk
dupe/oop
duplex/ex
duplicate/ate
duplication/ation
duplicator/ader
duplicity/icity
durability/ility
durable/urable
duration/ation
duress/ess

dusk/usk
dust/ust
dusted/usted
duster/uster
dustpan/an 1
duststorm/orm 1
dusty/usty
Dutch/utch
duty/oody
DVD/ee
dwarf/arf 2
dwell/ell
dweller/eller
Dwight/ight
dwindle/indle
dye/y
dyed/ide
dyes/ize
dynamite/ight
dynamo/o 1
dynamos/ose 2
dysfunction/unction

e

each/each
eager/eager
eagle/egal
ear/eer
earache/ake
eardrum/um
earful/earful
earl/url
earlobe/obe
early/urly
earmark/ark
earn/urn
Earp, Wyatt/urp
earplug/ug
earring/ing
earth/irth
earthbound/ound
earthquake/ake

earthworm/erm
earwax/ax
ease/eeze
east/east
easy/easy
easygoing/owing
eat/eet
eaten/eaten
eater/eeder
eavesdrop/op
eavesdropper/opper
eccentricity/icity
ecclesiastic/astic
ecologist/ologist
ecology/ology
economic/omic
economize/ize
economy/onomy
ecstatic/atic
Ecuador/ore
Ed/ed
Eddie/etty
edge/edge
edition/ition
editorial/orial
educate/ate
educator/ader
eel/eel
eerie/eery
effect/ect
effective/ective
effects/ex
effervescent/escent
efficient/icient
effuse/use 2
egad/ad 1
egg/eg
egghead/ed
eggplant/ant 1
eggshell/ell
egotism/ism
Egyptian/iption
Eiffel Tower/our 1

eight/ate
eighteen/een
eighty/ady
Einstein/ine 1
eject/ect
ejection/ection
ejects/ex
elaborate/ate
Elaine/ain
elastic/astic
elasticity/icity
elate/ate
elation/ation
elect/ect
election/ection
elective/ective
electrician/ition
electricity/icity
electrify/y
electrocute/ute
electrocution/ution
electrode/ode
electronic/onic
elects/ex
elemental/ental
elephant/unt
elevate/ate
elevation/ation
elevator/ader
eleven/even
elf/elf
elicit/icit
eliminate/ate
elimination/ation
elite/eet
Elizabeth/eath 1
Ella/ella
elope/ope
elsewhere/air
elude/ude
elusive/usive
emancipate/ate
embalm/alm, om

ember/ember
emblazon/azon
embody/ody
embrace/ace
embraced/aste
emcee/ee
emerge/erge
emergency/urgency
emergent/ergent
emigrate/ate
emotion/otion
emotional/otional
emperor/er
emphasize/ize
employ/oy
employed/oid
employee/ee
emporium/orium
empower/our 1
empowered/owered
enable/able
enact/act
enchant/ant 1
enchants/ance
enchilada/ada
enclose/ose 2
enclosure/osure
encore/ore
end/end
endeavor/ever
endorse/orse
endurable/urable
endurance/urance
endure/ure
energetic/etic
energize/ize
energizer/izer
enfold/old
enforce/orse
engage/age 1
engineer/eer
engorge/orge
engrave/ave

engross/ose 1
engrossed/ost 1
enhance/ance
enjoy/oy
enjoyed/oid
enjoys/oys
enlarge/arge
enlighten/ighten
enlist/ist
enmesh/esh
enough/uff
enrage/age 1
enrich/itch
enroll/ole
enrolled/old
ensure/ure
enter/enter
enterprise/ize
entertain/ain
enthrall/all
enthralled/alled
enthuse/use 2
enthusiasm/asm
enthusiast/ast, ist
enthusiastic/astic
entice/ice 1
enticed/iced
entire/ire
entitle/idle
entomb/oom
entourage/age 2
entrance/ance
entreaty/eedy
entrust/ust
entwine/ine 1
entwined/ind 1
envelope/ope
environmental/ental
envision/ision
enzyme/ime
episode/ode
equality/ality 2
equate/ate

equation/asion
equator/ader
equip/ip
equipped/ipped
erase/ace
erased/aste
erect/ect
erects/ex
erode/ode
erosion/osion
erosive/osive
err/er
erratic/atic
erred/erd
error/arer
erupt/upt
eruption/uption
escalate/ate
escalator/ader
escapade/ade 1
escape/ape
escort/ort
Eskimo Pie/y
Eskimos/ose 2
espionage/age 2
essay/ay
essays/aze
essential/ential
estate/ate
esteem/eem
Esther/ester
estimate/ate, it
etch/etch
eternal/ernal
Ethiopia/opia
ethnicity/icity
Eugene/een
euphoric/oric
Eurasian/asion
evacuate/ate
evaluate/ate
evaluation/ation
evaporate/ate

evasion/asion
eve/eave
event/ent
ever/ever
evergreen/een
evermore/ore
everybody/ody
everyday/ay
everyone/un
everyplace/ace
everything/ing
everywhere/air
evict/ict
eviction/iction
evicts/icks
evidence/ense
evident/ent
evidently/ently
evolution/ution
evolve/olve
ewe/ew
ex/ex
exact/act
exaggerate/ate
exaggerator/ader
exalt/alt
exam/am
exasperate/ate
exasperation/ation
excavate/ate
exceed/eed
excel/ell
excelled/eld
except/ept
exception/eption
excess/ess
excessive/essive
exchange/ange
excite/ight
exclaim/aim
exclude/ude
exclusion/usion
exclusive/usive

ex-con/awn
ex-cons/ons
excrete/eet
excursion/ersion
excusable/usable
excuse/use 1, use 2
execute/ute
execution/ution
exemplified/ide
exemplifies/ize
exemplify/y
exempt/empt
exercise/ize
exerciser/izer
exert/ert
exhale/ale 1
exhaust/ost 2
exhibit/ibit
exhibition/ition
exhilarate/ate
exhume/oom
exile/ile 1
exiled/ild
exist/ist
existence/istance
exotic/otic
expand/and
expanse/ance
expect/ect
expectation/ation
expects/ex
expedition/ition
expel/ell
expelled/eld
expense/ense
expensive/ensive
experiment/ent
experimental/ental
expire/ire
explain/ain
explanation/ation
explanatory/ory
explicit/icit

explode/ode
exploration/ation
explore/ore
explored/ord 1
explosion/osion
explosive/osive
export/ort
exporter/order
expose/ose 2
exposure/osure
express/ess
expressed/est
expression/ession
expressive/essive
extend/end
extension/ention
extensive/ensive
extent/ent
exterminate/ate
extermination/ation
exterminator/ader
external/ernal
extinct/inct
extol/ole
extolled/old
extract/act
extraction/action
extraordinary/ary
extreme/eem
extrovert/ert
exude/ude
exult/ult
eye/y
eyeball/all
eyebrow/ow 1
eyed/ide
eyedropper/opper
eyelash/ash 1
eyelid/id
eyeliner/iner
eyes/ize
eyesight/ight
eyesore/ore

fab/ab 1
fable/able
fabrication/ation
facade/awed
face/ace
faced/aste
facial/acial
facilitator/ader
facility/ility
fact/act
faction/action
facts/ax
fad/ad 1
faddy/atty
fade/ade 1
Fahrenheit/ight
fail/ale 1
fair/air
fairer/arer
fairy/ary
fairyland/and
fajita/ita
fake/ake
falafel/awful
fall/all
fallout/out
falsehood/ood 3
falsetto/etto
falsify/y
falter/alter
fame/aim
familiarity/arity
familiarize/ize
fan/an 1
fanatic/atic
fanfare/air
fang/ang
fanned/and
fantasize/ize
fantastic/astic
fantasyland/and

far/ar
faraway/ay
fare/air
farewell/ell
farm/arm 1
fascinate/ate
fascination/ation
fascism/ism
fast/ast
faster/aster
fastidious/idious
fat/at 1
fatalistic/istic
fatality/ality 1
fate/ate
father/ather 2
fatherhood/ood 3
fatigue/eague
fatten/atin
fatter/atter
fatty/atty
fault/alt
faults/alts
favor/aver
favoritism/ism
fawn/awn
fawned/ond
fawns/ons
fax/ax
faze/aze
FBI/y
fear/eer
fearful/earful
feast/east
feat/eet
feather/eather
featherbrain/ain
feature/eacher
February/ary
fed/ed
fedora/ora
fee/ee
feed/eed

feedback/ack
feeder/eeder
feel/eel
fees/eeze
feet/eet
feline/ine 1
fell/ell
fella/ella
feller/eller
fellow/ellow
fellowship/ip
felt/elt
female/ale 1
femininity/inity
fence/ense
fender/ender
fern/urn
ferocious/ocious
ferocity/ocity
Ferrari/arry 2
ferret/arrot
ferry/ary
fertile/urdle
fertilize/ize
fertilizer/izer
fester/ester
festivity/ivity
fetch/etch
fettuccine/ini
feud/ude
feudal/oodle
fever/eaver
few/ew
fiasco/asco
fib/ib
fickle/ickle
fiction/iction
fictitious/icious
fiddle/iddle
fiddlesticks/icks
field/ield
fifteen/een
fifty/ifty

fig/ig
fight/ight
fighter/ider
figurehead/ed
file/ile 1
filed/ild
filibuster/uster
Filipino/ino 2
fill/ill
filled/illed
filler/iller
filly/illy
fin/in
finale/olly
finality/ality 1
finance/ance
finch/inch
find/ind 1
fine/ine 1
fined/ind 1
finesse/ess
finessed/est
finger/inger 1
fingernail/ale 1
fingerprint/int
fingertip/ip
finite/ight
fink/ink
fir/er
fire/ire
firearm/arm 1
firefighter/ider
firefly/y
firehouse/ouse
firelight/ight
fireplace/ace
fireplug/ug
fireproof/oof 1
fireside/ide
firetrap/ap
firm/erm
first/irst
firsthand/and

fish/ish
fishbowl/ole
fishhook/ook 2
fishmonger/unger
fishpond/ond
fist/ist
fistfight/ight
fit/it
fits/its
five/ive 1
fix/icks
fixation/ation
fizz/iz
fizzle/izzle
fizzy/izzy
fjord/ord 1
flab/ab 1
flabbergast/ast
flabby/abby
flack/ack
flag/ag
flagpole/ole
flair/air
flake/ake
flame/aim
flamingo/ingo
flap/ap
flapjack/ack
flare/air
flash/ash 1
flashback/ack
flashlight/ight
flashy/ashy
flask/ask
flat/at 1
flatten/atin
flatter/atter
flattery/attery
flattop/op
flaunt/aunt
flavor/aver
flaw/aw
flawed/awed

flaws/ause
flea/ee
fleas/eeze
fleck/eck
flecked/ect
flecks/ex
fled/ed
flee/ee
fleece/ease 2
flees/eeze
fleet/eet
flesh/esh
flew/ew
flex/ex
flexed/ext
flexibility/ility
flibbertigibbet/ibit
flick/ick
flicked/ict
flicker/icker
flicks/icks
flies/ize
flight/ight
flighty/idy
flinch/inch
fling/ing
flint/int
flip/ip
flipped/ipped
flipper/ipper
flirt/ert
flirtation/ation
flirtatious/acious
flirty/irty
flit/it
flits/its
flitty/itty
float/ote
flock/ock
flocks/ox
flog/og
flood/ud
floodwater/otter

floor/ore
floored/ord 1
flop/op
floppy/oppy
floral/oral
floss/oss 2
flossed/ost 2
flounce/ounce
flour/our 1
flow/o 1
flowed/ode
flower/our 1
flowered/owered
flowerpot/ot
flowing/owing
flown/one 1
flows/ose 2
Floyd/oid
flu/ew
flub/ub
fluctuate/ate
fluff/uff
fluffy/uffy
fluke/uke
flung/ung
flunk/unk
fluorescent/escent
flurry/urry
flush/ush 1
fluster/uster
flute/ute
flutter/utter
flux/ucks
fly/y
FM/em
foal/ole
foam/ome 1
focal/ocal
fodder/otter
foe/o 1
foes/ose 2
fog/og
foggy/oggy

201

foghorn/orn
foil/oil
fold/old
folk/oke
folklore/ore
folks/okes
follow/allow 2
folly/olly
fond/ond
fonder/onder
food/ude
foodaholic/olic
fool/ool
foolhardy/ardy
foolproof/oof 1
foot/oot 2
football/all
foothold/old
footlocker/ocker
footloose/use 1
footmark/ark
footnote/ote
footprint/int
footprints/ince
footwork/erk
for/ore
forbid/id
forbidden/idden
force/orse
Ford/ord 1
forecast/ast
forecaster/aster
forefront/unt
foreground/ound
forehead/ed
foresees/eeze
foresight/ight
forever/ever
forevermore/ore
forewarn/orn
forgave/ave
forge/orge
forget/et

forgetter/etter
forgive/ive 2
forgiven/iven
forgot/ot
forgotten/otten
fork/ork 1
forlorn/orn
form/orm 1
formal/ormal
formality/ality 1
format/at 1
formation/ation
former/ormer
formulate/ate
fort/ort
forte/ort, ay
forthright/ight
fortify/ortify, y
fortune-teller/eller
forty/orty
forty-niner/iner
forward/erd
foster/oster
fought/ot
foul/owl
found/ound
foundation/ation
four/ore
fourteen/een
fourth/orth
four-wheeled/ield
fox/ox
foxhole/ole
foxy/oxy
fraction/action
fragmentary/ary
frail/ale 1
frame/aim
framework/erk
Fran/an 1
France/ance
franchise/ize
frank/ank

Frankenstein/ine 1
Frankfurt/ert
frankfurter/erter
Frankie/anky
frantic/antic
fraternal/ernal
fraud/awed
fray/ay
frayed/ade 1
freak/eek
freaky/eaky
freckle/eckle
Freddie/etty
free/ee
freed/eed
freelance/ance
freeload/ode
freely/eally
frees/eeze
freestyle/ile 1
free will/ill
freeze/eeze
freezer/eezer
freight/ate
freighter/ader
French/ench
frenetic/etic
frequent/ent
fresh/esh
freshen/ession
fret/et
Freud/oid
friction/iction
Friday/idy
fridge/idge
fried/ide
friend/end
friendship/ip
fries/ize
fright/ight
frighten/ighten
frill/ill
frilled/illed

frilly/illy
fringe/inge
fringy/ingy 2
Frisco/isco
frisk/isk
frisky/isky
Frito/edo
fritter/itter
frivolity/ality 2
frizz/iz
frizzy/izzy
frock/ock
frog/og
froggy/oggy
frolic/olic
from/um
front/unt
frontier/eer
fronts/unts
frost/ost 2
frostbite/ight
frostbitten/itten
froth/oth 2
frown/own 2
frowned/ound
froze/ose 2
frozen/ozen
fruit/ute
fruitcake/ake
fruity/oody
frumpy/umpy
frustrate/ate
frustration/ation
fry/y
fuddy-duddy/uddy
fudge/udge
fuel/uel
fulfill/ill
fulfilled/illed
full/ull 2
fullback/ack
fully/ully
fumble/umble

fumbling/umbling
fume/oom
fumigate/ate
fun/un
function/unction
fund/und
fundamental/ental
funk/unk
funky/unky
funnel/unnel
funny/unny
fur/er
furious/urious
furry/urry
furthermore/ore
fury/ury
fuse/use 2
fusion/usion
fuss/us
fussed/ust
futile/oodle
futility/ility
future/uture
futuristic/istic
fuzz/uzz

gab/ab 1
gabber/abber
gabby/abby
gag/ag
ga-ga/aw
gaily/aily
gain/ain
gait/ate
gal/al
Galahad/ad 1
gale/ale 1
gall/all
gallbladder/atter
galley/alley
gallivant/ant 1

galore/ore
game/aim
gang/ang
gangplank/ank
gangway/ay
gap/ap
gape/ape
garage/age 2
gargoyle/oil
garish/erish
garter/arter
Gary/ary
gas/ass
gash/ash
gasket/asket
gasoline/een
gasp/asp
gassed/ast
gastritis/itis
gate/ate
gather/ather 1
gator/ader
Gatorade/ade 1
gaudy/ody
gauge/age 1
gaunt/aunt
gauze/ause
gave/ave
gavel/avel
gawk/ock
gawks/ox
gawky/awky
gay/ay
Gaza Strip/ip
gaze/aze
gazelle/ell
gear/eer
gee/ee
geek/eek
geeky/eaky
geese/ease 2
geezer/eezer
gel/ell

gem/em
gender/ender
gene/een
generate/ate
generation/ation
generator/ader
generosity/ocity
genetic/etic
Genghis Khan/awn
genie/ini
gent/ent
genteel/eel
gentle/ental
gently/ently
gents/ense
geographic/aphic
geography/ography
geological/ogical
geologist/ologist
geology/ology
George/orge
Gepetto/etto
germ/erm
Geronimo/o 1
Gertie/irty
gesundheit/ight
get/et
Gettysburg Address/
    ess
geyser/izer
Ghana/onna
ghetto/etto
ghost/ost 1
ghostwriter/ider
ghoul/ool
giant/iant
giants/iance
gibe/ibe
Gibraltar/alter
giddy/itty
gift/ift
giftwrap/ap
gig/ig

gigantic/antic
giggle/iggle
giggly/iggly
gill/ill
Gina/ena
ginger/inger 2
gingerbread/ed
gingersnap/ap
Ginny/inny
giraffe/aff
girdle/urdle
girl/url
girlfriend/end
girth/irth
gist/ist
give/ive 2
given/iven
giver/iver 2
gizzard/izard
glacial/acial
gladder/atter
gladiola/ola
glance/ance
gland/and
glare/air
glass/ass
glassy/assy
glaze/aze
gleam/eem
glean/een
glee/ee
glib/ib
glide/ide
glider/ider
glimmer/immer
glint/int
glitch/itch
glitter/itter
glittery/ittery
glitzy/itzy
gloat/ote
glob/ob
global/oble

globe/obe
globetrotter/otter
glockenspiel/eel
gloom/oom
gloomy/oomy
glorified/ide
glorifies/ize
glorify/orify, y
glorious/orious
glory/ory
gloss/oss 2
glossed/ost 2
glossy/ossy
glove/ove 2
glow/o 1
glowed/ode
glowing/owing
glows/ose 2
glowworm/erm
glue/ew
glued/ude
glues/use 2
glug/ug
glum/um
glut/ut 1
gnash/ash 1
gnat/at 1
gnaw/aw
gnawed/awed
gnome/ome 1
gnu/ew
go/o 1
goad/ode
goal/ole
goalie/oly
goalpost/ost 1
goaltender/ender
goat/ote
gob/ob
gobble/obble
gobbledygook/
    ook 2, uke
gobbler/obbler

God/awed
godchild/ild
godfather/ather 2
Godiva/iva
godmother/other
goes/ose 2
go-getter/etter
goggle/oggle
going/owing
gold/old
golden retriever/
    eaver
goldenrod/awed
goldfish/ish
Goldilocks/ox
golly/olly
gone/awn
goner/onor
gong/ong
gonna/onna
goo/ew
good/ood 3
goodwill/ill
gooey/ewy
goof/oof 1
goofball/all
goofy/oofy
goon/oon
goop/oop
goopy/oopy
goose/use 1
gooseflesh/esh
gore/ore
gorge/orge
gorilla/illa
gory/ory
gosh/osh
got/ot
gotten/otten
Gouda/uda
gourd/ord 1
governmental/ental
gown/own 2

grab/ab 1
grabber/abber
grabby/abby
grace/ace
graced/aste
Gracie/acy
gracious/acious
grad/ad 1
grade/ade 1
graduate/ate, it
graduation/ation
graffiti/eedy
graft/aft
grain/ain
gram/am
Grammy/ammy
Granada/ada
grand/and
granddad/ad 1
granddaddy/atty
grandfather/ather 2
grandiose/ose 1
grandma/aw
grandmother/other
grandpa/aw
grandpappy/appy
grandparent/arent
grandson/un
grandstand/and
granny/anny
grant/ant 1
grants/ance
grape/ape
grapefruit/ute
grapevine/ine 1
graph/aff
graphic/aphic
grapple/apple
grasp/asp
grass/ass
grasshopper/opper
grassy/assy
grate/ate

Grateful Dead/ed
gratifies/ize
gratify/y
gratitude/ude
grave/ave
gravel/avel
graveyard/ard 1
gravitate/ate
gravity/avity
gravy/avy
gray/ay
grayed/ade 1
grayer/ayer
graze/aze
grease/ease 2
greased/east
great/ate
Great Britain/itten
Great Dane/ain
greater/ader
Greece/ease 2
greed/eed
greedy/eedy
Greek/eek
green/een
greenhorn/orn
greet/eet
Greg/eg
gregarious/arious
grenade/ade 1
Gretel/eddle
grew/ew
greyhound/ound
grid/id
griddle/iddle
gridlock/ock
grief/ief
grieve/eave
grill/ill
grilled/illed
grim/im
grime/ime
grimmer/immer

grin/in
grind/ind 1
grindstone/one 1
gringo/ingo
grinned/inned
grinner/inner
grip/ip
gripe/ipe
griper/iper
gristle/istle
grit/it
grits/its
gritty/itty
groan/one 1
grog/og
groggy/oggy
groin/oin
groom/oom
groomer/umor
groove/ove 3
grope/ope
gross/ose 1
grossed/ost 1
grotesque/esque
grotto/otto
grouch/ouch
ground/ound
groundhog/og
groundwork/erk
group/oop
grove/ove 1
grow/o 1
growing/owing
growl/owl
grown/one 1
grows/ose 2
growth/oth 1
gr-r-r/er
grub/ub
grubby/ubby
grudge/udge
gruel/uel
gruff/uff

gruffer/uffer
grumble/umble
grumbling/umbling
grump/ump
grumpy/umpy
grunt/unt
grunts/unts
guacamole/oly
Guam/om
guarantee/ee
guaranteed/eed
guarantees/eeze
guard/ard 1
guardianship/ip
guerrilla/illa
guess/ess
guessed/est
guesser/essor
guesswork/erk
guest/est
guide/ide
guideline/ine 1
guidepost/ost 1
guild/illed
guillotine/een
guilt/ilt
guise/ize
guitar/ar
gull/ull 1
gullibility/ility
gulp/ulp
gum/um
gumdrop/op
gummy/ummy
gumption/umption
gumshoes/use 2
gun/un
gung ho/o 1
Gunga Din/in
gunned/und
gunner/unner
gunnysack/ack
gunshot/ot

gunslinger/inger 1
gunsmith/ith
guppy/uppy
gush/ush 1
gushy/ushy
gust/ust
gusty/usty
gut/ut 1
gutter/utter
guttersnipe/ipe
guy/y
guys/ize
guzzle/uzzle
gymnast/ast, ist
gymnastic/astic
gyp/ip
gypped/ipped
gypsy/ipsy
gyrate/ate

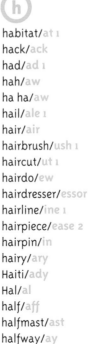

habitat/at 1
hack/ack
had/ad 1
hah/aw
ha ha/aw
hail/ale 1
hair/air
hairbrush/ush 1
haircut/ut 1
hairdo/ew
hairdresser/essor
hairline/ine 1
hairpiece/ease 2
hairpin/in
hairy/ary
Haiti/ady
Hal/al
half/aff
halfmast/ast
halfway/ay
halibut/ut 1

hall/all
hallow/allow 1
Halloween/een
hallucinate/ate
hallucination/ation
hallway/ay
hallways/aze
halt/alt
halter/alter
halts/alts
ham/am
hamper/amper
hand/and
handball/all
handbook/ook 2
handcuff/uff
handicap/ap
handiwork/erk
handkerchief/ief
handlebar/ar
handout/out
handpick/ick
handpicked/ict
handshake/ake
handstand/and
handwrite/ight
handwritten/itten
handyman/an 1
hang/ang
hangman/an 1
hangnail/ale 1
hangout/out
hangover/over
hankie/anky
hanky-panky/anky
Hans/ons
Hanukkah/onica
happy/appy
hara-kiri/eery
harangue/ang
harass/ass
harassed/ast
hard/ard 1

hard-boil/oil
harder/arter
hardhat/at 1
hardhead/ed
hardship/ip
hardy/ardy
hare/air
hark/ark
harm/arm 1
harmonic/onic
harmonica/onica
harmonize/ize
harpoon/oon
harpsichord/ord 1
Harry/ary
has/azz
hash/ash
haste/aste
hasten/ason
hasty/asty
hat/at 1
hatch/atch 1
hate/ate
hater/ader
haughty/ody
haul/all
hauled/alled
haunch/aunch
haunt/aunt
Havana/ana 1
Hawaiian/ion
hawk/ock
hawks/ox
hay/ay
haystack/ack
haystacks/ax
haywire/ire
haze/aze
hazy/azy
he/ee
head/ed
headache/ake
headband/and

headfirst/irst
headhunter/unter
headlight/ight
headline/ine 1
headlined/ind 1
headliner/iner
headlock/ock
headlong/ong
headmaster/aster
headphone/one 1
headstone/one 1
headstrong/ong
headway/ay
heady/etty
heal/eel
healed/ield
heap/eep
hear/eer
heard/erd
hearse/erse
heart/art 1
heartache/ake
heartbeat/eet
heartbreak/ake
heartbroken/oken
heartburn/urn
heartfelt/elt
heartsick/ick
heartstopper/opper
heartthrob/ob
hearty/ardy
heat/eet
heater/eeder
Heather/eather
heatstroke/oke
heave/eave
heave-ho/o 1
heaven/even
heavyweight/ate
heck/eck
heckle/eckle
Hector/ector
hedge/edge

heed/eed
heel/eel
Heidi/idy
height/ight
heighten/ighten
heir/air
heirloom/oom
heist/iced
held/eld
heliport/ort
hell/ell
hello/ellow, o 1
help/elp
helpmate/ate
Helsinki/inky
helter-skelter/elter
hem/em
hemisphere/eer
hemline/ine 1
hen/en
her/er
herb/urb
Hercules/eeze
herd/erd
herder/erter
here/eer
hereafter/after
hereditary/ary
heretic/ick
herewith/ith
hero/ero 1
heroic/oic
heroism/ism
heron/aron
herself/elf
hesitant/esident
hesitate/ate
hesitation/ation
hex/ex
hexagon/awn
hexed/ext
hey/ay
hi/y

hibernate/ate
hiccup/up
hiccupped/upt
hiccupper/upper
hid/id
hidden/idden
hide/ide
hideous/idious
hi-fi/y
high/y
high-heeled/ield
highlight/ight
highlighter/ider
highs/ize
high tech/eck
highway/ay
hijack/ack
hijacked/act
hike/ike
hiker/iker
hilarious/arious
hilarity/arity
hill/ill
hilltop/op
hilly/illy
hilt/ilt
him/im
himself/elf
hindsight/ight
hinge/inge
hint/int
hints/ince
hip/ip
hippie/ippy
hire/ire
his/iz
hiss/iss
hissed/ist
hissy/issy
historic/oric
history/istory
hit/it
hitch/itch

Hitchcock/ock
hitchhike/ike
hitchhiker/iker
hither/ither
hits/its
hitter/itter
hive/ive 1
hoard/ord 1
hoarder/order
hoarse/orse
hoax/okes
hobble/obble
hobbler/obbler
hobby/obby
hobnob/ob
Hoboken/oken
hockey/awky
hodgepodge/odge
hoedown/own 2
hog/og
hogwash/osh
hogwild/ild
hold/old
holdout/out
hole/ole
holey/oly
holiday/ay
holidays/aze
holistic/istic
holler/aller
hollow/allow 2
holly/olly
Hollywood/ood 3
holocaust/ost 2
holster/olster
holy/oly
Holy Grail/ale 1
home/ome 1
homebody/ody
homefront/unt
homegrown/one 1
homeland/and
homemade/ade 1

homeroom/oom
homesick/ick
homespun/un
homestead/ed
homestretch/etch
hometown/own 2
homework/erk
homicidal/idle
homonym/im
hon/un
honcho/oncho
hone/one 1
honey/unny
honeybun/un
honeybunch/unch
honeycomb/ome 1
honeymoon/oon
honeymooner/ooner
honeysuckle/uckle
Hong Kong/ong
honk/onk
honor/onor
honorary/ary
honorbound/ound
hood/ood 3
Hood, Robin/ood 3
hoodwink/ink
hoodwinked/inct
hoof/oof 2
hook/ook 2
hooky/ookie
hoop/oop
hoopla/aw
hoot/ute
hop/op
hope/ope
Hopi/opey
hopscotch/otch
Horatius/acious
hormone/one 1
horn/orn
horoscope/ope
horrific/ific

horrified/ide
horrifies/ize
horrify/orify, y
hors d'oeuvre/erve
horse/orse
horsefly/y
horsepower/our 1
horseshoe/ew
horticulture/ulture
hose/ose 2
hospital/iddle
hospitality/ality 1
host/ost 1
hostility/ility
hot/ot
hotel/ell
hotfoot/oot 2
hot rod/awed
hot rodder/otter
hotter/otter
hot-wire/ire
Houdini/ini
hound/ound
hound dog/og
hour/our 1
hourglass/ass
house/ouse
housebreak/ake
housebroken/oken
household/old
housekeeper/eeper
housewife/ife
housework/erk
how/ow 1
Howard/owered
Howdy Doody/oody
however/ever
howl/owl
hub/ub
hubbub/ub
hubby/ubby
hubcap/ap
huddle/uddle

hue/ew
hued/ude
hues/use 2
huff/uff
huffy/uffy
hug/ug
huge/uge
hulk/ulk
hull/ull 1
hullabaloo/ew
hum/um
humane/ain
humankind/ind 1
humble/umble
humbling/umbling
humbug/ug
humdinger/inger 1
humdrum/um
humidity/idity
humiliate/ate
humiliation/ation
humility/ility
hummer/ummer
hummingbird/erd
humor/umor
humorous/umorous
hump/ump
Hun/un
hunch/unch
hung/ung
hunger/unger
hunk/unk
hunker/unker
hunky-dory/ory
hunt/unt
hunter/unter
hunts/unts
hurdle/urdle
hurl/url
hurrah/aw
hurricane/ain
hurry/urry
hurt/ert

hurtle/urdle
hush/ush 1
hushaby/y
husk/usk
hustle/ustle
hut/ut 1
hutch/utch
hybrid/id
hydraulic/olic
hyena/ena
hygiene/een
hymn/im
hype/ipe
hyper/iper
hyperactive/active
hypertension/ention
hyphenate/ate
hypnotic/otic
hypnotism/ism
hypnotize/ize
hypocrisy/ocracy
hypocrite/it
hypocrites/its
hypocritical/itical
hysteria/area

I/y
ice/ice 1
iced/iced
icepack/ack
icicle/ickle
icky/icky
iconoclast/ast
icons/ons
icy/icy
ID/ee, idy
id/id
Idaho/o 1
ideal/eel
idealism/ism
idealistic/istic

idealize/ize
ideally/eally
identified/ide
identifies/ize
identify/y
idiosyncratic/atic
idiotic/otic
idle/idle
idol/idle
idolize/ize
if/iff
iffy/iffy
ignite/ight
ignition/ition
ignore/ore
ignored/ord 1
iguana/onna
ilk/ilk
I'll/ile 1
ill/ill
illegal/egal
illegality/ality 1
illicit/icit
Illinois/oy
illogical/ogical
illuminate/ate
illusion/usion
illusive/usive
illustrate/ate
illustration/ation
illustrator/ader
I'm/ime
imaginary/ary
imagination/ation
imbibe/ibe
imitate/ate
imitation/ation
imitator/ader
immature/ure
immaturity/urity
immense/ense
immensity/ensity
immerse/erse

immersed/irst
immersion/ersion
immigrate/ate
immigration/ation
immobile/oble
immoral/oral
immorality/ality 1
immortality/ality 1
immune/oon
immunity/unity
imp/imp
impact/act
impair/air
impale/ale 1
impart/art 1
impasse/ass
impeach/each
impede/eed
impeder/eeder
imperfection/ection
impersonate/ate
impersonation/ation
impersonator/ader
implant/ant 1
implement/ent
implicit/icit
implied/ide
implies/ize
implode/ode
implosion/osion
imply/y
impolite/ight
import/ort
importer/order
impose/ose 2
imposition/ition
impossibility/ility
imposter/oster
impractical/actical
impress/ess
impressed/est
impression/ession
impressive/essive

imprint/int
imprints/ince
impromptu/ew
improper/opper
improve/ove 3
improvise/ize
improviser/izer
impulsive/ulsive
impunity/unity
impure/ure
impurity/urity
in/in
inability/ility
inaction/action
inactive/active
inattention/ention
inborn/orn
inbound/ound
inbred/ed
incandescent/escent
incense/ense
incentive/entive
incessant/escent
inch/inch
incidental/ental
incidentally/ently
incision/ision
incisor/izer
incite/ight
incline/ine 1
include/ude
inclusion/usion
incognito/edo
incomplete/eet
inconclusive/usive
incorrect/ect
increase/ease 2
increased/east
incurable/urable
indecision/ision
indeed/eed
indent/ent
index/ex

indexed/ext
Indiana/ana 1
indicate/ate
indicator/ader
indict/ight
indigestion/estion
indirect/ect
indiscreet/eet
indiscretion/ession
individualism/ism
individuality/ality 1
indoor/ore
induce/use 1
indulge/ulge
industrialism/ism
ineffective/ective
inefficient/icient
inept/ept
inequality/ality 2
inexcusable/usable
infantile/ile 1
infect/ect
infection/ection
infects/ex
infer/er
inferiority/ority
inferred/erd
infiltrate/ate
infinity/inity
inflame/aim
inflammation/ation
inflate/ate
inflation/ation
inflection/ection
inflict/ict
influential/ential
info/o 1
inform/orm 1
informal/ormal
informality/ality 1
information/ation
informer/ormer

infraction/action
infrared/ed
infringe/inge
infuse/use 2
ingrate/ate
inhale/ale 1
inherent/arent
inherit/arrot
inhibit/ibit
inhibition/ition
inhumane/ain
initial/icial
initiate/ate
initiation/ation
inject/ect
injection/ection
injects/ex
injure/inger 2
injurious/urious
ink/ink
inkblot/ot
inked/inct
inkwell/ell
inmate/ate
inn/in
innate/ate
inner/inner
innermost/ost 1
innovation/ation
innovator/ader
inoculate/ate
input/oot 2
inquire/ire
inquisition/ition
insane/ain
inscribe/ibe
inscription/iption
insect/ect
insecticide/ide
insects/ex
insecure/ure
insecurity/urity
insensitivity/ivity

insert/ert
inside/ide
insider/ider
insidious/idious
insight/ight
insincere/eer
insincerity/arity
insinuate/ate
insist/ist
insistence/istance
insomniac/ack
inspect/ect
inspection/ection
inspector/ector
inspects/ex
inspiration/ation
inspire/ire
install/all
installed/alled
installer/aller
Instamatic/atic
instead/ed
instigate/ate
instigator/ader
instill/ill
instinct/inct
institute/ute
institution/ution
instruct/uct
instruction/uction
instructive/uctive
instructor/uctor
instrumental/ental
insufficient/icient
insult/ult
insurance/urance
insure/ure
insurgency/urgency
insurgent/ergent
intake/ake
integrate/ate
integration/ation
intellect/ect

intend/end
intense/ense
intensifies/ize
intensify/y
intensity/ensity
intensive/ensive
intent/ent
intention/ention
intently/ently
interact/act
interaction/action
interacts/ax
intercept/ept
interception/eption
interchange/ange
intercom/om
interfere/eer
interferer/earer
interjection/ection
interlaced/aste
interlude/ude
intermission/ition
intern/urn
internal/ernal
internship/ip
interpretation/ation
interracial/acial
interrogate/ate
interrogation/ation
interrupt/upt
interruption/uption
interscholastic/astic
intersect/ect
intersection/ection
intersects/ex
interspaced/aste
intersperse/erse
interstellar/eller
intertwine/ine 1
intertwined/ind 1
intervene/een
intervention/ention
interview/ew

209

interviewed/ude
interviews/use 2
intimidate/ate
intimidation/ation
into/ew
intoxicate/ate
intoxication/ation
intramural/ural
intrigue/eague
introduce/use 1
introduced/uced
introduction/uction
introvert/ert
intrude/ude
intrusion/usion
intrusive/usive
intuition/ition
invade/ade 1
invader/ader
invasion/asion
invent/ent
invention/ention
inventive/entive
inventor/enter
inverse/erse
invert/ert
invest/est
investigate/ate
investigation/ation
investigator/ader
investor/ester
invigorate/ate
invite/ight
involve/olve
iodine/ine 1
iota/ota
IQ/ew
Iran/awn
Iraq/ack
Irene/een
iridescent/escent
irk/erk
ironclad/ad 1

ironic/onic
ironical/onical
irregularity/arity
irrigate/ate
irritate/ate
irritation/ation
is/iz
Isabel/ell
Isabella/ella
isle/ile 1
isolate/ate
isolation/ation
Israeli/aily
issue/issue
Istanbul/ull 2
it/it
itch/itch
itinerary/ary
its/its
itself/elf
itsy-bitsy/itzy
Ivanhoe/o 1
I've/ive 1

j

jab/ab 1
jabber/abber
Jabberwocky/awky
jack/ack
jackal/ackle
jackknife/ife
jackpot/ot
jacks/ax
Jacques/ock
Jacques Cousteau/o 1
jade/ade 1
jag/ag
jaguar/ar
jail/ale 1
jailbird/erd
jailbreak/ake
Jake/ake

jalopy/oppy
jam/am
jamboree/ee
jamborees/eeze
James Bond/ond
Jan/an
Jane/ain
January/ary
Japan/an 1
Japanese/eeze
jar/ar
jarred/ard 1
Jason/ason
jaunt/aunt
jaw/aw
jawbone/one 1
jaws/ause
jaywalk/ock
jaywalker/ocker
jaywalks/ox
jazz/azz
jazzy/azzy
jealous/ealous
Jean/een
Jeanette/et
Jeanie/ini
jeep/eep
jeer/eer
Jeff/ef
Jekyll/eckle
jell/ell
jelled/eld
Jell-O/ellow
jelly/elly
jellyfish/ish
Jenny/enny
jeopardize/ize
jerk/erk
jerky/erky
Jessie/essy
jest/est
jester/ester
jet/et

jetliner/iner
jetsetter/etter
jewel/uel
jeweler/ooler
jiffy/iffy
jig/ig
jiggle/iggle
jiggly/iggly
jigsaw/aw
jigsaws/ause
Jill/ill
jilt/ilt
Jim/im
jingle/ingle
jitterbug/ug
jittery/ittery
jive/ive 1
Joan/one 1
Joan of Arc/ark
job/ob
Job/obe
jock/ock
jockey/awky
jocks/ox
Joe/o 1
Joel/ole
Joey/owy
jog/og
joggle/oggle
John/awn
John Doe/o 1
Johnny/awny
join/oin
joint/oint
joke/oke
joker/oker
jokes/okes
jolly/olly
jolt/olt
Jonah/ona
Josephine/een
josh/osh
jot/ot

journal/ernal
journalism/ism
joust/oust
joviality/ality 1
joy/oy
Joyce/oice
joyride/ide
joys/oys
Juanita/ita
Judah/uda
judge/udge
judgmental/ental
judicial/icial
judicious/icious
Judy/oody
jug/ug
juggle/uggle
juggler/uggler
juice/use 1
juiced/uced
jujitsu/ew
Jules Verne/urn
Juliet/et
July/y
July Fourth/orth
jumble/umble
jumbling/umbling
jump/ump
jumpy/umpy
junction/unction
June/oon
jungle/ungle
junk/unk
junk heap/eep
junky/unky
junkyard/ard 1
Jupiter/upiter
jurisdiction/iction
jury/ury
just/ust
justifiable/iable
justification/ation 1
justified/ide

justifies/ize
justify/y
jut/ut 1
juvenile/ile 1

kangaroo/ew
kangaroos/use 2
kaput/oot 2
karate/ody
Karen/aron
Kate/ate
Kathleen/een
Katie/ady
kayak/ack
kayaks/ax
kazoo/ew
kazoos/use 2
keel/eel
keen/een
keep/eep
keeper/eeper
keepsake/ake
keg/eg
Keith/eath 2
Kelly/elly
kelp/elp
Kenny/enny
Kentucky/ucky
kept/ept
kernel/ernal
kerosene/een
kerplop/op
kerplunk/unk
kettle/eddle
Kevin/even
key/ee
keyboard/ord 1
keyhole/ole
keynote/ote
keys/eeze
Khan, Genghis/awn

kibble/ibble
kick/ick
kicked/ict
kicker/icker
kickoff/off
kicks/icks
kickstand/and
kid/id
kidder/itter
kiddie/itty
kidnap/ap
kill/ill
killed/illed
killer/iller
killjoy/oy
killjoys/oys
kilometer/eeder,
   ometer
kilt/ilt
Kim/im
kimono/ona
kin/in
kind/ind 1
kindle/indle
kinfolk/oke
king/ing
King Kong/ong
King Tut/ut 1
kink/ink
kinked/inct
kinship/ip
Kirk/erk
kiss/iss
kissed/ist
kissy/issy
kit/it
kite/ight
kits/its
kitten/itten
kitty/itty
Kleenex/ex
knack/ack
knapsack/ack

knave/ave
knead/eed
knee/ee
kneecap/ap
kneed/eed
kneel/eel
knees/eeze
knelt/elt
knew/ew
knife/ife
knight/ight
knit/it
knits/its
knitter/itter
knob/ob
knobby/obby
knock/ock
knockabout/out
knockdown/own 2
knocker/ocker
knockout/out
knocks/ox
knockwurst/urst
knoll/ole
knot/ot
knotty/ody
know/o 1
knowing/owing
knowledge/
   owledge
known/one 1
knows/ose 2
knuckle/uckle
knucklehead/ed
konk/onk
kook/uke
Kool-Aid/ade 1
kowtow/ow 1
kowtowed/oud
Kringle, Kriss/ingle
Kriss Kringle/ingle
kung fu/ew

1

lab/ab 1
label/able
laboratory/ory
laborious/orious
lace/ace
laced/aste
lack/ack
lacked/act
lackluster/uster
lacks/ax
lacy/acy
lad/ad 1
ladder/atter
lady/ady
ladybird/erd
ladybug/ug
ladylike/ike
lag/ag
lagoon/oon
laid/ade 1
lair/air
lake/ake
lamb/am
lame/aim
lament/ent
lamp/amp
lampoon/oon
lampshade/ade 1
lance/ance
Lancelot/ot
land/and
landlord/ord 1
landlubber/ubber
landmark/ark
Land Rover/over
landscape/ape
landslide/ide
lane/ain
lanky/anky
lap/ap
lapel/ell

Lapland/and
lard/ard 1
large/arge
lark/ark
Larry/ary
laryngitis/itis
lash/ash 1
lass/ass
last/ast
latch/atch 1
late/ate
latecomer/ummer
later/ader
lather/ather 1
Latin/atin
Latino/ino 2
latitude/ude
latter/atter
laugh/aff
laughed/aft
laughingstock/ock
laughter/after
launch/aunch
launder/onder
Laundromat/at 1
laurel/oral
Laurie/ory
lavatory/ory
law/aw
lawful/awful
lawman/an 1
lawn/awn
lawns/ons
laws/ause
lawsuit/ute
lax/ax
lay/ay
layer/ayer
layover/over
layperson/erson
laze/aze
lazy/azy
lead/ed, eed

leader/eeder
leadership/ip
leaf/ief
league/eague
leak/eek
leaky/eaky
lean/een
leap/eep
leapfrog/og
learn/urn
lease/ease 2
least/east
leather/eather
leatherneck/eck
leave/eave
led/ed
ledge/edge
leech/each
leer/eer
leery/eery
left/eft
leftover/over
leg/eg
legal/egal
legality/ality 1
legalize/ize
legendary/ary
legion/egion
legislate/ate
legislation/ation
legislator/ader
legit/it
legwork/erk
lemonade/ade 1
lend/end
lender/ender
length/ength
Lenny/enny
Lent/ent
lentil/ental
leotard/ard 1
leprechaun/awn
leprechauns/ons

less/ess
lesser/essor
Lester/ester
letdown/own 2
letter/etter
letterhead/ed
level/evel
lever/ever
Levi's/ize
liability/ility
liable/iable
liaison/awn
liberate/ate
liberation/ation
liberator/ader
library/ary
libretto/etto
lice/ice 1
lick/ick
licked/ict
licks/icks
lid/id
lie/y
lied/ide
lies/ize
life/ife
lifeboat/ote
lifeguard/ard 1
lifelike/ike
lifeline/ine 1
lifelong/ong
lifesaver/aver
lifestyle/ile 1
lifetime/ime
lift/ift
liftoff/off
light/ight
lighten/ighten
lighter/ider
lighthouse/ouse
like/ike
likelihood/ood 3
likewise/ize

lilacs/ax
Lilliput/ut 1
lilt/ilt
lily/illy
limb/im
limbo/imbo
lime/ime
limelight/ight
limitation/ation
limousine/een
limp/imp
line/ine 1
lined/ind 1
lineup/up
linger/inger 1
lingo/ingo
linguine/ini
linguistic/istic
link/ink
linked/inct
lint/int
Linus/inus
lion/ion
lip/ip
lippy/ippy
lip-read/eed
lipstick/ick
lipsticks/icks
liqueur/ure
liquidate/ate
liquor/icker
lisp/isp
lisper/isper
list/ist
lit/it
liter/eeder
literary/ary
litter/itter
litterbag/ag
litterbug/ug
little/iddle
live/ive 1, ive 2
livelihood/ood 3

liver/iver 2
Liverpool/ool
livestock/ock
Liz/iz
lizard/izard
llama/ama 1
Lloyd/oid
load/ode
loaf/oaf
loan/one 1
lob/ob
lobby/obby
lobe/obe
local/ocal
locale/al
locality/ality 1
locate/ate
location/ation
Loch Ness/ess
lock/ock
locker/ocker
locket/ocket
locks/ox
locksmith/ith
loco/oco
locomotion/otion
lodge/odge
log/og
logical/ogical
loin/oin
Lola/ola
loll/all
lolled/alled
lollipop/op
lollygag/ag
lone/one 1
lonely/only
long/ong
Longfellow/ellow
longhand/and
longitude/ude
look/ook 2
lookout/out

loom/oom
loon/oon
loop/oop
loophole/ole
loose/use 1
loot/ute
looter/uter
lop/op
lope/ope
loquacious/acious
lord/ord 1
lore/ore
Lorraine/ain
lose/use 2
loser/user
loss/oss 2
lost/ost 2
lot/ot
lotion/otion
lottery/ottery
lotto/otto
loud/oud
louder/owder
loudmouth/outh 1
loudspeaker/eaker
Louise/eeze
Louisiana/ana 1
louse/ouse
love/ove 2
lovebird/erd
lovelorn/orn
lovesick/ick
lovestruck/uck
low/o 1
low-cal/al
lowdown/own 2
Lowell/ole
lows/ose 2
loyal/oil
Loyola/ola
luau/ow 1
lube/ube
lubricate/ate

luck/uck
lucky/ucky
lug/ug
Luke/uke
lukewarm/orm 1
lull/ull 1
lullabies/ize
lullaby/y
lumber/umber 1
lumberjack/ack
lump/ump
lumpy/umpy
lunar/ooner
lunatic/ick
lunch/unch
lunchbox/ox
lung/ung
lunge/unge
lurch/urch
lure/ure
lurk/erk
lush/ush 1
luster/uster
lute/ute
luxurious/urious
lynch/inch

ma/aw
ma'am/am
macabre/obber
macaroni/ony
macaroon/oon
Macbeth/eath 1
machete/etty
machine/een
mad/ad 1
madame/am
madcap/ap
madder/atter
made/ade 1
mademoiselle/ell

213

Mad Hatter/atter
madhouse/ouse
madman/an 1
Madrid/id
magazine/een
Maggie/aggy
magician/ition
magnetic/etic
magnetism/ism
magnified/ide
magnifies/ize
magnify/y
magpie/y
maid/ade 1
mail/ale 1
mailbag/ag
mailbox/ox
maim/aim
main/ain
Maine/ain
mainstream/eem
maintain/ain
majorette/et
majority/ority
make/ake
makeshift/ift
makeup/up
malaria/area
malcontent/ent
male/ale 1
malfunction/unction
Malibu/ew
malicious/icious
mall/all
malnutrition/ition
malt/alt
malts/alts
mama/ama 1
man/an 1
mañana/onna
mandate/ate
mandatory/ory
mandolin/in

mane/ain
Manhattan/atin
manhole/ole
manhunt/unt
manhunter/unter
maniac/ack
maniacs/ax
manicure/ure
manifest/est
Manila/illa
manipulate/ate
manipulation/ation
manipulator/ader
manner/anner
mannerism/ism
manor/anner
manslaughter/otter
manuscript/ipped
many/enny, inny
map/ap
mar/ar
marathon/awn
marathons/ons
March/arch
march/arch
Mardi Gras/aw
mare/air
Marge/arge
Marie/ee
marina/ina
marine/een
maritime/ime
mark/ark
Mark Twain/ain
Marlene/een
marmalade/ade 1
maroon/oon
marred/ard 1
marrow/arrow
marry/ary
marshmallow/
    allow 1, ellow
mart/art 1

martini/ini
Marty/ardy
martyr/arter
Marv/arve
Mary/ary
Mary Jo/o 1
Masai/y
mascara/ara
mascot/ot
masculinity/inity
mash/ash 1
mask/ask
mason/ason
masquerade/ade 1
masquerader/ader
mass/ass
massacred/erd
massage/age 2
masseur/ure
masseuse/use 1
mast/ast
master/aster
mastermind/ind 1
masterpiece/ease 2
mat/at 1
matador/ore
match/atch 1
mate/ate
materialism/ism
maternal/ernal
matey/ady
math/ath
mathematic/atic
mathematician/ition
matinee/ay
Matisse/ease 2
matrimonial/onial
matrimony/ony
matter/atter
Matterhorn/orn
mature/ure
maturity/urity
maul/all

mauled/alled
Maurice/ease 2
mauve/ove 1
Maxine/een
Maxwell/ell
may/ay
maybe/aby
Maybelline/een
Mayflower/our 1
mayonnaise/aze
mayor/ayer
Mazatlán/awn
maze/aze
me/ee
meadow/etto
meager/eager
meal/eel
mean/een
meant/ent
meantime/ime
meanwhile/ile 1
meany/ini
measure/easure
meat/eet
meatball/all
meaty/eedy
medal/eddle
meddle/eddle
mediator/ader
medicate/ate,
    edicate
medication/ation
mediocre/oker
meditate/ate
meditation/ation
meek/eek
meet/eet
Meg/eg
melancholy/olly
meld/eld
mellow/ellow
melodic/otic
melodious/odious

melodrama/ama 1
melodramatic/atic
melt/elt
meltdown/own 2
member/ember
membership/ip
memoir/ar
memorial/orial
memorize/ize
men/en
mend/end
menorah/ora
mental/ental
mentality/ality 1
mention/ention
mentor/enter, ore
meow/ow 1
meowed/oud
mercenary/ary
merchandise/ice 1
mere/eer
merge/erge
meringue/ang
merit/arrot
mermaid/ade 1
merry/ary
mesh/esh
mesmerize/ize
mess/ess
messed/est
messy/essy
met/et
metal/eddle
metaphor/ore
meteorite/ight
meteorology/ology
meter/eeder
metronome/ome 1
mew/ew
mewed/ude
mews/use 2
Mexico/o 1
mezzanine/een

Miami/ammy
mic/ike
mice/ice 1
Mickey/icky
microphone/one 1
microscope/ope
microscopic/opic
microwave/ave
midair/air
middle/iddle
midnight/ight
midriff/iff
midsummer/
   ummer
midterm/erm
midweek/eek
midwinter/inter
miff/iff
miffed/ift
might/ight
mighty/idy
migraine/ain
migrate/ate
migration/ation
mild/ild
mildewy/ewy
mile/ile 1
milestone/one 1
military/ary
milk/ilk
Milk Dud/ud
mill/ill
milled/illed
Millie/illy
milligram/am
million/illion
millionaire/air
Milwaukee/awky
mime/ime
Mimi/eamy
mince/ince
mind/ind 1
mine/ine 1

mined/ind 1
miner/iner
minestrone/ony
mingle/ingle
mini/inny
minimart/art 1
miniskirt/ert
minister/inister
mink/ink
Minnesota/ota
Minnie/inny
minor/iner
minority/ority
mint/int
mints/ince
minuet/et
minus/inus
minuscule/ool
minute/ute
mirage/age 2
mirror/earer
mirth/irth
misapprehension/
   ention
misbehave/ave
miscast/ast
misconception/
   eption
misconstrue/ew
misconstrued/ude
miscue/ew
miscued/ude
miscues/use 2
misdeal/eel
misdialed/ild
misdo/ew
miser/izer
misfiled/ild
misfit/it
misfits/its
misguide/ide
mishap/ap
mishmash/ash 1

misinform/orm 1
misjudge/udge
mislabel/able
mislead/eed
mismatch/atch 1
misplace/ace
misplaced/aste
misprint/int
misprints/ince
mispronounce/ounce
misquote/ote
misread/ed
misrepresent/ent
miss/iss
missed/ist
missile/istle
mission/ition
missionary/ary
Mississippi/ippy
missive/issive
Missouri/ury, urry
misspeak/eek
misspell/ell
misspelled/eld
misspent/ent
misspoken/oken
missy/issy
mist/ist
mistake/ake
Mister/ister
mistletoe/o 1
mistook/ook 2
mistreat/eet
mistrust/ust
mistrusted/usted
misunderstand/and
misunderstood/
   ood 3
misuse/use 1, use 2
mitt/it
mitten/itten
mitts/its
Mitzi/itzy

mix/icks
moan/one 1
moat/ote
mob/ob
Mobile/oble
mobile/oble, eel
mobility/ility
mobilize/ize
Moby Dick/ick
mock/ock
mockingbird/erd
mocks/ox
mod/awed
mode/ode
model/oddle
moderation/ation
moderator/ader
modernize/ize
modified/ide
modifies/ize
modify/y
module/ool
Mohawk/ock
Mohawks/ox
molar/olar
mold/old
mole/ole
molecule/ool
Molly/olly
mom/om
momentary/ary
mommy/ommy
Mona/ona
monarch/ark
monastery/ary
money/unny
mongoose/use 1
monk/unk
monkey/ee, unky
monkeys/eeze
monocle/onical
monologue/og
monopolize/ize

monorail/ale 1
monotone/one 1
monsoon/oon
monstrosity/ocity
Montana/ana 1
months/unts
Montreal/all
monumental/ental
moo/ew
mooch/ooch
moocher/uture
mood/ude
moody/oody
mooed/ude
moon/oon
moonbeam/eem
moonchild/ild
moonlight/ight
moonlighter/ider
moonlit/it
moonstruck/uck
moos/use 2
moose/use 1
moot/ute
mop/op
mope/ope
moped/ed
mopey/opey
moral/oral
morale/al
morality/ality 1
moratorium/orium
morbidity/idity
more/ore
morn/orn
morning/orning
moronic/onic
morons/ons
morose/ose 1
Morse code/ode
mortality/ality 1
mortar/order
mortifies/ize

mortify/ortify, y
mortuary/ary
Moscow/ow 1
mosey/osy
moss/oss 2
mossy/ossy
most/ost 1
motel/ell
moth/oth 2
mother/other
Mother Goose/use 1
motherhood/ood 3
motif/ief
motion/otion
motivate/ate
motivation/ation
motorbike/ike
motto/otto
mound/ound
mount/ount
mountaintop/op
mounts/ounce
mourn/orn
mourning/orning
mouse/ouse
Mouseketeer/eer
mousetrap/ap
mousse/use 1
mouth/outh 1
mouthwash/osh
move/ove 3
mow/o 1
mowed/ode
mowing/owing
mows/ose 2
Mozart/art 1
mozzarella/ella
Ms./iz
much/utch
muck/uck
mucky/ucky
mud/ud
muddle/uddle

muddy/uddy
mud hole/ole
muff/uff
muffle/uffle
mug/ug
mukluk/uck
mule/ool
multiplication/ation
multiplied/ide
multiplies/ize
multiply/y
multitude/ude
mum/um
mumble/umble
mumbling/umbling
mummify/y
mummy/ummy
munch/unch
mundane/ain
municipality/ality 1
mural/ural
murder/erter
murky/erky
muscle/ustle
musclebound/ound
muse/use 2
muser/user
mush/ush 1
mushroom/oom
musicale/al
musician/ition
musk/usk
musketeer/eer
muskrat/at 1
muss/us
mussed/ust
mussel/ustle
must/ust
mustache/ash 1
mustang/ang
muster/uster
musty/usty
mute/ute

n

mutilate/ate
mutilation/ation
mutineer/eer
mutt/ut 1
mutter/utter
muumuu/ew
muumuus/use 2
muzzle/uzzle
my/y
myself/elf
mysterious/erious
mystery/istory
mystic/istic
mysticism/ism
mystifies/ize
mystify/y
mystique/eek
myth/ith
mythological/ogical
mythology/ology

n

nab/ab 1
Nabisco/isco
nadir/ader
nag/ag
nail/ale 1
naive/eave
name/aim
namesake/ake
name tag/ag
Nan/an 1
nanny/anny
nap/ap
napalm/alm
narcotic/otic
narrate/ate
narrator/ader
narrow/arrow
nation/ation
nationality/ality 1
nationalize/ize

nativity/ivity
naughty/ody
nauseate/ate
Navajo/o 1
navigate/ate
navigator/ader
navy/avy
nay/ay
nays/aze
Neanderthal/all
near/eer
nearby/y
Near East/east
nearer/earer
neat/eet
neaten/eaten
neater/eeder
neat-o/edo
necessary/ary
neck/eck
neckline/ine 1
necks/ex
necktie/y
neckties/ize
nectar/ector
nectarine/een
need/eed
needle/eedle
needlepoint/oint
needy/eedy
neglect/ect
neglects/ex
negotiator/ader
neigh/ay
neighborhood/ood 3
neighed/ade 1
Nell/ell
Nellie/elly
neophyte/ight
Neptune/oon
nerdy/urdy
Nero/ero 1
nerve/erve

nest/est
net/et
network/erk
neurotic/otic
neuter/uter
neutrality/ality 1
neutralize/ize
neutrons/ons
never/ever
nevermore/ore
nevertheless/ess
new/ew
newborn/orn
newcomer/ummer
New Delhi/elly
newfound/ound
New Guinea/inny
newly/uly
newlywed/ed
New Mexico/o 1
Newport/ort
news/use 2
newsbreak/ake
newscast/ast
newscaster/aster
newsletter/etter
newsprint/int
newsreel/eel
newt/ute
New York/ork 1
next/ext
NFL/ell
nib/ib
nibble/ibble
nice/ice 1
nicey-nicey/icy
niche/itch
nick/ick
nicked/ict
nickel/ickle
nickname/aim
nicks/icks
Nicky/icky

nicotine/een
niece/ease 2
nifty/ifty
Nigeria/eria
night/ight
nightclub/ub
nightfall/all
nightgown/own 2
nightie/idy
nightingale/ale 1
nightlife/ife
nightmare/air
nightshirt/ert
nighttime/ime
nil/ill
Nile/ile 1
nimble/imble
nincompoop/oop
nine/ine 1
ninny/inny
nip/ip
nipped/ipped
nippy/ippy
nitpick/ick
nitpicked/ict
nitpicker/icker
nitpicks/icks
nitwit/it
nitwits/its
nix/icks
no/o 1
Nobel Prize/ize
nobility/ility
noble/oble
nobody/ody
nocturnal/ernal
nocturne/urn
nod/awed
Noel/ell
noise/oys
Nolan/olen
nomad/ad 1
nominate/ate

217

nomination/ation, omination
nominee/ee
nominees/eeze
nonbeliever/eaver
nonchalant/aunt
noncommittal/iddle
nondescript/ipped
none/un
nonetheless/ess
nonfat/at 1
nonfiction/iction
nonplus/us
nonplussed/ust
nonsense/ense
nonstop/op
nonuser/user
noodle/oodle
nook/ook 2
noon/oon
noose/use 1
nope/ope
nor/ore
Nora/ora
norm/orm 1
normal/ormal
normality/ality 1
north/orth
North Carolina/ina 2
North Dakota/ota
North Pole/ole
Norway/ay
Norwegian/egion
nose/ose 2
nosebleed/eed
nosedive/ive 1
nose-thumber/ummer
nosh/osh
nosy/osy
not/ot
notch/otch
note/ote

notebook/ook 2
notification/ation
notified/ide
notifies/ize
notify/y
notion/otion
notoriety/iety
notorious/orious
Notre Dame/aim
noun/own 2
November/ember
Novocain/ain
now/ow 1
nowadays/aze
nowhere/air
nubby/ubby
nude/ude
nudge/udge
nuke/uke
null/ull 1
nullify/y
numb/um
number/umber 1
numerous/umorous
numskull/ull 1
nun/un
nurse/erse
nursed/irst
nursemaid/ade 1
nut/ut 1
nutrition/ition
nutritious/icious
nutshell/ell
nutty/uddy
nuzzle/uzzle

oaf/oaf
Oahu/ew
oak/oke
oaken/oken
oaks/okes

oar/ore
oat/ote
oath/oth 1
oatmeal/eel
obese/ease 2
obey/ay
obeyed/ade 1
obeys/aze
obituary/ary
object/ect
objection/ection
objective/ective
objectivity/ivity
objects/ex
obligation/ation
obligatory/ory
oblique/eek
oblong/ong
O'Brien/ion
obscene/een
obscure/ure
obscurity/urity
observation/ation
observatory/ory
observe/erve
obsessed/est
obsession/ession
obsessive/essive
obstetrician/ition
obstruct/uct
obstruction/uction
obtain/ain
obtrusive/usive
occasion/asion
occult/ult
occupation/ation
occupied/ide
occupies/ize
occupy/y
occur/er
occurred/erd
ocean/otion
oceanography/

ography
o'clock/ock
octagon/awn
octopus/uss 1
odd/awed
oddball/all
odder/otter
ode/ode
odious/odious
odometer/ometer
Oedipus/uss 1
of/ove 2
off/off
offend/end
offender/ender
offense/ense
offensive/ensive
offhand/and
official/icial
officiate/ate
offspring/ing
offstage/age 1
offtrack/ack
often/often
ogle/oggle
oh/o 1
oil/oil
okay/ay
okayed/ade 1
okays/aze
okey-doke/oke
Oklahoma/oma
old/old
older/older
Old King Cole/ole
Oldsmobile/eel
oldster/olster
Olympiad/ad 1
Omaha/aw
omit/it
omniscient/icient
on/awn
once/unts

one/un
ongoing/owing
only/only
ooze/use 2
opaque/ake
operate/ate
operation/ation
operator/ader
opossum/ossum
opportune/oon
opportunistic/istic
opportunity/unity
oppose/ose 2
oppress/ess
oppressed/est
oppression/ession
oppressive/essive
oppressor/essor
optician/ition
optimism/ism
optimistic/istic
option/option
or/ore
oral/oral
orangoutang/ang
orangutan/an 1
ordeal/eel
order/order
ordinary/ary
Oreo/o 1
Oreos/ose 2
organism/ism
organization/ation
organize/ize
organizer/izer
origami/ommy
originality/ality 1
oriole/orial
Orion/ion
ornamental/ental
ornate/ate
orthodox/ox
orthopedic/edic

ostentatious/acious
ostracize/ize
other/other
otherwise/ize
otter/otter
ouch/ouch
ought/ot
ounce/ounce
our/our 1
oust/oust
out/out
outbid/id
outbound/ound
outbreak/ake
outburst/irst
outcast/ast
outclassed/ast
outcome/um
outcries/ize
outcry/y
outdid/id
outdo/ew
outdone/un
outdoor/ore
outdraw/aw
outfit/it
outfits/its
outfox/ox
outgoing/owing
outgrew/ew
outgrossed/ost 1
outgrow/o 1
outguess/ess
outguessed/est
outhouse/ouse
outlast/ast
outlaw/aw
outlawed/awed
outlaws/ause
outline/ine 1
outlined/ind 1
outlive/ive 2
outlook/ook 2

outloud/oud
outnumber/umber 1
outpost/ost 1
output/oot 2
outrage/age 1
outrageous/ageous
outran/an 1
outrank/ank
outreach/each
outright/ight
outrun/un
outscore/ore
outscored/ord 1
outshine/ine 1
outshone/one 1
outshoot/ute
outside/ide
outsider/ider
outsmart/art 1
outspoken/oken
outswam/am
outtalk/ock
outvote/ote
outwear/air
outweighed/ade 1
outweighs/aze
outwit/it
outwits/its
outworn/orn
ovation/ation
over/over
overachiever/eaver
overact/act
overactive/active
overacts/ax
overall/all
overate/ate
overbite/ight
overboard/ord 1
overbuild/illed
overcame/aim
overcast/ast
overcharge/arge

overcoat/ote
overcome/um
overcrowd/oud
overdid/id
overdo/ew
overdone/un
overdrawn/awn
overdress/ess
overdressed/est
overdue/ew
overeager/eager
overeat/eet
overeater/eeder
overexert/ert
overexpose/ose 2
overfed/ed
overfeed/eed
overflow/o 1
overflowed/ode
overflowing/owing
overflows/ose 2
overgrown/one 1
overgrowth/oth 1
overhang/ang
overhaul/all
overhauled/alled
overhead/ed
overhear/eer
overheard/erd
overindulge/ulge
overjoy/oy
overjoyed/oid
overkill/ill
overlap/ap
overload/ode
overlook/ook 2
overmuch/utch
overnight/ight
overpaid/ade 1
overpass/ass
overpower/our 1
overpowered/owered
overpriced/iced

219

overprotective/ective
overran/an 1
overrate/ate
overreact/act
overreacts/ax
overridden/idden
overripe/ipe
overrule/ool
overseas/eeze
oversee/ee
oversees/eeze
overshoot/ute
oversight/ight
oversleep/eep
overslept/ept
overspend/end
overstate/ate
overstep/ep
overstepped/ept
overstuff/uff
overt/ert
overtake/ake
overtime/ime
overtire/ire
overture/ure
overturn/urn
overweight/ate
overwork/erk
overzealous/ealous
ow/ow 1
owe/o 1
owed/ode
owes/ose 2
owl/owl
own/one 1
ownership/ip
ox/ox
ozone/one 1

p

pa/aw
pace/ace

paced/aste
pachyderm/erm
Pacific/ific
pacified/ide
pacifies/ize
pacifism/ism
pacify/y
pack/ack
packed/act
packs/ax
Pac-Man/an 1
pact/act
pad/ad 1
paddle/attle
padlock/ock
page/age 1
pagoda/ota
paid/ade 1
pail/ale 1
pain/ain
pair/air
pajama/ama 1,
        ama 2
Pakistan/an 1
pal/al
pale/ale 1
Palestine/ine 1
palindrome/ome 1
pallbearer/arer
palm/alm, om
palomino/ino 2
Pam/am
pamper/amper
pan/an 1
Panama/aw
Panasonic/onic
pancake/ake
pane/ain
panic-stricken/icken
panned/and
panorama/ama 2
pant/ant 1
pantomime/ime

pants/ance
paperback/ack
paperweight/ate
papoose/use 1
pappy/appy
par/ar
parachute/ute
parade/ade 1
paradise/ice 1
paradox/ox
paragon/awn
paragons/ons
paragraph/aff
Paraguay/y
parakeet/eet
parallel/ell
paralyze/ize
paramount/ount
paranoid/oid
paraphrase/aze
parasite/ight
parasitic/itic
parasol/all
paratrooper/ooper
parch/arch
Parcheesi/easy
parent/arent
parental/ental
park/ark
Parmesan/awn
parole/ole
paroled/old
parolee/oly
parrot/arrot
part/art 1
participate/ate
participation/ation
party/ardy
partygoing/owing
Pasadena/ena
pass/ass
passed/ast
passerby/y

passport/ort
password/erd
past/ast
paste/aste
pastel/ell
pasteurize/ize
pastime/ime
pastor/aster
pastoral/oral
pastrami/ommy
pat/at 1
patch/atch 1
patchwork/erk
patchy/atchy
paternal/ernal
path/ath
pathetic/etic
pathology/ology
patriotic/otic
patriotism/ism
patrol/ole
patrolled/old
patroller/olar
patronize/ize
patty/atty
Paul/all
Paulette/et
Paul Revere/eer
paunch/aunch
pauper/opper
pause/ause
pave/ave
pavilion/illion
paw/aw
pawed/awed
pawn/awn
pawnbroker/oker
pawned/ond
pawns/ons
pawnshop/op
paws/ause
pay/ay
paycheck/eck

220

payoff/off
payola/ola
payroll/ole
pays/aze
pea/ee
peace/ease 2
Peace Corps/ore
peacetime/ime
peach/each
peacock/ock
peacocks/ox
peak/eek
peanutty/uddy
pear/air
pearl/url
pearly/urly
peas/eeze
peashooter/uter
pebble/ebble
pecan/awn
pecans/ons
peck/eck
pecks/ex
peculiarity/arity
pedal/eddle
peddle/eddle
pediatrician/ition
pedicure/ure
pedigree/ee
pedigrees/eeze
peek/eek
peek-a-boo/ew
peeker/eaker
peel/eel
peeled/ield
peep/eep
peephole/ole
peer/eer
peewee/ee
peg/eg
pelt/elt
pen/en
penalize/ize

pencil/encil
penetrate/ate
penmanship/ip
penned/end
penny/enny
pension/ention
pensive/ensive
pentagon/awn
penthouse/ouse
pep/ep
pepped/ept
peppermint/int
pepperoni/ony
Pepsi-Cola/ola
per/er
perceive/eave
percent/ent
percents/ense
perception/eption
perch/urch
percolate/ate
percussion/ussion
perfect/ect
perfection/ection
perfects/ex
perform/orm 1
performer/ormer
perfume/oom
perfumy/oomy
periscope/ope
perish/erish
periwinkle/inkle
perk/erk
perky/erky
perm/erm
permission/ition
permissive/issive
permit/it
permits/its
perpetrator/ader
perplex/ex
perplexed/ext
persecute/ute

persecution/ution
persecutor/uter
persevere/eer
Persian/ersion
persist/ist
persistence/istance
person/erson
personality/ality 1
personified/ide
personifies/ize
personify/y
personnel/ell
perspective/ective
perspiration/ation
perspire/ire
persuade/ade 1
persuader/ader
persuasion/asion
pert/ert
perturb/urb
Peru/ew
peruse/use 2
pessimism/ism
pest/est
pester/ester
pet/et
petal/eddle
Pete/eet
Peter/eeder
Peter Pan/an 1
petite/eet
petition/ition
petrified/ide
petrify/y
petticoat/ote
petty/etty
pew/ew
pewter/uter
pharaoh/arrow
phase/aze
PhD/ee
phenomenon/awn
Phil/ill

phone/one 1
phonetic/etic
phonic/onic
phonograph/aff
phony/ony
phony-baloney/ony
phooey/ewy
photograph/aff
photographed/aft
photographic/aphic
photography/
    ography
phrase/aze
physician/ition
physique/eek
picaresque/esque
piccolo/o
pick/ick
picked/ict
picker/icker
picker-upper/
    upper
picket/icket
pickle/ickle
pickpocket/ocket
picks/icks
pickup/up
picky/icky
picnic/ick
picnicked/ict
picnicker/icker
picnics/icks
pictorial/orial
picturesque/esque
piddle/iddle
pie/y
piece/ease 2
pieced/east
piecemeal/eel
pier/eer
Pierre/air
pies/ize
piety/iety

221

pig/ig
pigeonhole/ole
pigeonholed/old
pigeon-toed/ode
piggyback/ack
pigpen/en
pigskin/in
pigsties/ize
pigsty/y
pigtail/ale 1
pike/ike
pile/ile 1
piled/ild
pill/ill
pillar/iller
pillow/illow
pimple/imple
pin/in
piñata/ada
pinball/all
pinch/inch
pine/ine 1
pinecone/one 1
pined/ind
ping/ing
Ping-Pong/ong
pink/ink
pinkie/inky
pinned/inned
Pinocchio/o 1
pinochle/uckle
pinpoint/oint
pinpricks/icks
pinstripe/ipe
pioneer/eer
pip/ip
pipe/ipe
pipeline/ine 1
piper/iper
pip-squeak/eek
pique/eek
piranha/onna
pirouette/et

pistachio/o 1
pit/it
pita/ita
pitch/itch
pitchfork/ork 1
pitfall/all
pits/its
pitter-patter/atter
pity/itty
pizzazz/azz
place/ace
placed/aste
plagiarism/ism
plagiarize/ize
plaid/ad 1
plain/ain
plainspoken/oken
plan/an 1
plane/ain
planetary/ary
plank/ank
planned/and
planner/anner
plant/ant 1
plantation/ation
plants/ance
plaque/ack
plaques/ax
plaster/aster
plastic/astic
plate/ate
platform/orm 1
Platonic/onic
platoon/oon
platter/atter
platypus/uss 1
play/ay
played/ade 1
player/ayer
playground/ound
playmate/ate
play-off/off
playpen/en

plays/aze
plaything/ing
playwright/ight
plea/ee
plead/eed
pleas/eeze
please/eeze
pleasure/easure
pleat/eet
pledge/edge
pliable/iable
pliant/iant
plight/ight
plod/awed
plop/op
plot/ot
plotter/otter
plow/ow 1
plowed/oud
ploy/oy
ploys/oys
pluck/uck
plucked/uct
plucks/ucks
plucky/ucky
plug/ug
plum/um
plumber/ummer
plume/oom
plump/ump
plunder/under
plunge/unge
plunk/unk
plural/ural
plus/us
plush/ush 1
PM/em
pneumonia/onia
poach/oach
pocket/ocket
pod/awed
poem/ome 1
poetic/etic

point/oint
poise/oys
poke/oke
poker/oker
pokes/okes
polar/olar
Polaroid/oid
pole/ole
police/ease 2
policed/east
polish/olish
polite/ight
political/itical
politician/ition
politics/icks
poll/ole
polled/old
pollster/olster
pollute/ute
polluter/uter
pollution/ution
Polly/olly
Pollyanna/ana 1
polo/olo
poltergeist/iced
polyester/ester
pompom/om
poncho/oncho
pond/ond
ponder/onder
ponds/ons
pontoon/oon
pony/ony
pooch/ooch
poodle/oodle
poof/oof 1
poofy/oofy
pooh/ew
poohed/ude
pool/ool
poop/oop
pooper/ooper
poor/ore, ure

pop/op
popcorn/orn
pope/ope
Popeye/y
popper/opper
poppy/oppy
poppycock/ock
Popsicle/ickle
Pop Tart/art 1
popularity/arity
popularize/ize
populate/ate
population/ation
porch/orch
porcupine/ine 1
por favor/or
pork/ork 1
port/ort
porter/order
portfolio/o 1
porthole/ole
portion/ortion
portrayed/ade 1
portrays/aze
pose/ose 2
posh/osh
position/ition
posse/ossy
possess/ess
possessed/est
possession/ession
possessive/essive
possessor/essor
possibility/ility
possum/ossum
post/ost 1
postcard/ard 1
posterity/arity
postmark/ark
postmaster/aster
postpone/one 1
postscript/ipped
postwar/ore

pot/ot
potbelly/elly
potential/ential
pothole/ole
potion/otion
potluck/uck
potter/otter
pottery/ottery
potty/ody
pouch/ouch
pounce/ounce
pound/ound
pour/ore
poured/ord 1
pout/out
pouter/owder
pow/ow 1
powder/owder
power/our 1
power-driven/iven
powered/owered
powerhouse/ouse
powwow/ow 1
pox/ox
practical/actical
practicality/ality 1
prairie/ary
praise/aze
prance/ance
prank/ank
prattle/attle
pray/ay
prayed/ade 1
prayer/air
prays/aze
preach/each
preacher/eacher
prearrange/ange
precarious/arious
precautionary/ary
precede/eed
precinct/inct
precise/ice 1

precision/ision
precocious/ocious
precut/ut 1
predecessor/essor
predict/ict
prediction/iction
predictor/ictor
predicts/icks
preemie/eamy
prefer/er
preferential/ential
preferred/erd
prehistoric/oric
prejudge/udge
prejudicial/icial
preliminary/ary
premature/ure
premier/eer
premonition/ition
preoccupied/ide
preoccupies/ize
preoccupy/y
prep/ep
preparation/ation
prepare/air
preposition/ition
preschool/ool
preschooler/ooler
prescribe/ibe
prescription/iption
present/ent
presentation/ation
presenter/enter
presents/ense
preservation/ation
preserve/erve
preshrunk/unk
president/esident
presidential/ential
press/ess
pressed/est
presume/oom
presumption/umption

preteen/een
pretend/end
pretender/ender
pretense/ense
pretension/ention
pretty/iddy
prevail/ale 1
prevent/ent
prevention/ention
preventive/entive
prey/ay
price/ice 1
priced/iced
pricey/icy
prick/ick
pricked/ict
prickly/ickly
pricks/icks
pride/ide
pried/ide
priest/east
prim/im
prima donna/onna
primary/ary
primate/ate
prime/ime
primp/imp
prince/ince
principality/ality 1
print/int
printer/inter
prints/ince
priority/ority
Priscilla/illa
prism/ism
prissy/issy
prize/ize
prizefight/ight
prizewinner/inner
pro/o 1
probability/ility
probation/ation
probe/obe

223

problematic/atic
proceed/eed
procession/ession
processor/essor
procrastinate/ate
procrastination/ation
procrastinator/ader
prod/awed
prodder/otter
produce/use 1
produced/uced
production/uction
productive/uctive
productivity/ivity
profane/ain
profess/ess
professed/est
profession/ession
professionalism/ism
professor/essor
profile/ile 1
profound/ound
program/am
progress/ess
progressed/est
progression/ession
progressive/essive
prohibit/ibit
prohibition/ition
project/ect
projector/ector
projects/ex
prolific/ific
prologue/og
prolong/ong
prom/om
promenade/ade 1,
  awed
promote/ote
promotion/otion
promotional/otional
prone/one 1
pronoun/own 2

pronounce/ounce
pronto/onto
pronunciation/ation
proof/oof 1
proofread/ed, eed
proofreader/eeder
prop/op
propel/ell
propelled/eld
propeller/eller
proper/opper
proportion/ortion
proposal/osal
propose/ose 2
proposition/ition
propriety/iety
pros/ose 2
prose/ose 2
prosecute/ute
prosecution/ution
prosecutor/uter
prospect/ect
prospects/ex
prosperity/arity
protect/ect
protection/ection
protector/ector
protects/ex
protégé/ay
protein/een
protest/est
protestor/ester
protocol/all
prototype/ipe
protrude/ude
protrusion/usion
proud/oud
prouder/owder
prove/ove 3
proverb/urb
provide/ide
provider/ider
provision/ision

provoke/oke
provoker/oker
provokes/okes
prowl/owl
proxy/oxy
prude/ude
prudent/udent
prune/oon
pry/y
psalm/alm, om
pseudonym/im
psych/ike
psychological/ogical
psychologist/ologist
psychology/ology
psychopath/ath
psychosomatic/atic
psychotic/otic
PTA/ay
PU/ew
pub/ub
publicity/icity
publicize/ize
puck/uck
pucker/ucker
pucks/ucks
puddle/uddle
pueblo/o 1
puff/uff
puffy/uffy
pug/ug
puke/uke
pull/ull 2
pulley/ully
pulp/ulp
pulsate/ate
pump/ump
pumpernickel/ickle
pumpkin/umpkin
pun/un
punch/unch
punctuality/ality 1
punctuate/ate

punctuation/ation
punk/unk
punker/unker
punky/unky
punned/und
punner/unner
punt/unt
punter/unter
punts/unts
pup/up
pupil/uple
puppy/uppy
pure/ure
purebred/ed
purgatory/ory
purge/erge
purify/y
purity/urity
purloin/oin
Purple Heart/art 1
purr/er
purred/erd
purse/erse
pursue/ew
pursued/ude
pursues/use 2
pursuit/ute
pus/us
push/ush 2
pushover/over
pushy/ushy
puss/uss 1
pussycat/at 1
pussyfoot/oot 2
put/oot 2
put-down/own 2
putt/ut 1
putter/utter
putty/uddy
puzzle/uzzle
pyramid/id
python/awn
pythons/ons

q

Q-tip/ip
quack/ack
quacked/act
quacks/ax
quad/awed
quadruple/uple
quail/ale 1
quake/ake
qualification/ation
qualified/ide
qualifies/ize
qualify/y
quality/ality 2
qualm/alm, om
quarantine/een
quarrel/oral
quarry/ory
quart/ort
quarter/order
quarterback/ack
quartet/et
quash/osh
queasy/easy
Quebec/eck
queen/een
quelled/eld
quench/ench
quencher/enture
query/eery
quest/est
question/estion
questionnaire/air
quibble/ibble
quick/ick
quicken/icken
quicker/icker
quickie/icky
quickly/ickly
quicksand/and
quiet/iet
quilt/ilt

quip/ip
quipped/ipped
quirk/erk
quirky/erky
quit/it
quite/ight
quits/its
quitter/itter
quiver/iver 2
quixotic/otic
quiz/iz
quota/ota
quotation/ation
quote/ote

r

rabbi/y
rabble/abble
racoon/oon
race/ace
raced/aste
racehorse/orse
racetrack/ack
racial/acial
racism/ism
rack/ack
racketeer/eer
racks/ax
radiate/ate
radiation/ation
radiator/ader
radio/o 1
radioactive/active
radioactivity/ivity
radios/ose 2
raft/aft
rafter/after
rag/ag
rage/age 1
ragtag/ag
raid/ade 1
raider/ader

rail/ale 1
railroad/ode
railway/ay
railways/aze
rain/ain
rainbow/o 1
rainbows/ose 2
raincheck/eck
raincoat/ote
raindrop/op
rainfall/all
rainswept/ept
raise/aze
raisin/azon
rake/ake
rally/alley
ram/am
Rama/ama 1
Ramon/one 1
ramp/amp
rampage/age 1
rampageous/ageous
ramshackle/ackle
ran/an 1
rang/ang
range/ange
Rangoon/oon
rank/ank
ransack/ack
ransacked/act
rant/ant 1
rap/ap
Raphael/ell
rapport/ore
Raquel/ell
rare/air
rarer/arer
rarity/arity
rash/ash 1
rasp/asp
raspberry/ary
rat/at 1
rate/ate

rather/ather 1
ratifies/ize
ratify/y
ratio/o 1
rationale/al
rationality/ality 1
rattle/attle
rattlesnake/ake
ratty/atty
ravage/avage
rave/ave
ravine/een
ravioli/oly
raw/aw
ray/ay
rays/aze
razz/azz
razzmatazz/azz
reach/each
react/act
reaction/action
reactive/active
reacts/ax
read/ed, eed
reader/eeder
ready/etty
real/eel
realism/ism
realistic/istic
reality/ality 1
realization/ation
realize/ize
really/eally
ream/eem
reap/eep
reaper/eeper
reappear/eer
rear/eer
rearrange/ange
reason/eason
reassurance/urance
reassure/ure
reattach/atch 1

225

rebate/ate
rebel/ebble, ell
rebelled/eld
rebirth/irth
reborn/orn
rebound/ound
rebuff/uff
rebuild/illed
rebuke/uke
rebut/ut 1
recall/all
recalled/alled
recap/ap
recede/eed
receipt/eet
receive/eave
receiver/eaver
reception/eption
recess/ess
recessed/est
recession/ession
recharge/arge
reciprocity/ocity
recital/idle
recite/ight
reclaim/aim
recline/ine 1
recliner/iner
recluse/use 1
reclusive/usive
recognition/ition
recognize/ize
recoil/oil
recollect/ect
recollection/ection
recommend/end
recommendation/
    ation
reconcile/ile 1
reconsider/itter
reconstruct/uct
reconstruction/
    uction

record/ecord, ord 1
recorder/order
recreation/ation
recruit/ute
recruiter/uter
rectify/y
recuperate/ate
red/ed
redder/etter
redeem/eem
red-faced/aste
redhead/ed
redid/id
redo/ew
redone/un
redshirt/ert
reduce/use 1
reduced/uced
reduction/uction
redwood/ood 3
Reeboks/ox
reed/eed
reef/ief
reek/eek
reel/eel
reelect/ect
reelects/ex
reeled/ield
reenter/enter
ref/ef
refer/er
referee/ee
refereed/eed
referees/eeze
referred/erd
refill/ill
refine/ine 1
refined/ind 1
reflect/ect
reflection/ection
reflective/ective
reflector/ector
reflects/ex

reflex/ex
reform/orm 1
reformatory/ory
reformer/ormer
refrain/ain
refresh/esh
refreshen/ession
refrigerator/ader
refuge/uge
refugee/ee
refund/und
refuse/use 1, use 2
refute/ute
regain/ain
regal/egal
regard/ard 1
regatta/ada
regime/eem
region/egion
registrar/ar
registration/ation
regress/ess
regret/et
regroup/oop
regrowth/oth 1
regularity/arity
regulate/ate
regulation/ation
regulator/ader
rehab/ab 1
rehearse/erse
rehearsed/irst
reign/ain
reimburse/erse
reimbursed/irst
rein/ain
reindeer/eer
reinforce/orse
reiterate/ate
reject/ect
rejection/ection
rejects/ex
rejoice/oice

rejoin/oin
relate/ate
relation/ation
relativity/ivity
relax/ax
relaxation/ation
relay/ay
release/ease 2
released/east
reliable/iable
reliance/iance
reliant/iant
relied/ide
relief/ief
relies/ize
relieve/eave
relive/ive 2
rely/y
remain/ain
remake/ake
remark/ark
remarry/ary
Rembrandt/ant 1
remember/ember
remind/ind 1
reminisced/ist
remorse/orse
remote/ote
remove/ove 3
render/ender
rendezvous/ew
rendezvoused/ude
rendition/ition
renegade/ade 1
renege/eg
renew/ew
renewal/uel
renewed/ude
Reno/ino 2
Renoir/ar
renounce/ounce
renown/own 2
renowned/ound

rent/ent
rental/ental
reoccurred/erd
reorganize/ize
repaid/ade 1
repair/air
repay/ay
repays/aze
repeat/eet
repeater/eeder
repel/ell
repelled/eld
repent/ent
repercussion/ussion
repetition/ition
repetitious/icious
rephrase/aze
replace/ace
replaced/aste
replied/ide
replies/ize
reply/y
report/ort
reporter/order
repossess/ess
represent/ent
represents/ense
repress/ess
repressed/est
repression/ession
reprimand/and
reproach/oach
reproduce/use 1
reproduced/uced
reproduction/uction
reproductive/uctive
reptile/ile 1
reptilian/illion
repulsive/ulsive
reputation/ation
repute/ute
request/est
require/ire

rerun/un
research/urch
resemble/emble
resent/ent
resents/ense
reservation/ation
reserve/erve
reservoir/ar, ore
reset/et
reshape/ape
reside/ide
resident/esident
residential/ential
residue/ew
resign/ine 1
resignation/ation
resigned/ind 1
resist/ist
resistance/istance
resolute/ute
resolution/ution
resolve/olve
resort/ort
resource/orse
respect/ect
respects/ex
respond/ond
responds/ons
responsibility/ility
rest/est
restart/art 1
restaurant/aunt
restore/ore
restored/ord 1
restrain/ain
restrict/ict
restriction/iction
restricts/icks
result/ult
resurrection/ection
retail/ale 1
retain/ain
retaliate/ate

retaliation/ation
retch/etch
retell/ell
rethink/ink
retire/ire
retold/old
retouch/utch
retrace/ace
retraced/aste
retreat/eet
retribution/ution
retrieve/eave
retroactive/active
retrospective/ective
return/urn
reunion/union
reunite/ight
reusable/usable
reveal/eel
revealed/ield
revel/evel
revelation/ation
revenue/ew
revenues/use 2
reverberate/ate
Revere, Paul/eer
reverse/erse
reversed/irst
review/ew
reviewed/ude
reviews/use 2
revise/ize
revision/ision
revitalize/ize
revival/ival
revive/ive 1
revolt/olt
revolution/ution
revolutionary/ary
revolve/olve
revue/ew
reward/ord 1
rewrote/ote

rhinestone/one 1
rhino/ino 1
rhyme/ime
rib/ib
rice/ice 1
rich/itch
ricotta/ota
ricocheted/ade 1
rid/id
riddle/iddle
ride/ide
rider/ider
ridge/idge
ridicule/ool
riffraff/aff
rift/ift
rig/ig
rigatoni/ony
right/ight
rigor/igger
rile/ile 1
riled/ild
rim/im
rind/ind 1
ring/ing
ringer/inger 1
ringleader/eeder
Ringo/ingo
rink/ink
rinky-dink/ink
rinky-dinky/inky
rinse/ince
Rin Tin Tin/in
Rio de Janeiro/arrow
Rio Grande/and
riot/iet
rip/ip
ripe/ipe
rip-off/off
ripped/ipped
ripple/ipple
riptide/ide
Rip Van Winkle/inkle

227

rise/ize
riser/izer
risk/isk
risky/isky
Rita/ita
rite/ight
ritualistic/istic
ritzy/itzy
rival/ival
river/iver 2
roach/oach
road/ode
roadblock/ock
roadblocks/ox
roadrunner/unner
roadside/ide
roam/ome 1
roar/ore
roared/ord 1
roast/ost 1
rob/ob
robber/obber
robe/obe
Robin Hood/ood 3
robot/ot
robust/ust
rock/ock
rockaby/y
Rockefeller/eller
rocker/ocker
rocket/ocket
rocks/ox
rocky/awky
rod/awed
rode/ode
rodeo/o 1
rodeos/ose 2
rogue/ogue 1
role/ole
roll/ole
rolled/old
roller/olar
Rolls-Royce/oice

roly-poly/oly
romance/ance
romantic/antic
romanticism/ism
romanticize/ize
Rome/ome 1
Romeo/o 1
romp/omp
Ron/awn
roof/oof 1, oof 2
rooftop/op
rook/ook 2
rookie/ookie
room/oom
roomy/oomy
roost/uced
rooster/ooster
root/oot 2, ute
rooter/uter
rope/ope
rose/ose 2
Rose Bowl/ole
rosebud/ud
rosebush/ush 2
Rosemarie/ee
Rosemary/ary
Rose Parade/ade 1
Rosie/osy
Ross/oss 2
roster/oster
rosy/osy
rot/ot
rotate/ate
rotation/ation
rotten/otten
rouge/uge
rough/uff
rougher/uffer
roughhouse/ouse
roughneck/eck
round/ound
roundabout/out
roundup/up

roust/oust
rout/out
route/out, ute
routine/een
rover/over
row/o 1, ow 1
rowboat/ote
rowed/ode
rowing/owing
rows/ose 2
Roy/oy
royal/oil
rub/ub
rubber/ubber
rubberneck/eck
rubbernecks/ex
rubble/ouble
rudder/utter
rude/ude
rue/ew
rued/ude
ruffle/uffle
rug/ug
rule/ool
ruler/ooler
rum/um
rumble/umble
rumbling/umbling
rummy/ummy
rumor/umor
rumormonger/unger
rump/ump
Rumpelstiltskin/in
run/un
runabout/out
runaround/ound
runaway/ay
runaways/aze
rung/ung
runner/unner
runny/unny
runt/unt
runts/unts

runway/ay
rural/ural
ruse/use 2
rush/ush 1
Russell/ustle
Russian/ussion
rust/ust
rusted/usted
rustle/ustle
rusty/usty
rut/ut 1
Ruth/ooth
Ruth, Babe/ooth
RV/ee
Ryan/ion
rye/y

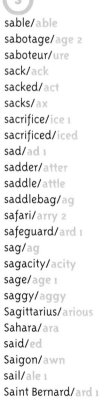

S

sable/able
sabotage/age 2
saboteur/ure
sack/ack
sacked/act
sacks/ax
sacrifice/ice 1
sacrificed/iced
sad/ad 1
sadder/atter
saddle/attle
saddlebag/ag
safari/arry 2
safeguard/ard 1
sag/ag
sagacity/acity
sage/age 1
saggy/aggy
Sagittarius/arious
Sahara/ara
said/ed
Saigon/awn
sail/ale 1
Saint Bernard/ard 1

S

sainthood/ood 3
Saint Jude/ude
Saint Nick/ick
Saint Patrick's
   Day/ay
Saint Peter/eeder
sake/ake
sale/ale 1
salesmanship/ip
saliva/iva
Sally/alley
salon/awn
saloon/oon
salt/alt
Salt Lake City/itty
salts/alts
salute/ute
Sam/am
same/aim
samurai/y
sanctimony/ony
sanctuary/ary
sand/and
sandbag/ag
sandblast/ast
sandblaster/aster
sandbox/ox
sandman/an 1
sandpiper/iper
sane/ain
San Francisco/isco
sang/ang
sanitary/ary
San Jose/ay
sank/ank
Santa Anita/ita
Santa Claus/ause
Santa Fe/ay
Santa Monica/onica
sap/ap
sapphire/ire
sappy/appy
Sarah/ara

sarcasm/asm
sarcastic/astic
sardine/een
sarge/arge
sari/arry 2
sarong/ong
sash/ash 1
sashimi/eamy
Saskatchewan/awn
sass/ass
sassafras/ass
sassed/ast
sassy/assy
sat/at 1
satellite/ight
satin/atin
satire/ire
satirize/ize
satisfaction/action
satisfied/ide
satisfies/ize
satisfy/y
sauce/oss 2
saucy/ossy
Saudi/ody
sauerkraut/out
Saul/all
sauna/onna
savage/avage
Savannah/ana 1
save/ave
savor/aver
savory/avery
saw/aw
sawdust/ust
sawed/awed
sax/ax
saxophone/one 1
say/ay
scab/ab 1
scald/alled
scale/ale 1
scaly/aily

scam/am
scamp/amp
scamper/amper
scan/an 1
scanner/anner
scant/ant 1
scapegoat/ote
scar/ar
scare/air
scarecrow/o 1
scarecrows/ose 2
scarf/arf 1
scarred/ard 1
scary/ary
scatter/atter
scatterbrain/ain
scene/een
scent/ent
scents/ense
scheme/eem
schism/ism
schlep/ep
scholar/aller
scholarship/ip
scholastic/astic
school/ool
schoolbell/ell
schoolmaster/aster
schoolwork/erk
schooner/ooner
schuss/uss 1
science/iance
scientific/ific
sci-fi/y
scoff/off
scold/old
scoop/oop
scooper/ooper
scoot/ute
scooter/uter
scope/ope
scorch/orch
score/ore

scoreboard/ord 1
scorecard/ard 1
scored/ord 1
scorn/orn
Scot/ot
Scotch/otch
Scottie/ody
scour/our 1
scoured/owered
scout/out
scoutmaster/aster
scowl/owl
Scrabble/abble
scram/am
scrap/ap
scrapbook/ook 2
scrape/ape
scrappy/appy
scratch/atch 1
scratchy/atchy
scrawl/all
scrawled/alled
scrawny/awny
scream/eem
screech/each
screecher/eacher
screen/een
screw/ew
screwdriver/iver 1
screws/use 2
screwy/ewy
scribble/ibble
scribe/ibe
script/ipped
scroll/ole
Scrooge/uge
scrub/ub
scrubber/ubber
scruff/uff
scrunch/unch
scruple/uple
scrutinize/ize
scud/ud

scuff/uff
scuffle/uffle
scum/um
scummy/ummy
scurry/urry
scuttle/uddle
scuttlebutt/ut 1
sea/ee
seafarer/arer
seafood/ude
seal/eel
sealed/ield
seam/eem
seaport/ort
search/urch
searchlight/ight
seas/eeze
seashore/ore
seasick/ick
season/eason
seat/eet
Seattle/attle
seaweed/eed
seclude/ude
seclusion/usion
seclusive/usive
secondary/ary
secondhand/and
secretary/ary
secrete/eet
sect/ect
section/ection
securable/urable
secure/ure
security/urity
sedan/an 1
sedate/ate
sedentary/ary
see/ee
seed/eed
seedy/eedy
seek/eek
seem/eem

seen/een
seep/eep
sees/eeze
seesaw/aw
seesawed/awed
seesaws/ause
seethe/eethe
segregate/ate
segregation/ation
seize/eeze
select/ect
selection/ection
selective/ective
selects/ex
self/elf
sell/ell
seller/eller
semester/ester
semiautomatic/atic
semicolon/olen
semiformal/ormal
seminar/ar
send/end
sender/ender
senile/ile 1
senility/ility
seniority/ority
señor/ore
señora/ora
señorita/ita
sensationalism/ism
sense/ense
sensibility/ility
sensitivity/ivity
sensitize/ize
sent/ent
sentimental/ental
sentimentality/ality 1
separate/ate, it
separation/ation
September/ember
serape/oppy
serenade/ade 1

serenader/ader
serene/een
serf/urf
serious/erious
serpentine/een
serve/erve
servitude/ude
Sesame Street/eet
session/ession
set/et
setback/ack
settle/eddle
setup/up
Seuss, Dr./use 1
seven/even
seventeen/een
7-Up/up
sever/ever
severe/eer
severer/earer
severity/arity
sew/o 1
sewed/ode
sewing/owing
sewn/one 1
sews/ose 2
sex/ex
shabby/abby
shack/ack
shackle/ackle
shacks/ax
shade/ade 1
shadowbox/ox
shady/ady
shaft/aft
shag/ag
shaggy/aggy
shake/ake
Shake 'n Bake/ake
Shakespeare/eer
shall/al
shallow/allow 1
sham/am

shame/aim
shampoo/ew
shampooed/ude
shampoos/use 2
shamrock/ock
shamrocks/ox
Shanghai/y
shape/ape
share/air
sharecropper/opper
shareholder/older
shark/ark
Sharon/aron
sharpshooter/uter
shatter/atter
shave/ave
shaver/aver
shawl/all
she/ee
shed/ed
sheen/een
sheep/eep
sheepskin/in
sheer/eer
sheet/eet
shelf/elf
shell/ell
shelled/eld
Shelley/elly
shelter/elter
shelve/elve
Sherlock/ock
shied/ide
shield/ield
shies/ize
shift/ift
shifty/ifty
shillelagh/aily
shimmer/immer
shin/in
shindig/ig
shine/ine 1
shiner/iner

shingle/ingle
shiny/iny
ship/ip
shipped/ipped
shipper/ipper
shipshape/ape
shipwreck/eck
shipwrecked/ect
shipyard/ard 1
shirk/erk
Shirley/urly
shirt/ert
shirtsleeve/eave
shirttail/ale 1
shish kebab/ob
shiver/iver 2
shock/ock
shocker/ocker
shocks/ox
shockwave/ave
shoddy/ody
shoe/ew
shoehorn/orn
shoelace/ace
shoes/use 2
shoeshine/ine 1
shoeshiner/iner
shoestring/ing
shone/one 1
shook/ook 2
shoot/ute
shooter/uter
shop/op
shoplift/ift
shopper/opper
shore/ore
short/ort
shortcake/ake
shortchange/ange
shortcut/ut 1
shorter/order
shorthand/and
shortstop/op

shorty/orty
Shoshone/ony
shot/ot
shotgun/un
shotput/oot 2
should/ood 3
shoulder/older
shout/out
shouter/owder
shove/ove 2
show/o 1
showbiz/iz
showed/ode
shower/our 1
showered/owered
showing/owing
shown/one 1
show-off/off
shows/ose 2
showtime/ime
showy/owy
shrank/ank
shred/ed
shredder/etter
shrewd/ude
shriek/eek
shrill/ill
shrilly/illy
shrimp/imp
shrimpy/impy
shrine/ine 1
shrink/ink
shrivel/ivel
shroud/oud
shrub/ub
shrug/ug
shrunk/unk
shrunken/unken
shucks/ucks
shudder/utter
shuffle/uffle
shun/un
shunned/und

shush/ush 1
shut/ut 1
shutter/utter
shuttle/uddle
shy/y
shyness/inus
Siamese/eeze
Siberia/eria
Sibyl/ibble
Sicilian/illion
sick/ick
sickbed/ed
sicken/icken
sicker/icker
sickle/ickle
sickly/ickly
Sid/id
side/ide
sidekick/ick
sideline/ine 1
sidesaddle/attle
sideshow/o 1
sideshows/ose 2
sidestep/ep
sidestepped/ept
sideswipe/ipe
sidetrack/ack
sidetracked/act
sidewalk/ock
sideways/aze
sieve/ive 2
sift/ift
sigh/y
sighed/ide
sighs/ize
sight/ight
sightsee/ee
sign/ine 1
signed/ind 1
signifies/ize
signify/y
signpost/ost 1
silhouette/et

silicon/awn
silk/ilk
silkworm/erm
sill/ill
silly/illy
Silly Putty/uddy
silverware/air
similarity/arity
simmer/immer
simple/imple
simplicity/icity
simplifies/ize
simplify/y
simplistic/istic
sin/in
Sinbad/ad 1
since/ince
sincere/eer
sincerer/earer
sincerity/arity
sing/ing
Singapore/ore
singe/inge
singer/inger 1
single/ingle
Sing Sing/ing
sinister/inister
sink/ink
sinned/inned
sinner/inner
sinus/inus
sip/ip
sipped/ipped
sipper/ipper
sir/er
sire/ire
sirloin/oin
sis/iss
sissy/issy
sister/ister
sisterhood/ood 3
sit/it
sitcom/om

site/ight
sits/its
sitter/itter
Sitting Bull/ull 2
situate/ate
situation/ation
six/icks
sixteen/een
size/ize
sizzle/izzle
skate/ate
skateboard/ord 1
skater/ader
skedaddle/attle
skepticism/ism
sketch/etch
ski/ee
skid/id
skied/eed
skies/ize
skill/ill
skilled/illed
skim/im
skimp/imp
skimpy/impy
skin/in
skinned/inned
skinny/inny
skintight/ight
skip/ip
skipped/ipped
skipper/ipper
Skippy/ippy
skirt/ert
skis/eeze
skit/it
skits/its
skittery/ittery
skulk/ulk
skull/ull 1
skunk/unk
sky/y
skydive/ive 1

skydiver/iver 1
skylark/ark
skyline/ine 1
skyrocket/ocket
slack/ack
slacks/ax
slain/ain
slam/am
slang/ang
slant/ant 1
slap/ap
slaphappy/appy
slapstick/ick
slash/ash 1
slate/ate
slaughter/otter
slave/ave
slavery/avery
slay/ay
slays/aze
sled/ed
sleek/eek
sleep/eep
sleepaholic/olic
sleeper/eeper
Sleeping Beauty/
    oody
sleepwalk/ock
sleepwalker/ocker
sleepwalks/ox
sleepy/eepy
sleepyhead/ed
sleet/eet
sleeve/eave
sleigh/ay
sleighbell/ell
slender/ender
slept/ept
sleuth/ooth
slew/ew
slice/ice 1
sliced/iced
slick/ick

slicked/ict
slicker/icker
slid/id
slide/ide
slight/ight
slighter/ider
slim/im
slime/ime
slimmer/immer
sling/ing
slingshot/ot
slink/ink
slinky/inky
slip/ip
slipped/ipped
slipper/ipper
slipshod/awed
slit/it
slither/ither
slits/its
sliver/iver 2
slob/ob
slobber/obber
sloop/oop
slop/op
slope/ope
sloppy/oppy
Sloppy Joe/o 1
slosh/osh
slot/ot
sloth/oth 2
slouch/ouch
slow/o 1
slowdown/own 2
slowed/ode
slowly/oly
slowpoke/oke
slows/ose 2
sludge/udge
slug/ug
slum/um
slumber/umber 1
slumlord/ord 1

slump/ump
slunk/unk
slur/er
slurp/urp
slurred/erd
slush/ush 1
sly/y
slyness/inus
smack/ack
smacked/act
smacks/ax
small/all
smaller/aller
smallish/olish
smart/art 1
smarter/arter
smarty/ardy
smash/ash 1
smear/eer
smell/ell
smelly/elly
smelter/elter
smile/ile 1
smiled/ild
smirk/erk
smith/ith
smitten/itten
smock/ock
smocks/ox
smoggy/oggy
smoke/oke
smoker/oker
smokes/okes
smokescreen/een
Smokey the Bear/air
smolder/older
smooch/ooch
smorgasbord/ord 1
smother/other
smudge/udge
smug/ug
smuggle/uggle
smuggler/uggler

Smurf/urf
smut/ut 1
snack/ack
snacked/act
snacks/ax
snafu/ew
snag/ag
snaggletooth/ooth
snail/ale 1
snake/ake
snakebite/ight
snakeskin/in
snap/ap
snappy/appy
snapshot/ot
snare/air
snatch/atch 1
snazzy/azzy
sneak/eek
sneaker/eaker
sneaky/eaky
sneer/eer
sneeze/eeze
sneezy/easy
snide/ide
sniff/iff
sniffed/ift
snigger/igger
snip/ip
sniper/iper
snipped/ipped
snippy/ippy
snitch/itch
snivel/ivel
snob/ob
snobby/obby
snoop/oop
snooper/ooper
snoopy/oopy
snoot/ute
snooty/oody
snooze/use 2
snoozer/user

snore/ore
snored/ord 1
snort/ort
snot/ot
snotty/ody
snout/out
snow/o 1
snowball/all
snowballed/alled
snowbound/ound
snowdrift/ift
snowed/ode
snowfall/all
snowflake/ake
snowing/owing
snowplow/ow 1
snows/ose 2
snowstorm/orm 1
Snow White/ight
snowy/owy
snub/ub
snuff/uff
snuffle/uffle
snug/ug
snuggle/uggle
snuggler/uggler
so/o 1
soak/oke
soap/ope
soapy/opey
soar/ore
soared/ord 1
sob/ob
sobber/obber
soccer/ocker
socialism/ism
socialite/ight
socialize/ize
society/iety
sociologist/ologist
sociology/ology
sock/ock
socket/ocket

socks/ox
Socrates/eeze
soda/ota
soften/often
soggy/oggy
soil/oil
sojourn/urn
solar/olar
Solarcaine/ain
sold/old
sole/ole
solely/oly
solicit/icit
solidarity/arity
solidifies/ize
solidify/y
solitaire/air
solitary/ary
solitude/ude
solo/olo
solution/ution
solve/olve
sombrero/arrow
some/um
somebody/ody
somehow/ow 1
someone/un
somersault/alt
somersaults/alts
something/ing
sometime/ime
someway/ay
somewhat/ot, ut 1
somewhere/air
son/un
song/ong
songbird/erd
songwriter/ider
Sonia/onia
sonic/onic
sonny/unny
Sony/ony
soon/oon

sooner/ooner
soot/oot 2
soothsayer/ayer
sophistication/ation
sophomore/ore
sophomoric/oric
sore/ore
sorority/ority
sorry/arry 2
sort/ort
SOS/ess
sought/ot
soul/ole
sound/ound
soundproof/oof 1
soundtrack/ack
soup/oop
soupy/oopy
sour/our 1
source/orse
sourdough/o 1
soured/owered
sourpuss/uss 1
south/outh 1
South Carolina/ina 2
South Dakota/ota
southpaw/aw
souvenir/eer
Soviet/et
sow/ow 1
sox/ox
soy/oy
spa/aw
space/ace
spacecraft/aft
spaced/aste
spaceship/ip
spacey/acy
spacious/acious
spackle/ackle
spade/ade 1
spaghetti/etty
Spain/ain

span/an 1
spank/ank
spanned/and
spar/ar
spare/air
sparerib/ib
spark/ark
sparred/ard 1
sparrow/arrow
spasm/asm
spastic/astic
spat/at 1
spatial/acial
spawn/awn
speak/eek
speaker/eaker
spear/eer
spearhead/ed
spearmint/int
specialize/ize
specific/ific
specifies/ize
specify/y
speck/eck
spectator/ader
specter/ector
speculate/ate
speculation/ation
speculator/ader
sped/ed
speech/each
speed/eed
speeder/eeder
speedometer/ometer
speed-read/eed
speedy/eedy
spell/ell
spellbound/ound
spelled/eld
speller/eller
spend/end
spendthrift/ift
spent/ent

spewed/ude
sphere/eer
spice/ice 1
spiced/iced
spicy/icy
spider/ider
spied/ide
spies/ize
spiffy/iffy
spike/ike
spill/ill
spilled/illed
spillover/over
spilt/ilt
spin/in
spindle/indle
spinal cord/ord
spine/ine 1
spinner/inner
spiny/iny
spire/ire
spiritualism/ism
spit/it
spitball/all
spite/ight
spitfire/ire
spits/its
spitter/itter
spittoon/oon
splash/ash 1
splashdown/own 2
splashy/ashy
splat/at 1
splatter/atter
splendor/ender
splice/ice 1
splint/int
splinter/inter
split/it
splits/its
splurge/erge
spoil/oil
spoilsport/ort

Spokane/an 1
spoke/oke
spoken/oken
spokes/okes
spokesperson/erson
sponge/unge
spoof/oof 1
spoofy/oofy
spook/uke
spool/ool
spoon/oon
spoonfed/ed
sport/ort
sportsmanship/ip
sporty/orty
spot/ot
spot-check/eck
spotlight/ight
spotty/ody
spouse/ouse
spout/out
sprain/ain
sprang/ang
sprawl/all
sprawled/alled
spray/ay
sprayed/ade 1
sprays/aze
spread/ed
spree/ee
sprees/eeze
spring/ing
springtime/ime
springy/ingy 1
sprinkle/inkle
sprint/int
sprinter/inter
sprints/ince
sprite/ight
spritz/its
sprout/out
spruce/use 1
spruced/uced

sprung/ung
spry/y
spryness/inus
spud/ud
spun/un
spunk/unk
spunky/unky
spur/er
spurred/erd
spurt/ert
sputter/utter
spy/y
spyglass/ass
squabble/obble
squabbler/obbler
squad/awed
squall/all
squalled/alled
squalor/aller
squander/onder
square/air
squash/osh
squat/ot
squawk/ock
squawks/ox
squeak/eek
squeaky/eaky
squeal/eel
squeezer/eezer
squelch/elch
squid/id
squiggle/iggle
squiggly/iggly
squint/int
squire/ire
squirm/erm
squirrel/url
sqirt/ert
squirter/erter
squirty/irty
squish/ish
stab/ab 1
stabilize/ize

stability/ility	starvation/ation	stereotype/ipe	stomachache/ake
stable/able	starve/arve	sterilize/ize	stomp/omp
stack/ack	stash/ash 1	stern/urn	stone/one 1
stacked/act	state/ate	stethoscope/ope	stonewall/all
stacks/ax	static/atic	Steve/eave	stony/ony
staff/aff	station/ation	stew/ew	stood/ood 3
staffed/aft	stationary/ary	stewed/ude	stooge/uge
stag/ag	stationery/ary	stews/use 2	stool/ool
stage/age 1	statistic/istic	stick/ick	stoolie/uly
stagecoach/oach	status quo/o 1	sticker/icker	stoop/oop
stagestruck/uck	staunch/aunch	sticks/icks	stop/op
stagnate/ate	stay/ay	stickup/up	stoplight/ight
stain/ain	stayed/ade 1	sticky/icky	stopper/opper
stair/air	stays/aze	stiff/iff	stopwatch/otch
staircase/ace	steadfast/ast	stiletto/etto	store/ore
stairway/ay	steady/etty	still/ill	stored/ord 1
stake/ake	steak/ake	stilled/illed	stork/ork 1
stakeout/out	steal/eel	stilt/ilt	storm/orm 1
stale/ale 1	steam/eem	stimulate/ate	story/ory
stalemate/ate	steamboat/ote	stimulation/ation	storyline/ine 1
stall/all	steamroll/ole	sting/ing	stout/out
stalled/alled	steamrolled/old	stinger/inger 1	stouter/owder
stamp/amp	steamroller/olar	stingray/ay	stove/ove 1
stampede/eed	steamy/eamy	stingy/ingy 2	stow/o 1
Stan/an 1	steed/eed	stink/ink	stowaway/ay
stance/ance	steel/eel	stinkaroo/ew	stowed/ode
stand/and	steep/eep	stinky/inky	straddle/attle
standby/y	steeper/eeper	stint/int	straight/ate
standout/out	steer/eer	stir/er	straighter/ader
standstill/ill	Stella/ella	stirred/erd	strain/ain
star/ar	stellar/eller	stitch/itch	strait/ate
starch/arch	steam/eem	stock/ock	straitlaced/aste
stardust/ust	stench/ench	stockbroker/oker	strand/and
stare/air	stencil/encil	Stockholm/ome 1	strange/ange
stargaze/aze	step/ep	stockpile/ile 1	stranglehold/old
stark/ark	stepchild/ild	stockpiled/ild	strangulate/ate
starlight/ight	stepdaughter/otter	stocks/ox	strap/ap
starred/ard 1	stepmother/other	stocky/awky	stratosphere/eer
starry/arry 2	stepped/ept	stoic/oic	straw/aw
starstruck/uck	stepsister/ister	stoke/oke	strawberry/ary
start/art 1	stereo/o	stokes/okes	straws/ause
starter/arter	stereophonic/onic	stole/ole	stray/ay
Star Trek/eck	stereos/ose 2	stolen/olen	strays/aze

235

streak/eek
stream/eem
streamline/ine 1
streamlined/ind 1
street/eet
streetcar/ar
strength/ength
strep/ep
stress/ess
stressed/est
stressful/essful
stretch/etch
strewn/oon
stricken/icken
strict/ict
stricter/ictor
stride/ide
strife/ife
strike/ike
striker/iker
string/ing
strip/ip
stripe/ipe
stripped/ipped
strive/ive 1
striven/iven
strode/ode
Stroganoff/off
stroke/oke
strokes/okes
stroll/ole
strolled/old
stroller/olar
strong/ong
stronghold/old
struck/uck
strudel/oodle
struggle/uggle
struggler/uggler
strum/um
strummer/ummer
strut/ut 1
stub/ub

stubble/ouble
stubby/ubby
stuck/uck
student/udent
studio/o 1
study/uddy
stuff/uff
stuffy/uffy
stumble/umble
stumbling/umbling
stump/ump
stumpy/umpy
stun/un
stung/ung
stunk/unk
stunned/und
stunner/unner
stunt/unt
stunts/unts
stupefies/ize
stupefy/y
stupid/upid
stupider/upiter
stupidity/idity
stupor/ooper
sturdy/urdy
stutter/utter
sty/y
style/ile 1
styled/ild
sub/ub
subdue/ew
subdued/ude
subdues/use 2
subject/ect
subjective/ective
subjects/ex
sublime/ime
submarine/een
submerge/erge
submerse/erse
submersion/ersion
submission/ition

submissive/issive
submit/it
subpoena/ena
subscribe/ibe
subscription/iption
subside/ide
substitute/ute
substitution/ution
subterfuge/uge
subtitle/idle
subtle/uddle
subtopic/opic
subtract/act
subtraction/action
subtracts/ax
suburb/urb
subvert/ert
subway/ay
subways/aze
succeed/eed
success/ess
successful/essful
succession/ession
successor/essor
succinct/inct
succotash/ash 1
succumb/um
such/utch
suck/uck
sucked/uct
sucker/ucker
sucks/ucks
suction/uction
Sudafed/ed
sue/ew
sued/ude
suede/ade 1
sues/use 2
suffer/uffer
suffice/ice 1
sufficed/iced
sufficient/icient
suffocate/ate

suffragette/et
sugarcoat/ote
suggest/est
suggestion/estion
suit/ute
suitcase/ace
suite/eet
suitor/uter
sulk/ulk
sum/um
summarize/ize
summation/ation
summer/ummer
summertime/ime
sun/un
sunbeam/eem
sunblock/ock
sunburn/urn
sunburst/irst
sundown/own 2
sung/ung
sunk/unk
sunken/unken
sunlight/ight
sunlit/it
sunned/und
sunny/unny
sunrise/ize
sunscreen/een
sunset/et
Sunset Strip/ip
sunshine/ine 1
sunstroke/oke
suntan/an 1
suntanned/and
super/ooper
superb/urb
supercool/ool
Superdome/ome 1
super-duper/ooper
superficial/icial
superiority/ority
Superman/an 1

supermom/om
superpower/our 1
supersede/eed
supersonic/onic
superstar/ar
superstition/ition
superstitious/icious
supervise/ize
supervision/ision
supervisor/izer
supper/upper
supplant/ant 1
supplied/ide
supplies/ize
supply/y
support/ort
supporter/order
suppose/ose 2
suppress/ess
suppressed/est
suppression/ession
supreme/eem
Supreme Court/ort
sure/ure
surefire/ire
surety/urity
surf/urf
surfboard/ord 1
surge/erge
surly/urly
surname/aim
surpass/ass
surpassed/ast
surprise/ize
surrender/ender
surround/ound
survey/ay
surveyed/ade 1
surveyor/ayer
surveys/aze
survival/ival
survive/ive 1

survivor/iver 1
Susanna/ana 1
suspect/ect
suspects/ex
suspend/end
suspender/ender
suspense/ense
suspension/ention
suspicion/ition
suspicious/icious
sustain/ain
suture/uture
svelte/elt
Svengali/olly
swab/ob
Swahili/eally
swallow/allow 2
swam/am
swami/ommy
swamp/omp
swan/awn
swanky/anky
swans/ons
swap/op
swarm/orm 1
swashbuckle/uckle
swat/ot
swatch/otch
sway/ay
swayed/ade 1
sways/aze
swear/air
swearword/erd
sweat/et
sweater/etter
sweaty/etty
sweep/eep
sweeper/eeper
sweet/eet
sweeten/eaten
sweeter/eeder
sweetheart/art 1

sweetie/eedy
swell/ell
swelter/elter
swept/ept
swerve/erve
swift/ift
swig/ig
swim/im
swimmer/immer
swindle/indle
swine/ine 1
swing/ing
swipe/ipe
swirl/url
swirly/urly
swish/ish
Swiss/iss
switch/itch
switcheroo/ew
swivel/ivel
swollen/olen
swoon/oon
swoop/oop
sword/ord 1
swore/ore
sworn/orn
swung/ung
symbol/imble
symbolic/olic
symbolism/ism
sympathetic/etic
sympathize/ize
symphonic/onic
symptomatic/atic
synagogue/og
syndrome/ome 1
synonym/im
synthetic/etic
Syria/eria
syringe/inge
systematic/atic
Szechwan/awn

t

tab/ab 1
Tabasco/asco
tabby/abby
tabernacle/ackle
table/able
tabloid/oid
taboo/ew
taboos/use 2
tack/ack
tacked/act
tackle/ackle
tact/act
tactical/actical
tad/ad 1
tadpole/ole
tag/ag
tagalong/long
Tahiti/eedy
tail/ale 1
tailgate/ate
tailgater/ader
tailpipe/ipe
tailspin/in
tailwind/inned
Taipei/ay
Taiwan/awn
Taj Mahal/all
take/ake
tale/ale 1
talk/ock
talkathon/awn
talker/ocker
talks/ox
tall/all
Tallahassee/assy
taller/aller
tallish/olish
tally/alley
tamale/olly
tambourine/een
tame/aim

237

Tammy/ammy
tamper/amper
tan/an 1
Tang/ang
tangerine/een
tank/ank
tanned/and
tanner/anner
tantalize/ize
tantamount/ount
tap/ap
tape/ape
tar/ar
tardy/ardy
tarred/ard 1
tarry/ary
tart/art 1
Tartar/arter
tarter/arter
task/ask
taste/aste
tasty/asty
tatter/atter
tattle/attle
tattletale/ale 1
tattoo/ew
tattooed/ude
tattoos/use 2
taught/ot
taunt/aunt
taupe/ope
taut/ot
tauter/otter
tawny/awny
tax/ax
taxation/ation
taxi/axi
taxicab/ab 1
taxpayer/ayer
tea/ee
teach/each
teacher/eacher
teacup/up

teakettle/eddle
teal/eel
team/eem
teamwork/erk
teapot/ot
tear/air, eer
teardrop/op
tearful/earful
tearstain/ain
teary/eery
teas/eeze
tease/eeze
technicality/ality 1
technician/ition
technique/eek
technology/ology
Ted/ed
Teddy/etty
tee/ee
team/eem
teen/een
teenage/age 1
teeny/ini
teenybopper/opper
teeny weeny/ini
teeter/eeder
teeth/eath 2
teethe/eethe
Tel Aviv/eave
telecast/ast
telegram/am
telegraph/aff
telephone/one 1
telephonic/onic
telescope/ope
telescopic/opic
televise/ize
television/ision
tell/ell
teller/eller
telltale/ale 1
Tell, William/ell
temperamental/ental

temporary/ary
tempt/empt
ten/en
tenacious/acious
tenacity/acity
tend/end
tender/ender
tenderfoot/oot 2
tenderize/ize
tenderloin/oin
Tennessee/ee
tense/ense
tension/ention
tent/ent
tents/ense
tepee/ee, eepy
tepees/eeze
teriyaki/awky
term/erm
terminate/ate
terminator/ader
terminology/ology
termite/ight
terrain/ain
terrific/ific
terrified/ide
terrifies/ize
terrify/y
territorial/orial
territory/ory
terror/arer
terrorism/ism
terrorize/ize
Terry/ary
terse/erse
Tess/ess
test/est
tester/ester
testify/y
testimonial/onial
testimony/ony
tether/eather
text/ext

textbook/ook 2
Thailand/and
than/an 1, en
thank/ank
that/at 1
thatch/atch 1
thaw/aw
theft/eft
their/air
them/em
theme/eem
then/en
Theodore/ore
theorize/ize
theory/eery
there/air
thereafter/after
therefore/ore
thermometer/ometer
thermostat/at 1
these/eeze
they/ay
thick/ick
thicken/icken
thicker/icker
thicket/icket
thickly/ickly
thief/ief
thigh/y
thighs/ize
thimble/imble
thin/in
thing/ing
thingamabob/ob
thingamajig/ig
think/ink
thinned/inned
thinner/inner
third/erd
thirst/irst
thirteen/een
thirty/irty
this/iss

thistle/istle
thong/ong
thorn/orn
thoroughbred/ed
those/ose 2
though/o 1
thought/ot
thrash/ash 1
thread/ed
threadbare/air
threat/et
three/ee
threshold/old
threw/ew
thrift/ift
thrifty/ifty
thrill/ill
thrilled/illed
thriller/iller
thrive/ive 1
throat/ote
throb/ob
throne/one 1
throng/ong
throttle/oddle
through/ew
throughout/out
throw/o 1
throwaway/ay
throwing/owing
thrown/one 1
throws/ose 2
thrust/ust
thud/ud
thug/ug
thumb/um
thumbnail/ale 1
thumbtack/ack
thumbtacks/ax
thump/ump
thunder/under
thundercloud/oud
thunderstorm/orm 1

thunderstruck/uck
thus/us
thwart/ort
thyme/ime
Tibet/et
tick/ick
ticked/ict
ticker/icker
ticket/icket
tickle/ickle
tickly/ickly
ticks/icks
Tic Tac/ack
ticktock/ock
ticktocks/ox
tidal/idle
tidbits/its
tide/ide
tidepool/ool
tidy/idy
tie/y
tied/ide
tier/eer
ties/ize
tiff/iff
tight/ight
tighten/ighten
tighter/ider
tight-lipped/ipped
tightrope/ope
tightwad/awed
Tijuana/onna
tile/ile 1
tiled/ild
till/ill
tilled/illed
tilt/ilt
Tim/im
Timbuktu/ew
time/ime
timekeeper/eeper
timepiece/ease 2
time-saver/aver

times table/able
timetable/able
timeworn/orn
timidity/idity
tin/in
Tina/ena
tinfoil/oil
tinge/inge
tingle/ingle
Tinkertoys/oys
tinny/inny
tint/int
tints/ince
tiny/iny
tip/ip
tipped/ipped
tipper/ipper
tippytoe/o 1
tipsy/ipsy
tiptoe/o 1
tiptoed/ode
tiptoeing/owing
tiptoes/ose 2
tiptop/op
tirade/ade 1
tire/ire
'tis/iz
tissue/issue
titanosaur/ore
title/idle
titter/itter
tizzy/izzy
to/ew
toad/ode
toadstool/ool
toast/ost 1
today/ay
Todd/awed
toddle/oddle
toe/o 1
toehold/old
toenail/ale 1
toes/ose 2

together/eather
toil/oil
token/oken
Tokyo/o 1
told/old
Toledo/o 1
tolerate/ate
toll/ole
tom/om
tomahawk/ock
tomahawks/ox
tomb/oom
tombstone/one 1
tomcat/at 1
Tommy/ommy
ton/un
tone/one 1
tongue/ung
tonic/onic
tonight/ight
tonsillitis/itis
Tonto/onto
Tony/ony
too/ew
toodle-oo/ew
took/ook 2
tool/ool
toot/ute
tooth/ooth
toothache/ake
toothbrush/ush 1
toothpaste/aste
toothpick/ick
toothpicks/icks
top/op
topaz/azz
topic/opic
topmost/ost 1
topnotch/otch
topper/opper
torch/orch
torchbearer/arer
tore/ore

239

torment/ent
tormentor/enter
torn/orn
Toronto/onto
torpedo/edo
torrential/ential
tortellini/ini
toss/oss 2
tossed/ost 2
tostada/ada
tot/ot
totality/ality 1
tote/ote
totter/otter
touch/utch
touchdown/own
tough/uff
tougher/uffer
toughie/uffy
tour/ure
tow/o 1
toward/ord 1
towed/ode
towel/owl
tower/our 1
towered/owered
towing/owing
town/own 2
towrope/ope
tows/ose 2
toxicity/icity
toy/oy
toyed/oid
Toyota/ota
toys/oys
trace/ace
traced/aste
track/ack
tracked/act
tracks/ax
tract/act
traction/action
Tracy/acy

trade/ade 1
trademark/ark
trader/ader
tradition/ition
traffic/aphic
trail/ale 1
trailblaze/aze
train/ain
trait/ate
traitor/ader
tram/am
tramp/amp
trampoline/een
trance/ance
tranquilize/ize
tranquillity/ility
transact/act
transaction/action
transatlantic/antic
transcend/end
transcendental/ental
transcribe/ibe
transcript/ipped
transferred/erd
transfix/icks
transform/orm 1
transformer/ormer
transfusion/usion
transistor/ister
transition/ition
translate/ate
translator/ader
transmission/ition
transmit/it
transmits/its
transmittal/iddle
transparent/arent
transpire/ire
transplant/ant 1
transplants/ance
transport/ort
transportation/ation
transporter/order

transverse/erse
trap/ap
trapdoor/ore
trapeze/eeze
trash/ash 1
trash can/an 1
trashy/ashy
trauma/ama 1
traumatic/atic
traumatize/ize
travel/avel
travelogue/og
tray/ay
trays/aze
tread/ed
treadmill/ill
treason/eason
treasure/easure
treat/eet
treaty/eedy
treble/ebble
tree/ee
treed/eed
trees/eeze
treetop/op
trek/eck
trekked/ect
treks/ex
tremble/emble
trench/ench
trend/end
trendsetter/etter
trespass/ass
Trevor/ever
trial/ile 1
tribe/ibe
tribute/ute
trick/ick
tricked/ict
trickle/ickle
tricks/icks
tricky/icky
tricycle/ickle

tried/ide
tries/ize
trigger/igger
trill/ill
trilled/illed
trillion/illion
trim/im
trimmer/immer
Trinidad/ad 1
trinity/inity
trip/ip
triple/ipple
tripod/awed
tripped/ipped
tripper/ipper
trite/ight
triviality/ality 1
trod/awed
troll/ole
trolley/olly
trombone/one 1
tromp/omp
troop/oop
trooper/ooper
tropic/opic
trot/ot
trotter/otter
troubadour/ore
trouble/ouble
troubleshoot/ute
troubleshooter/uter
trough/off
trounce/ounce
troupe/oop
trouper/ooper
trout/out
Troy/oy
truce/use 1
truck/uck
trucked/uct
trucker/ucker
truckload/ode
trucks/ucks

trudge/udge
Trudy/oody
true/ew
truffle/uffle
truism/ism
truly/uly
trump/ump
trunk/unk
trust/ust
trusted/usted
trustee/usty
truth/ooth
try/y
tryout/out
tsk tsk/isk
tsunami/ommy
tub/ub
tube/ube
tucked/uct
Tucson/awn
tug/ug
tuition/ition
tumble/umble
tumbleweed/eed
tumbling/umbling
tummy/ummy
tumor/umor
tumult/ult
tune/oon
tuner/ooner
tunnel/unnel
turf/urf
Turk/erk
turkey/erky
turmoil/oil
turn/urn
turncoat/ote
turnover/over
turnstile/ile 1
turquoise/oice, oys
turtle/urdle
turtledove/ove 2
turtleneck/eck

tusk/usk
tussle/ustle
Tut, King/ut 1
tutor/uter
tutorial/orial
tutti-frutti/oody
tutu/ew
tux/ucks
tuxedo/edo
TVs/eeze
twang/ang
tweak/eek
tweed/eed
tweet/eet
tweezer/eezer
twelve/elve
twice/ice 1
twiddle/iddle
twig/ig
twilight/ight
twin/in
twine/ine 1
twined/ind 1
twinge/inge
Twinkie/inky
twinkle/inkle
twirl/url
twirly/urly
twist/ist
twister/ister
twitch/itch
twitter/itter
two/ew
two-seater/eeder
tycoon/oon
tyke/ike
Tylenol/all
type/ipe
typecast/ast
typewriter/iter
typewritten/itten
typhoon/oon

u

udder/utter
ugh/ug
Ukraine/ain
ukulele/aily
umbrella/ella
ump/ump
umpire/ire
unable/able
unafraid/ade 1
unapparent/arent
unaware/air
unbend/end
unborn/orn
unbroken/oken
uncanny/anny
unchain/ain
uncivil/ivel
unclear/eer
unclench/ench
uncontrolled/old
uncouth/ooth
uncut/ut 1
undeniable/iable
under/under
underachiever/eaver
underarm/arm
undercut/ut 1
underdog/og
underdone/un
underfed/ed
underfoot/oot 2
undergrad/ad 1
underground/ound
underlie/y
underline/ine 1
underlined/ind 1
undermine/ine 1
undermined/ind 1
underneath/eath 2
underpaid/ade 1
underpants/ance

underrate/ate
underscore/ore
undershirt/ert
understand/and
understood/ood 3
understudy/uddy
undertow/o 1
underwater/otter
underway/ay
underwear/air
underweight/ate
underwent/ent
undo/ew
undone/un
undress/ess
undressed/est
unearth/irth
uneasy/easy
unemotional/otional
unemployed/oid
unexplored/ord 1
unfair/air
unfit/it
unfold/old
unfulfilled/illed
unfurl/url
unglued/ude
unhappy/appy
unheard/erd
unhitch/itch
unholy/oly
unhook/ook 2
unhurt/ert
unicorn/orn
unifies/ize
uniform/orm 1
unify/y
unimpressed/est
union/union
unique/eek
unite/ight
unity/unity
universe/erse

university/ersity
unjust/ust
unkind/ind 1
unknown/one 1
unlace/ace
unlaced/aste
unlatch/atch 1
unlawful/awful
unless/ess
unlike/ike
unload/ode
unlock/ock
unlocks/ox
unlucky/ucky
unmade/ade 1
unnecessary/ary
unnerve/erve
unobtrusive/usive
unofficial/icial
unorthodox/ox
unpack/ack
unpacked/act
unpacks/ax
unpaid/ade 1
unparalleled/eld
unpin/in
unplug/ug
unproductive/uctive
unravel/avel
unreal/eel
unrealistic/istic
unrefined/ind 1
unrehearsed/irst
unreliable/iable
unripe/ipe
unroll/ole
unromantic/antic
unruly/uly
unsaid/ed
unsatisfied/ide
unsavory/avery
unscrew/ew
unseen/een

unsettle/eddle
unskilled/illed
unspoken/oken
unstable/able
unsteady/etty
unsung/ung
unsure/ure
unsurpassed/ast
untidy/idy
untie/y
untied/ide
unties/ize
until/ill
unto/ew
untold/old
untrue/ew
untruth/ooth
unusable/usable
unveil/ale 1
unwed/ed
unwell/ell
unwind/ind 1
unwise/ize
unwrap/ap
unwritten/itten
unzip/ip
up/up
upbeat/eet
update/ate
upend/end
upgrade/ade 1
upheld/eld
uphill/ill
uplift/ift
upon/awn
upped/upt
uppercut/ut 1
upright/ight
uproar/ore
uproarious/orious
uproot/ute
upscale/ale 1
upset/et

upstage/age 1
upstart/art 1
uptight/ite
up-to-date/ate
upturn/urn
urge/erge
urgency/urgency
urgent/ergent
urn/urn
Uruguay/y
us/us
USA/ay
usable/usable
use/use 1, use 2
user/user
usurp/urp
Utah/aw
utensil/encil
utility/ility
utilize/ize
utmost/ost 1
utopia/opia
utter/utter

vacate/ate
vacation/ation
vaccinate/ate
vaccine/een
vagabond/ond
vagabonds/ons
vain/ain
valentine/ine 1
validate/ate
validity/idity
valley/alley
vamoose/use 1
vamoosed/uced
vamp/amp
vampire/ire
van/an 1
vandalism/ism

vane/ain
vanguard/ard 1
vanilla/illa
Van Winkle, Rip/inkle
vaporizer/izer
variation/ation
variety/iety
various/arious
vary/ary
vase/ace
Vaseline/een
vast/ast
vaster/aster
vat/at 1
vaudeville/ille
vault/alt
vaulter/alter
vaults/altz
VCR/ar
veal/eel
veer/eer
veg/edge
vegetarianism/ism
vehicle/ickle
veil/ale 1
vein/ain
velocity/ocity
velour/ure
vendor/ender
vent/ent
ventilator/ader
vents/ense
venture/enture
veracity/acity
verb/urb
verbalize/ize
verbose/ose 1
verge/erge
verification/ation
verified/ide
verifies/ize
verify/y
Vermont/aunt

Verne, Jules/urn
Veronica/onica
versatility/ility
verse/erse
version/ersion
verve/erve
very/ary
vest/est
vet/et
veto/edo
vex/ex
vexed/ext
viable/iable
vibrate/ate
vibration/ation
vicarious/arious
vice/ice 1
vicinity/inity
vicious/icious
Vicki/icky
victimize/ize
victor/ictor
victorious/orious
video/o 1
videos/ose 2
vied/ide
Vietnam/om
view/ew
viewed/ude
viewpoint/oint
views/use 2
vigor/igger
vile/ile 1
villa/illa
vindicate/ate
vine/ine 1
viola/ola
violate/ate
violation/ation
violin/in
VIP/ee
viper/iper
vise/ize

vision/ision
visionary/ary
visor/izer
visualize/ize
vital/idle
vitality/ality 1
vitalize/ize
vivacious/acious
vocabulary/ary
vocal/ocal
vocalize/ize
vogue/ogue 1
voice/oice
void/oid
volley/olly
volleyball/all
voluntary/ary
volunteer/eer
volunteerism/ism
voodoo/ew
vote/ote
vouch/ouch
vow/ow 1
vowed/oud
vowel/owl
vulgarity/arity
vulture/ulture

wad/awed
waddle/oddle
wade/ade 1
waffle/awful
wag/ag
wage/age 1
wail/ale 1
waist/aste
wait/ate
waiter/ader
waive/ave
waiver/aver
wake/ake

walk/ock
walker/ocker
walkie-talkie/awky
walks/ox
wall/all
walled/alled
wallflower/our 1
wallow/allow 2
Wally/olly
Walter/alter
waltz/alts
wand/ond
wander/onder
wanderlust/ust
wands/ons
wane/ain
wanna/onna
want/aunt
war/ore
ward/ord 1
wardrobe/obe
ware/air
warehouse/ouse
warfare/air
warlike/ike
warm/orm 1
warmer/ormer
warmonger/unger
warn/orn
warning/orning
warpath/ath
warred/ord 1
wart/ort
wartime/ime
warty/orty
wary/ary
was/uzz
wash/osh
washboard/ord 1
Washington, DC/ee
washrag/ag
waste/aste
wasteland/and

watch/otch
watchdog/og
watchword/erd
water/otter
waterbed/ed
waterfall/all
Waterloo/ew
watery/ottery
wave/ave
waver/aver
wavy/avy
wax/ax
waxy/axi
way/ay
wayfarer/arer
ways/aze
we/ee
weak/eek
weaker/eaker
wear/air
weary/eery
weather/eather
weatherbeaten/eaten
weather vane/ain
weatherworn/orn
weave/eave
weaver/eaver
wed/ed
wedge/edge
weed/eed
weeder/eeder
weedy/eedy
week/eek
weekday/ay
weep/eep
weeper/eeper
weepy/eepy
weigh/ay
weighed/ade 1
weighs/aze
weight/ate
weighty/ady
welch/elch

weld/eld
welfare/air
well/ell
well-versed/irst
welt/elt
went/ent
wept/ept
were/er
west/est
wet/et
wetter/etter
we've/eave
whack/ack
whacked/act
whale/ale 1
wham/am
whammy/ammy
wharf/arf 2
what/ot, ut 1
whatever/ever
whatnot/ot
wheat/eet
wheedle/eedle
wheel/eel
wheelbarrow/arrow
wheelchair/air
wheelie/eally
wheeze/eeze
when/en
whenever/ever
where/air
wherever/ever
whet/et
whether/eather
which/itch
whichever/ever
whiff/iff
whiffed/ift
while/ile 1
whim/im
whine/ine 1
whined/ind 1
whiner/iner

whinny/inny
whiny/iny
whip/ip
whiplash/ash 1
whipped/ipped
whippoorwill/ill
whirl/url
whirlpool/ool
whirlwind/inned
whisk/isk
whiskey/isky
whisper/isper
whistle/istle
white/ight
whiten/ighten
whiter/ider
whitewash/osh
whittle/iddle
whiz/iz
who/ew
whoa/o 1
whoever/ever
whole/ole
wholesale/ale 1
wholly/oly
whom/oom
whomp/omp
whoop/oop
whoopee/oopy
whoosh/ush 2
whopper/opper
whose/use 2
why/y
Wichita/aw
wicker/icker
wicket/icket
wicks/icks
wide/ide
wider/ider
widespread/ed
wienie/ini
wife/ife
wig/ig

wiggle/iggle
wiggly/iggly
wigwam/om
wild/ild
wildcat/at 1
wildebeast/east
wildflower/our 1
wildlife/ife
will/ill
willed/illed
William Tell/ell
willow/illow
willpower/our 1
willy-nilly/illy
wilt/ilt
wimp/imp
wimpy/impy
win/in
wince/ince
wind/ind 1, inned
windbag/ag
windblown/one 1
windmill/ill
windowpane/ain
windowsill/ill
windpipe/ipe
windshield/ield
windswept/ept
wine/ine 1
wing/ing
wingding/ing
wingdinger/inger 1
wink/ink
winked/inct
winner/inner
Winnie the Pooh/ew
Winnipeg/eg
winter/inter
wipe/ipe
wiper/iper
wire/ire
wiretap/ap
wise/ize

wisecrack/ack
wisecracked/act
wisecracks/ax
wiser/izer
wish/ish
wishbone/one 1
wisp/isp
wit/it
witch/itch
witchcraft/aft
with/ith
withdraw/aw
withdrawn/awn
withdrew/ew
wither/ither
withheld/eld
withhold/old
within/in
without/out
wits/its
witticism/ism
witty/itty
wizard/izard
Wizard of Oz/ause
wobble/obble
wobbler/obbler
woe/o 1
woebegone/awn
woes/ose 2
wok/ock
woke/oke
woks/ox
womb/oom
wombat/at 1
won/un
wonder/under
wonton/awn
woo/ew
wood/ood 3
woodblock/ock
woodchopper/opper
woodchuck/uck
woodcutter/utter

woodpile/ile 1
woodwind/inned
woodwork/erk
wooed/ude
woof/oof 2
wool/ull 2
woolly/ully
word/erd
wordy/urdy
wore/ore
work/erk
workaholic/olic
workload/ode
workout/out
workplace/ace
workshop/op
worldwide/ide
worm/erm
worn/orn
worry/urry
worrywart/ort
worse/erse
worsen/erson
worst/irst
worth/irth
worthwhile/ile 1
would/ood 3
wound/ound
wove/ove 1
wow/ow 1
wowed/oud
wrap/ap
wrath/ath
wreath/eath 2
wreck/eck
wrecked/ect
wrecks/ex
wrench/ench
wretch/etch
wring/ing
wrinkle/inkle
wrist/ist
wristwatch/otch

write/ight
writer/ider
written/itten
wrong/ong
wrote/ote
wrung/ung
wry/y
Wyatt Earp/urp

Xerox/ox
x-ray/ay
x-rayed/ade 1
x-rays/aze
xylophone/one 1

yacht/ot
yak/ack
yakked/act
yaks/ax
Yale/ale 1
yam/am
yank/ank
Yankee/anky
Yankee Doodle/oodle
yap/ap
yard/ard 1
yardstick/ick
yarn/arn
yawn/awn
yawned/ond
yawner/onor
yawns/ons
year/eer
yearn/urn
yeast/east
yell/ell
yelled/eld
yeller/eller
yellow/ellow
Yellowstone/one 1

yelp/elp
yen/en
yep/ep
yes/ess
yesterday/ay
yet/et
yield/ield
yippee/ippy
yokel/ocal
Yokohama/ama 1
yolk/oke
yolks/okes
yonder/onder
yoo-hoo/ew
you/ew
young/ung
younger/unger
your/ore, ure
you're/ure
yourself/elf
youth/ooth
you've/ove 3
yo-yo/o 1
yo-yos/ose 2
yuck/uck
yucky/ucky
Yukon/awn
yule/ool
yum/um
yummy/ummy
yuppie/uppy
Yvonne/awn

z

zag/ag
Zambezi/easy
Zanzibar/ar
zap/ap
zeal/eel
zealous/ealous
zero/ero 1
zest/est

Zeus/use 1
zigzag/ag
zillion/illion
zinc/ink
zing/ing
zinger/inger 1
zingy/ingy 1
zip/ip
zipped/ipped
zipper/ipper
zippy/ippy
zit/it
zither/ither
zits/its
zone/one 1
zonk/onk
zoo/ew
zoologist/ologist
zoology/ology
zoom/oom
zoos/use 2
zucchini/ini

Make your words sing!

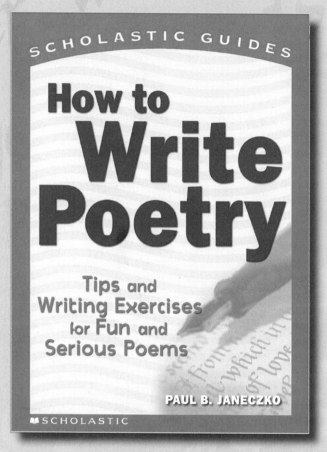

SCHOLASTIC GUIDES

How to Write Poetry

Tips and Writing Exercises for Fun and Serious Poems

PAUL B. JANECZKO

SCHOLASTIC

Paperback ISBN: 0-590-10078-5
128 Pages • $8.95 • Ages 9–14

A celebrated poet shares his tips on the art of writing poems. This is the perfect introduction for aspiring young writers, with advice from different poets, inspiring examples of verse, and helpful suggestions to turn any first draft into a work of art.

"A practical and inspiring guide." —*School Library Journal*, starred review

"[Janeczko] shares the joy, wonder, and music of words." —*Booklist*

Available wherever books are sold.

SCHOLASTIC